HOW TO GET YOUR BOOK PUBLISHED

HOW TO GET YOUR BOOK PUBLISHED

_____ Herbert W. Bell

Cincinnati, Ohio

Library of Congress Cataloging-in-Publication Data
Bell, Herbert W., 1922-
    How to get your book published.

    Bibliography: p.
    Includes index.
    1. Authors and publishers. I. Title.
PN155.B45   1985   808'.02   85-17796
ISBN 0-89879-193-6

Design by Joan Ann Jacobus

To Shirley

Contents

PREFACE

I wrote this book to help authors through the complexities of book publishing: preparing acceptable projects, selecting the best publisher, negotiating favorable terms, and ensuring that their manuscripts are published in a satisfactory way.

In part, I wanted to package for the guidance of others an unusual experience that included sales, editorial, and executive assignments in trade, professional, and college textbook publishing. Another motive, I suspect, was to do penance for those times when as an editor I may have dealt unfairly with authors or not risen effectively to their defense.

In discussing issues on which publishers and authors frequently disagree, I have attempted to present both points of view and to be objective in making judgments between them. If I have been evenhanded, I have achieved one of my major goals.

Although much of this book is based on personal experience, I am indebted to many others who have written on publishing before me, and in particular to the Authors Guild for the valuable material it publishes for its members.

And I am appreciative of several people who have been especially helpful. Georges Borchardt and Claire Smith were generous in explaining the role of agents, Matthew Hodgson supplied valuable information on university presses, and Edward Rosenblum reviewed the section on book production and made many useful suggestions.

Special thanks are due Carol Cartaino, who reviewed the material, identifying serious omissions and inconsistencies, and Margaret Miner, who worked hard to make my writing more readable.

All omissions and errors still existing are solely my responsibility, and I'd like having them pointed out to me, so I can correct them in any future edition.

Herbert W. Bell

Long Beach, North Carolina
June 14, 1985

HOW TO GET YOUR BOOK PUBLISHED

_____ Chapter 1

The Author-Publisher Relationship

Most writers sooner or later want to see their work published in book form. A book can get its "arms" around a subject or story in a way that is impossible in other media, such as newspapers or periodicals. Even more important, books have a degree of permanence that no other medium enjoys. Once read, they can later be revisited, like old friends, or shared with others. Even books with modest sales find their way into libraries to wait patiently for months, years, or decades for opportunities to entertain or enlighten. And they can be rediscovered by a whole new generation to whom they speak a forgotten truth or illuminate a dark corner of the past.

Writing a book and getting it published is a pentathlon event, requiring determination and endurance in meeting a variety of challenges. Whatever your objectives—financial gain, critical acclaim, or merely a sense of accomplishment—the process involves a relationship with a publisher that may begin early in the writing process and last for many years.

Authors and publishers need each other. Although authors occasionally publish their own books, the problems in doing so are not only burdensome but financially risky as well. And publishers have not been able to replace authors with full-time staffs of writers to turn out best sellers. So authors and publishers each bring needed talents to the relationship, and each assume a set of responsibilities.

Simply put, the author is responsible for the content, or message, i.e., the basic work to be published. The publisher's responsibilities are to provide at least some editorial advice and assistance with respect to substance and style, to produce the book to appeal to the audi-

1

ence for which it is written, to market it effectively, and to share the profits from the venture with the author by paying him or her a percentage of the income from sales. In practice, however, the lines are not always so clearly drawn. A publisher may play a major role in helping to shape the content, and an author may, through an intimate knowledge of the audience for whom the book was written, provide valuable marketing suggestions, even contributing personally to the marketing effort through television appearances, lectures, and so forth. Therefore, to be most successful, authors and publishers must be flexible and cooperative, taking advantage of each other's strengths and respecting the contribution that each can make to the venture.

Unfortunately, authors—especially new authors—suffer a considerable disadvantage in the partnership. While publishers have years of experience in publishing books and dealing with authors, new authors usually have only a hearsay knowledge of the publishing process, what is expected of them, and what they should reasonably expect from their publishers. This lack of experience makes authors heavily dependent on the good faith and trustworthiness of their publishers. While this trust is usually justified, it is unhealthy in any relationship to be at such a disadvantage.

Nothing dramatizes this disadvantage more than the contracts authors must sign in order to have their works published, contracts that dictate the terms by which authors must abide for the entire lives of their books. These documents, usually consisting of four or more pages, spell out the rights and obligations of both parties. However, since they are written by publishers, they tend to emphasize the rights of publishers and the obligations of authors. There is no malice or lack of ethics in this; parties to any agreement must look out for their own interests. It is simply that publishers, based on their years of experience, are acutely aware of the pitfalls of publishing, and authors usually are not. Nor will a lawyer be of much help to an author, unless he knows the publishing business.

Many authors of trade books (that is, books of general interest) use the services of literary agents, most of whom have a solid knowledge of trade book publishing, and who oversee their clients' relationships with publishers. Over the years, agents have played a significant role in getting authors a fairer deal from publishers. A recent example is their success in persuading many publishers to provide authors with insurance against losses from libel suits. However, since most literary agents are reluctant to take unpublished authors as clients, they are of limited help to those who need it most. Furthermore, authors of textbooks, professional books, and scholarly books rarely use the services of literary agents, primarily because agents do not have the knowledge and experience to evaluate projects for these more specialized markets.

The Authors Guild, which was also instrumental in getting libel insurance protection for authors, plays a valuable role in author-publisher relations by educating members through its quarterly bulletin, through the work of its special committees and seminars, and by taking public positions on unfair practices. However, membership in the Guild is limited to authors who are published or who have books under contract, again leaving those who most need help without professional guidance. In addition, most members are authors of trade books, and issues of concern to professional and textbook authors are not addressed by the Guild unless they also happen to be of interest to the majority of its members.

The chapters ahead explain the whole publishing process, from manuscript development through publication and sale, with an emphasis on issues that are vital to authors. These issues are examined from the point of view of both author and publisher, so that an author can understand the reasons for certain publishing practices and either accept them or suggest practical alternatives. By understanding the process and the issues, authors may be better able to write publishable manuscripts, select the right publishers for their projects, negotiate better publishing terms, and in so doing, be more fully rewarded for their creative work.

Chapter 2

Books,
Book Markets,
and Types
of Publishing:
an Orientation

Book publishing encompasses a variety of publishing ventures that are in many ways different businesses. There is trade book publishing, textbook publishing, publishing of professional and scholarly books, encyclopedia publishing, and each of these in turn consists of further subdivisions. For example, trade books include adult trade, juvenile, and religious books. Textbook publishers may publish for the elementary school, high school, or college markets. Medical and legal books are separate types of professional publishing. Some publishers do just one kind of publishing, while others are active in two or more areas.

The key differences among these types of publishing lie in the markets for which they publish and the techniques employed in reaching those markets. How this affects authors will be highlighted in the following sections.

TRADE BOOKS

Trade books are those written for the general public and are sold primarily through retail bookstores, department stores, specialty stores (pet shops, garden centers, sporting goods stores, and so forth), and book clubs; and they are sold to libraries. Retail stores and libraries may order directly from each publisher, or if they prefer, through book wholesalers (who serve as regional sources for trade, professional, and scholarly books).

Large trade publishers have their own sales forces that call on bookstores and wholesalers as well as department stores and specialty stores. Smaller trade publishers use independent commissioned sales people who represent a number of publishers or they arrange to have their books sold by the sales force of another, larger publisher.

Timing

Most trade publishers group their new books into spring and fall lists, though some publish a third-season list. The spring list is published from January through May and the fall list from September until mid-November. Very few trade books are published during the summer months because book sales are generally slow then, and few are published in late November and December because bookstores do not want to handle new books once the Christmas selling season begins. Spring and fall lists are sold by the sales forces months in advance of publication, with the objective of getting sizable orders from as many accounts as possible prior to publication.

In other types of publishing, the publication date is generally considered the date when finished books are available for shipment from the publisher's warehouse. In trade book publishing, however, the publication date is usually six weeks after finished books are scheduled to be available. The books are then shipped to book reviewers and bookstores as soon as available, and, if all goes very well, reviews will appear in newspapers on or near the day the book is officially published, and bookstores will then have the book on their shelves. Publishers also schedule the initial advertising (often the only advertising) for the publication date, and sometimes even a press conference for the author. Trade publishers plan publication days as events—and hope that is what they turn out to be.

Timing is such a critical factor in trade publishing that effective production scheduling is very important, and it is essential to be sensitive and responsive to the publisher's deadlines for turning in manuscripts, processing proofs, and so on. Delays are frequently damaging to sales, and they can be disastrous for a book of timely importance, or a book that has a special seasonal appeal, as a Christmas gift, for summer activities, or the like.

Libraries

Libraries are an important market for trade books, and account for 10 percent of the copies of trade books sold. However, about 80 percent of their purchases are made indirectly, through wholesalers. As a result, libraries are a phantom market to publishers, who have little idea how many copies of any title or what portion of their entire business is done with any one library or with libraries in general. Unfortunately, this tends to make publishers insensitive to the library market. There are a number of different kinds of libraries, each of which buys a different mix of books. Academic libraries at colleges and universities and public libraries, are both large purchasers of trade and professional books. There are also libraries in schools that purchase large quantities of juveniles and special libraries (serving businesses, government agencies, research facilities, museums, medical facilities, law offices, and so forth) which purchase a good number of trade and professional books of all kinds.

Returns

A burdensome but seemingly necessary practice throughout the book industry is that unsold books in bookstores and at wholesalers may be returned for credit. It seems necessary so that bookstores can stock books they have no assurance they can sell. The packing and shipping costs back and forth, however, are burdensome to all concerned, especially to publishers. Furthermore, most returned books are somewhat scuffed, and need new jackets if they are to be resold, or may be too damaged by their travels to be resold at all. In addition, there is paperwork for the original sale, and more paperwork to credit the accounts for the returns. The result is much activity and expense, but no income for publishers or booksellers and no royalties to authors.

Returns are a major problem for trade books. Although the volume of returns differs from book to book and from year to year, it is likely to average between 12 and 25 percent of sales, and on an individual book may be much higher. Although the processing of returns is costly for everyone, no one as yet has found a good solution to the problem. However, as more and more bookstores install computer systems that record sales and inventory information, stores will place smaller but more frequent orders based on historical sales information, and the volume of returns is almost certain to diminish. Most trade publishers hold back a portion of their authors' royalties, usually 15 percent, in anticipation of heavy returns.

Bookstore Chains

In trade book publishing today, a major factor is the growth and importance of bookstore chains. Two in particular, B. Dalton Booksellers and Waldenbooks, each with over 700 stores, now hold dominant positions in the retail book business and in some areas represent a threat to independently owned stores. The chains, located primarily in shopping centers and malls, place all initial orders for new books from their central office, and the decisions of the large chains to take or not take a new book can make the difference between its success and failure, not only because of the number of stores they control, but also because they are aggressive marketers. As a result, some publishers will occasionally call the chain marketing director in advance of signing up a book to determine if the chain will be likely to order it. Publishers and authors are concerned that this can give the chains an editorial veto over what is published. However, to the extent that chains make it easier to determine what books the market can absorb, their size would appear to be beneficial. In addition, the chains have outlets in many areas not previously served by bookstores, some of which probably could not have been served profitably by privately owned stores which often lack the efficiency of the chains. On balance, therefore, the growth of bookstore chains has been good for trade publishers and good for authors.

Book Surplus

There is little doubt that one of the problems plaguing the book industry, and trade book publishing in particular, is that more books are published than the market can absorb in profitable quantities. There are in excess of 600,000 books of all kinds in print, and over forty thousand new books and new editions are published each year. About one-third of these are trade books. There are limited dollars and limited hours available for purchasing and reading of books, especially in competition with the free and effortless entertainment offered by television. There is limited shelf space in retail stores on which to display the many good books already in print and the flood of new titles published each year. And finally, the number of people who are regular trade book buyers is but a small fraction of the population. However, unless the federal government can be persuaded to pay authors and publishers to reduce the size of their annual output, as they do farmers, this would appear to be a problem that can only be held in check by the operation of the free market and the failures that result from too many books chasing too few readers.

This superabundance of books, especially those written for the general reader, certainly contributes to the problems trade book authors face in attempting to earn a living from their writing.

Adult Trade

These are books of general interest to adult readers—fiction, memoirs of well-known persons or events, biography, popular science, mysteries, adventure, romance, travel, recreation, health, hobbies, cookbooks, and popular reference works of all types.

Some of these are "backlist" books—that is, books that enjoy modest but steady sales over a number of years. These provide publishers with a base of continuing income. Fiction, biography, memoirs, and fad-type books (sometimes referred to as nonbooks) are generally "frontlist" books, that is, books that will usually have a life of between six and twelve months, and some of which, for reasons not always well understood, may make the various best-seller lists for a period of time (and may even become backlist). These frontlist books are the books whose sales are most difficult to predict. Even the most experienced editors are regularly surprised both by dramatic successes and equally dramatic failures.

Juveniles

Books written for young people are a separate and important part of trade book publishing. Within a publishing house, these books are published by a separate editorial unit that understands the interests and language skills of children. However, juvenile books are usually marketed by the same sales force and advertising and promotion staffs as adult trade books. Juveniles are usually written and advertised for specific age groups, such as ages two to five, six to eight, eight to twelve, and twelve and up. Books for the youngest group consist more of illustrations than text, and the proportion of illustrations decreases as the age of the group for which they are written increases. Publishers like to select the illustrators for juvenile books, so it is best to avoid making commitments to illustrators prior to getting a publisher's approval. Although there are occasional best sellers, books for juveniles usually have modest but steady sales, and sales to school and public libraries are especially important. Because juvenile books suffer a good deal of abuse in schools and libraries, they are usually published in library editions (with reinforced bindings) as well as in trade editions for sale through bookstores. There may also be a paperback edition sold through bookstores.

Religious Books

This is another large and generally lucrative kind of publishing. A number of trade houses such as Harper & Row, Prentice-Hall, William Morrow, and others have religious book departments and publishing programs, but the majority of religious books are published by houses specializing in them. Many of these are denominational and affiliated with the major Christian and Jewish groups, but a number are not. Their books include not only Bibles, hymnals, prayer books, and books on theology, but also books on social problems, and inspirational books that sometimes sell hundreds of thousands of copies. As one might imagine, the Bible is the all-time best seller among books, and is available in many versions, and in editions specially bound for every sacred occasion and family event. Religious books of broad interest are sold by general bookstores, but religious bookstores are responsible for a major portion of their sales.

Trade Paperbacks

Not to be confused with mass-market paperbacks found in racks in drugstores and supermarkets, trade paperbacks are sold through retail bookstores and are identical to traditional trade books except that they are bound in soft covers and sold at lower prices. The lower price is made possible in part by the cheaper binding, but also by the expectation that a lower price will enlarge the market, making the lower price feasible. In practice, sometimes it does and sometimes it doesn't.

Trade paperbacks may be published simultaneously with the hard-cover edition, or they may be published months or even years later. If the publisher believes there is a two-tier market, that is, a library, bookstore, and mail-order market for the hard-cover edition, and a price-sensitive trade market for a trade paperback edition, the publisher may publish both editions at the same time. Otherwise, he is likely to wait until the hard-cover edition has had a good sale before issuing the paperback.

In some publishing houses, there is a separate department responsible for trade paperbacks, but in others they are handled by the department publishing the hard-cover edition. Libraries do not like trade paperbacks because they are not as durable as hard-cover books, and book reviewers are less likely to review them, which explains in part why they have not entirely replaced hard-cover books.

Imprints

Some trade book publishing houses include an editorial "imprint" division, a semiautonomous editorial unit. An editor, usually one with a distinguished record and a group of loyal authors, runs an independent editorial enterprise that signs up authors and develops and edits projects which are then turned over to the publishing house for production, marketing, and order processing. The books are published under the joint imprint of the editor or editors and the publishing house. Examples are "A Cornelia and Michael Bessie Book, Harper & Row, Publishers" or "A Helen and Kurt Wolff Book, Harcourt Brace Jovanovich, Publishers." In exchange for their editorial services, the editorial imprint receives a portion of the profit generated by their books on some agreed-upon formula. These arrangements are attractive in those cases where first-class editors find the constraints of a large organization burdensome or intolerable, but lack the funds or the desire to establish their own publishing house.

Editors with their own imprints frequently provide more editorial guidance and polish, but there is also a risk that their books may be treated as stepchildren and receive less attention, or that the separateness of their programs will result in poorer coordination of editorial, production, and marketing operations that is so critical to effective publishing. And if there is a logjam in production, are the imprint books more likely to be delayed? This depends largely on the ability and aggressiveness of the editor.

Packagers

Trade book houses also use "packagers" who are not affiliated with any one publishing house. The packager, often a former editor, will typically develop an idea for a book, usually a complex nonfiction book requiring a lot of illustrations, and then find an author with whom to work in creating it. Armed with a book proposal, the packager will then seek a publisher for the project, and will either contract to deliver an edited manuscript, or a designed and typeset book ready for printing, or even bound books. If the publisher handles the printing and binding, the publisher will normally pay the packager a royalty on sales. If the packager delivers bound books, the publisher pays a fixed amount per copy as agreed in advance. In either case, the packager usually wants an advance large enough to cover expenses, including payment to the author, and at least a small profit.

Working with packagers has its advantages, since they provide both the ideas for books and their publishers, but because of that, packagers pay authors less than they would normally receive working directly with publishers on the same projects. It is probably useful to know some packagers in order to be considered for their projects. A number of them are listed in *Literary Market Place* under the heading of "Book Producers."

MASS-MARKET PAPERBACKS

Mass-market paperbacks are low-cost editions of trade books produced in large quantities, and distributed primarily through independent distributors and jobbers who stock racks in drugstores, supermarkets, newsstands, and chain stores. They are also sold through retail bookstores and stores serving colleges and universities, where paperbacks are frequently used as textbooks or for supplementary reading. It is through these widely available lower-priced editions that trade books have the opportunity to reach a truly large readership, with sales in the millions of copies.

For many years, most mass-market paperback publishers were independent houses, who purchased the rights to publish mass paperback editions of successful hard-cover books as well as publishing original editions of mysteries, westerns, and romances. Today most mass paperback publishers are owned by publishing conglomerates, but they still compete openly for the mass paperback rights, and trade publishers will sell the rights to the highest bidder even if a mass-market paperback house is owned by their parent organization.

Mass-market paperbacks are reset in a smaller type size and in a smaller format that will fit into a paperback rack, and they are printed on less expensive paper in a long press run of 100,000 copies or more. Usually the entire press run is sent out to the distributors, who place a portion of them into display racks, displacing other titles that are no longer selling well. If the distributor still has an excessive stock of these displaced titles, he tears off the covers and returns them to the publisher for credit, and destroys what remains of the books. A mass paperback publisher may print and distribute 500,000 copies of a work, and end up selling only 300,000 copies. (There have been a few unfortunate cases of distributors selling books without covers, or counterfeiting covers and returning them to publishers for credit.)

Mass-market paperback publishers purchase the rights to a paperback edition from the original publisher for an advance against royalties—usually 6 to 8 percent of the list price of all copies sold, sometimes stepping up to 10 percent on sales in excess of 150,000 copies. This income is usually divided equally between the original publisher and the author. In the 1970s, due to highly competitive auctions, books that were best sellers in their hard-cover editions were being purchased for advances in excess of a million dollars. In 1981, Pocket Books paid $2.3 million for John Irving's *The Hotel New Hampshire* and later reported a loss of $1 million on the book. Nevertheless, some paperbacks have had phenomenal sales by book industry standards. Mario Puzo's *The Godfather* sold 14 million copies over the life of the paperback edition, Eric Segal's *Love Story* sold over 10 million copies, and *The Thorn Birds* sold over 4 million copies. Sales of these magnitudes will support advances in excess of a million dollars, but given that advances are not returnable, what if a book doesn't achieve a large enough sale to cover the advance? The mass-market paperback publisher can suffer big losses, and that is what happened increasingly during the late 1970s and early 1980s.

Paperback publishers have done original publishing, especially of mysteries, romances, and westerns for many years. Recently, however, as the purchase of paperback rights at auctions became more and more perilous, paperback publishers began competing with hard-cover publishers in signing up authors directly, and either publishing a hard-cover edition themselves, or selling the rights to the hard-cover edition to a trade publisher, or forgoing the hard-cover edition entirely. If a book is likely to have a modest sale in hardcovers and a large sale in paperback, it will generally be more rewarding to have it published by a paperback house at the outset. This is discussed in greater detail in Chapter 6 on selecting a publisher. Thus, in the struggle to survive, trade publishing and mass-market paperback publishing have been moving into each other's territory. In the 1950s, publishing was highly structured. Trade book publishers produced hard-cover trade books, and sold the rights to paperback editions to mass paperback publishers. Mass-market paperbacks were sold through different outlets than hard-cover books. Currently, trade publishers are not only publishing trade paperbacks, at least one publisher is experimenting with the publication of its own mass-market paperbacks. And the mass-market paperback publishers are moving increasingly into the areas once served only by the trade book publishers both editorially and in marketing to retail outlets. Whether each of these types of publishers will successfully master the other's business remains to be seen.

TECHNICAL AND PROFESSIONAL BOOKS

These are books written for people who are seeking additional information about their chosen vocation—books for accountants, engineers, architects, contractors, business managers and executives, doctors, lawyers, computer technicians, programmers, and so forth.

Although editors of technical and professional books know a good deal about the markets for their publishing programs, the content of such works is usually too specialized for them to evaluate alone. Therefore, editors pay outside consultants who are experts in their fields to advise them on book proposals and manuscripts. The editor's role is to judge how a project will sell based on the technical appraisal of its content by his or her advisors.

Professional books sell well through retail and college bookstores, and to company and academic libraries. The more specialized books are usually stocked by only a small number of stores in places with a relatively large population of technical and professional people. They are sold by publishers' representatives usually specializing in these types of books. If a house publishes both trade and professional books, both lines may be handled by the same or by separate sales forces.

Direct-mail campaigns are vital to the successful marketing of technical and professional books. They not only result in orders by mail, but also account for many of the sales to libraries and through bookstores, since a person receiving the mailing may ask the company librarian to order the work, or go to a bookstore to acquire it.

There is also an international market for certain kinds of professional books—those in fields in which practices and standards are not significantly different in other countries. By contrast, some engineering books, for example, are burdened by differences in engineering and building codes, and by our use of the English system of measurement versus the metric system. And books on accounting and law have almost no international sales since they are based on U.S. law. On the other hand, books on electronics, computers, management, and architecture, to mention a few, enjoy excellent international sales.

Among professional publishers is a small group of technical and scientific houses who publish highly specialized books in the physical and biological sciences, as well as scientific periodicals. Since most university presses do not publish scholarly works in the sciences, these publishers serve as the university presses of the scientific community. Because of the high costs of typesetting technical books and the small markets that exist for them domestically, they are heavily dependent on international sales for their survival.

Law books present a special problem, because in every area of law, the most recent court decision can be an important precedent in a current case. Therefore, to be useful, law books must be as up to date as possible, yet it is impractical to revise them every few months. The most common solution is to provide supplements on a subscription basis that fit into a pocket at the back of the book. Publishing contracts for law books stipulate that the author will provide updating material for these supplements, and a portion of the author's royalties is based on the income from their sale. In fact, because most law books do not have large sales, the sale of supplements is an important part of the publisher's and author's income.

One favorable feature of publishing professional books is that, unlike trade book buyers, professional people are willing to pay a high price for books. The cost can be treated as a business expense for tax purposes, and the value of the information is usually well in excess of the price of the book. In addition, many professional books sell steadily for years and can be a long-term source of income for their authors.

TEXTBOOKS

Although the general public is most aware of trade book publishing and its best sellers, the textbook segment of the publishing industry is actually the largest. Many large companies publish texts for both schools (elementary and high school) and colleges, but these are actually very different businesses, and there are few advantages to being active in both areas.

College Textbooks

These are for students taking specific courses in colleges and universities. They are sold by salaried representatives who call on instructors to promote their list of titles and arrange for them to receive sample copies of texts for the courses they teach. The instructors then select from among the many texts available the ones that most closely fit their needs. They notify the college bookstores of their selections and the number of students they expect in the courses. The bookstores then order the texts from the publishers. And the students buy the texts that are required for the courses they have enrolled in. (College publishing is unusual in that the person who buys the product is different from the person who chooses it.)

International sales may be significant, depending on the subject, the academic level of the text, and the reputation of the author. (International sales are discussed further at the end of this chapter.)

Representatives are also the eyes and ears of the editorial staff, reporting not only on changing trends within the curriculum and needs for texts with different approaches, but also on instructors who either might be encouraged to prepare a new text or who may already have one in preparation. Anyone writing a new text or interested in doing so may be encouraged to submit an outline and sample material to the appropriate editor in the home office. Since it is impractical for editors to be experts in the range of subjects for which they are responsible, editors use advisors—usually instructors who teach the courses for whom the texts are being written, and who have demonstrated good judgment about trends and needs. The editor sends the sample material to one or more of these advisors, and then makes a decision to publish or not publish a work based on their reviews.

Textbooks are frequently published with separate materials to supplement the book and make it easier to use. Some of these supplements are profitable; others are not but are considered part of the cost of strengthening a textbook's position among competing books. Because of the high stakes, textbooks for the big freshman-level college courses are likely to have more supplementary materials than texts for more advanced courses with smaller enrollments. Among the materials that may supplement texts are soft cover books of readings, for purchase by students, containing selections that students might otherwise have to find in the library in a number of different volumes. Texts also frequently have instructors' manuals on how to use the text most effectively, as well as tests and solution manuals all of which are usually free to instructors. Some texts will have study guides that are for sale to students to help them in using the text. Accounting textbooks usually have practice sets, and some texts have overhead transparencies or filmstrips as teaching aids. All of these materials are developed to make a textbook more attractive to the instructor.

Introductory texts with large sales potential are usually heavily illustrated with photographs and drawings that are to be provided by the author, unless the publisher agrees to provide them.

One of the problems in publishing and distributing college textbooks is the large secondhand market. There are several organizations that buy up used textbooks from students at the end of each year at a fraction of their original price, and resell them to college stores who in turn sell them to students for several dollars less than the price of new texts. College textbook publishers deplore this secondhand market, because it drastically reduces the sales of textbooks after their first year, and authors naturally also suffer since they receive no royalties on the second and third sales of their books. However, students pay high prices for new books, and there is no good reason why such books should not be reused. Perhaps publishers should engage in the repurchase and resale of their own books and pay authors a small royalty on the resales. Publishers attempt to minimize the resale problem by publishing revised editions as frequently as practical, usually every four or five years, in order to make the used books obsolete. Revisions are made to bring the material up to date and sometimes the quality of the design and production is upgraded to make the text more competitive, but frequently the only socially redeeming value in a new edition is the added employment it provides typesetters.

College textbook publishing also suffers from a high level of returns, because college bookstores have difficulty predicting sales volume. There are a number of reasons for this. Instructors have a tendency to overestimate enrollments. Some students taking a course don't buy texts. Occasionally instructors will tell the bookstore that a given text is required, then tell their classes that it is only recommended. In addition, if the text has been out for a year or more, the bookstore will probably be stocking both new and used books—and the used books will sell out first. Finally, if there is more than one bookstore serving the campus, which is frequently the case, both stores may order enough books for a majority of the enrollment in each course, because if one store runs out of books, the other store gets the business. These conditions taken together cause very heavy returns in a market where the needs should be quite predictable.

Elementary and High School Textbooks

These are for students in classes from kindergarten through grade twelve. El-hi publishers play a major role in determining the content of these texts, and generally speaking, it is not a business in which a teacher submits sample material to a publisher and is given a contract for its development and publication. More commonly, a publisher decides, after a good deal of research, that it wants to develop a book or a program of books of a certain type for some part of the school curriculum. It will then seek out one or more members of the educational community, perhaps curriculum supervisors, to work with the publisher in developing those materials. At the elementary-school level, the project is most likely to be a whole program of coordinated books for grades one through four in math, for example, or grades six through eight in science or social studies. Millions of dollars are then invested in editorial work, design, artwork, and composition in an effort to make the new program as competitive as possible both in instructional content and visual appeal. These works usually include teachers' editions that carry annotated instructions for the teacher in the margins, or have a separate insert of instructions to the teacher bound into the volumes.

At the high school level, individual books are more common than programs. However, the stakes are high in these individual books as well, so a good deal is invested in their development.

The marketing of el-hi textbooks differs from state to state depending on state law. In some states, texts are selected and purchased by the state; in others, the decisions are made by city or county school systems either wholly on their own initiative or from a list approved at the state level; and in yet others, the decisions are made at the individual schools. Where the state does the purchasing, individual school systems will be polled regarding their preferences, and then a state textbook committee makes the final decision. That decision may be in favor of a single title, or four or five titles from which the individual school systems can make their choice. Some states require by law that the publisher maintain an inventory of the selected texts within the state; typically, the inventory is held in state-owned textbook depositories prior to being ordered by the individual schools. Depositories usually order books for delivery in the spring, but the books are not paid for until the following November or December—and the state only pays for copies that are distributed to schools, not for those that may still remain in the depository.

The texts are sold by salaried representatives who call on instructors, department heads, curriculum supervisors, members of textbook selection committees, and anyone else who has a voice in determining the textbooks to be used in a state or school system. Representatives must also be prepared to give elaborate presentations to textbook committees, detailing how their book differs from the competing texts.

Both states and school systems usually go through the textbook selection process about once every four years for each course or program of courses, and prior to the selection is the time of peak selling activity. The size of the sales effort depends on the state, but when a state such as Texas is about to select a text, it is not uncommon for publishers to put their entire sales forces into the state. When a text is finally selected, the publisher signs a contract with the state or school system that specifies the price at which the texts are to be bought for the entire period of the contract. These contracts can be painful during periods of high inflation, especially if small reprints are required.

Once purchased, the textbooks are owned by the state or the local school system or school, and are loaned to the students each year. As a result, the publisher of an adopted textbook has a large sale in the first year, and then small sales of replacement copies for lost and damaged books in the following three or four years. However, workbooks are a publisher's delight since they must be reordered every year.

A complication in el-hi publishing is that when a publisher brings out a new edition of a book or a program, which he will normally do about every four years, the company must still keep the old edition in print so long as there are any adoption contracts in force.

Sometimes a state likes a publisher's book, with the exception of a few items or sections in the book. In such cases, because of the size of the state markets, it is not uncommon for the publisher to modify the book to meet the desires of the state, and that modified version then becomes a special edition for that state, and known, for example, as the Texas edition or the North Carolina edition. (Some years ago, one state that disapproved of an amendment to the Constitution would only purchase a civics text that omitted it. The publisher took out the offending amendment.) Authors may object to the requested changes, but they normally agree to them for the sake of the sale.

School textbooks usually have no sales at all through wholesalers, trade bookstores, and by direct mail, and few sales in international markets.

MAIL-ORDER PUBLISHING

Although many trade books, textbooks, and professional books can be sold in some quantities by direct mail, there is also a special kind of publishing in which mail-order selling is the dominant marketing technique. These are books that are carefully designed to appeal to a large audience whose names are readily available on a mailing list of at least several million names. The books, usually printed in full color, can be either single, large, expensive books or a whole program of books at a relatively lower price, such as *The Southern Living Cookbook Library*. As in this example, many of these publishing programs are built around magazine subscription lists and are related to the magazines' contents. From readership surveys the publisher knows those features in the magazine that are popular with the subscribers, and the subscribers know what to expect when they are offered a book by the publisher of that magazine.

These programs can be very successful, but they are also high risk ventures for the publisher, since success or failure can turn on a very small difference in the percentage of responses to the mail-order offering—for example, the difference between 3 and 2½ percent.

BOOK CLUBS

Book clubs are really a special type of mail-order selling, in which the club offers prospective members a book free or at a very low price, plus periodic selections at a discount from the publisher's list price, in exchange for the member's agreement to take a specified number of selections each year.

There are a wide variety of clubs, from the Literary Guild and the Book-of-the-Month Club, which offer trade adult books, to highly specialized clubs for engineers, scientists, writers, accountants, and so forth. Most clubs today are operated by book publishers, but none limit their selections to books they publish, instead acquiring the book club rights from other publishers whenever books are available that will be of interest to their memberships. The club purchases the rights in return for a royalty on sales to members and an advance against those royalties.

Book clubs can play an important role in the marketing of trade and professional books, and occasionally of scholarly works. Textbooks are rarely book club selections.

UNIVERSITY PRESSES

University presses play a small but important role in the world of publishing, since they publish works of academic value that, because of their limited markets, probably would not be published by commercial publishers. Whereas a commercial publisher is primarily concerned with the marketability of a manuscript, the university press is primarily concerned with its scholarship and originality.

University presses play an especially valuable role for the academic community whose members find it necessary to publish scholarly works in order to establish their reputations and advance professionally. However, as noted earlier, they do not generally publish scientific works, leaving these to the small group of commercial publishers who specialize in science and technology.

Many publishing ventures are unprofitable, but university presses are nonprofit by plan, a situation made possible by the financial support they receive from their universities. This may take the form of free rent, light, heat, and other miscellaneous services, or the annual provision for a deficit of a given size, or both. Also, some university presses have endowments. In addition, a press may seek and obtain funds from another university or from a foundation for a specific project in which that organization has an interest.

The financial support that university presses receive enables them to publish books that will sell as few as one or two thousand copies, whereas commercial publishers will rarely publish works whose expected sales are less than five thousand.

Literary Market Place lists eighty-two university presses, some of whom publish only a half dozen books a year, while a few large presses such as Princeton, Harvard, and Columbia publish over 100 books a year, and are in many ways indistinguishable from commercial houses.

University presses, especially those affiliated with state universities, also frequently serve as publishers of works of regional interest—books on local history and natural history, regional cooking, and biographies of regional heroes and statesmen. While these works must be academically sound for acceptance by a university press, they may be written in a more popular style, less encumbered by the trappings of scholarship. Occasionally these works will achieve exceptionally large sales. For example, *Marion Brown's Southern Cookbook*, published by the University of North Carolina Press, has sold over half a million copies since its first publication in 1951. And some books that are assumed to have limited academic appeal enjoy a very large sale, such as Eudora Welty's *One Writer's Beginnings*, which was published in 1984 by Harvard University Press and listed by *The New York Times* as number six on their hard-cover nonfiction best-seller list for 1984.

Although university presses generally do not publish textbooks and are not set up to market them, some will on occasion publish senior or graduate-level textbooks whose potential sales are too modest to interest a commercial publisher. Because of their specialized nature and the limited competition, these books do not need the efforts of a sales force and can be sold to the college market by direct mail.

A majority of the works published by each press is prepared by the faculty at the university with which the press is affiliated, but faculty members and the university press are not limited to working with each other. Instructors frequently publish with presses at other institutions if they have established programs in the authors' fields, and some presses seek out works on other campuses.

University presses also publish paperback editions of books being discontinued by commercial publishers if the works have continuing sales as texts or supplementary readings. And they may serve as distributors of books and periodicals developed by learned societies.

Manuscripts submitted to a university press are critically reviewed by several authorities in the field who may or may not be members of the faculty at the university. If these reviews are favorable, it is then considered by the press's editorial board, which is made up of members of the university faculty, and only those works that the board considers academically sound are approved for publication. In that regard, the publication by a university press is more a seal of approval than commercial publication.

University presses employ the same marketing techniques as commercial publishers. They normally have sales representatives calling on bookstores and wholesalers (who in turn sell to the important library market); they employ direct mail to reach the academic faculties; and they usually use export sales agencies for the international markets.

ENCYCLOPEDIAS

There are a variety of works published that are called encyclopedias. Some are single-volume reference works, organized alphabetically, for either the general public or for professional audiences. Examples of popular works are the *Encyclopedia of Gardening* and the *Illustrated Encyclopedia of Animals*. For professionals, there is for example, the *Encyclopedia of Professional Management* and the *Encyclopedia of Instrumentation and Control*. These volumes may be collective works with many contributors, or they may be the work of a single author. Encyclopedias of this type are marketed through bookstores and by direct mail as though they were trade or professional books—and, indeed, that is what they really are. A single author or an editor in chief responsible for overseeing contributions is usually paid a royalty and can make out well financially. Contributors are usually paid a small fee either by the publisher or by the editor in chief from an advance against royalty earnings.

Other encyclopedias are large multi-volume reference works either on all branches of knowledge such as *The Encyclopaedia Britannica* or covering a more limited area such as in the *Encyclopedia of Science and Technology*. Because of their size and scope, these sets of necessity are the work of many contributors and consultants, and require investments of many millions of dollars. General encyclopedias are sold by large sales forces calling on libraries, schools, and door-to-door on individual families. The more specialized multi-volume encyclopedias are also sold to libraries and educational institutions, but rely on direct mail to reach individual buyers. Attempts to sell multi-volume encyclopedias through bookstores have generally been unsuccessful. In recent years, sales directly to individual homes have been made more difficult by Federal Trade Commission regulations that permit purchasers to reconsider and cancel their orders within a given period of time.

INTERNATIONAL MARKETS

Trade books, technical and professional books, college textbooks, scholarly books, mail-order books, and encyclopedias all have potential international sales in their U.S. editions, the size of which depends on the subject matter and the level of each book. Generally speaking, books at the craftsman and technician levels have poorer international sales than higher level books, because cultural, procedural and terminological differences are too great. For example, medical books have a good international sale, but nursing books do not; some engineering books have a good international sale, but building trades books do not. Trade books will have good sales in English-speaking countries, but poor sales in their English-language edition in the rest of the world. In contrast, advanced textbooks, professional, scientific, and scholarly books will generally have some sales even in countries where English is not the indigenous language, because English has become the second language for educated persons throughout the world.

Effective marketing to international markets, however, is no easy task. Sales are plagued by currency regulations and fluctuations, credit problems, customs regulations and duties, unreliable postal systems, theft, and the logistical problems of delivering books in a reasonable time. In short, it is a business for specialists.

Publishers solve the problems of international sales in a variety of ways depending on the volume of sales they expect to generate in each area or country. Larger companies may operate their own subsidiaries in their larger markets such as in Canada, the United Kingdom, Australia, New Zealand, and possibly South Africa and a few other major markets. In the balance of the world, they generally use regional sales representatives, book export agents, or have arrangements with other publishers to stock and promote their books. Small publishers rely almost entirely on the services of export agents and wholesalers who serve international markets. Many medium-sized publishers develop a crazy quilt of arrangements that looks disorganized and haphazard, but which nevertheless may represent their best way of reaching each segment of the international markets.

In addition to the sale of U.S. editions, most publishers try to sell translation rights to foreign publishers for foreign-language editions, and it is through these foreign-language editions that maximum penetration of international markets is achieved. In addition, adaptations of U.S. editions are sometimes made for other English-speaking countries that are, in effect, cultural translations. For example, a text on economics may be rewritten for the British market, incorporating their currency, banking and economic system, and their laws and regulations.

The foregoing suggests a rational neatness in publishing as in, "A place for everything, and everything in its place." It is not always so. Some professional books, especially business books, have a broad enough sale to be treated as trade books. Some trade books are used as textbooks, especially in the humanities and social sciences. The same is true of professional books; medical books, for example, are generally treated as both professional books and textbooks. And some textbooks, especially advanced texts in the sciences and engineering, occasionally sell well to scientists and engineers. These are exceptions that cannot generally be counted on, but neither should they be ignored, since they represent extra opportunities for sales, and extra income for both publisher and author.

Chapter 3

The Financial Rewards of Publishing

Although few people write books solely to make money, professional writers need it to pay their bills, for additional income to help send children to college, to buy a new car or boat (of better yet, a new car *and* boat), or at the very least to cover out-of-pocket expenses incurred while writing. How do you get paid for your work, and what can you expect to make by writing books? Do publishers keep an unfair share of the income from their authors' work?

These are the questions we will be examining in this chapter.

HOW AUTHORS FARE

Because the media tend to publicize the unusual, many people believe that authors make a great deal of money. It is true, of course, that the authors of very successful books—trade books, professional books, and textbooks alike—make out very well, just as do those at the top of their professions in sports, business, medicine and law. But these are the exceptions. On average, authors do not get rich writing books.

Authors are generally paid by getting a share of what their publishers receive from selling copies of their books, and a share of what their publishers receive from selling subsidiary rights—the rights granted to others to prepare other editions or forms of the work, such as book club editions, paperback editions, foreign language editions, dramatizations, and so forth.

On hard-cover trade books, the author's share, or royalty, is usually between 10 and 15 percent of the list price of all copies sold, and at least 50 percent of the publisher's receipts from the sale of subsidiary rights. Although royalty arrangements are usually much more complex than this (different rates for different kinds of sales are spelled out in Chapter 11), these simplified terms will provide a rough guide to an author's earnings. For example, assuming a royalty of 10 percent of the list price on a 350-page trade book selling fifteen thousand copies at $18, an author will earn $27,000 from the sale of copies, and perhaps an additional $13,000 from the sale of subsidiary rights, for a total of $40,000 for a book that may have required two or more years of work. On the other hand, if the book sells only five thousand copies, the author will earn only $9,000 from the sale of copies, and perhaps only $2,000 from the sale of subsidiary rights, for a total of $11,000. Since there is no way of knowing in advance how well any book will sell, book authors cannot know how well they are to be paid until long after the work is completed.

A study sponsored by the Author's Guild Foundation surveyed a large number of book authors, the majority of whom were members of the Guild, regarding income earned in 1979. Much of the data is difficult to evaluate, because some book authors write primarily as a hobby, and may write part time either to supplement their income or for professional advancement. An academician, for example, may write mainly to advance a particular thesis or for professional recognition; a consultant may write to gain a reputation as an authority and increase business. For these reasons, the royalty earnings of part-time authors do not tell us very much.

However, the survey data on authors whose sole income was derived from writing books is more significant, since we can assume that most of these authors were striving for commercial success and a reasonably good standard of living. The median income of this group was $6 per hour and $11,000 a year. In order to earn this hourly rate annually, they would have to work 7½ hours a day for five days a week, forty-nine weeks a year. On average, therefore, these authors were writing full time. This income is considerably less than an entry-level postal worker earns at work requiring no advanced education and no special training or skill —and postal workers are entitled to pensions and other benefits paid for by the government, perquisites that authors must purchase themselves. Therefore, although writing books may provide nonfinancial rewards such as recognition or a flexible lifestyle, or provide part-time authors with a modest supplementary income, for most authors it is not a way to acquire wealth.

John Sayles, novelist and film-maker, said it well in a piece for the September 6, 1981, *New York Times Book Review:*

> *The money I got for my first novel came to around $2.50 an hour. I worked on a movie once where the producers wanted the screenplay so fast and so desperately that I made about $500 an hour. It wasn't any better than things I've never been able to sell. Getting paid for writing is a bad joke that has nothing to do with the value of what you've written. I feel that writing is its own reward, and anything beyond that, like getting published or making money, is a combination of luck, timing and advertising. Writing isn't easy, but it beats working for a living. If I stop doing it tomorrow, it will be because it isn't fun any more, and I hope whatever new job I get doesn't require that I get up too early.*

Although there is no survey data available on the amounts earned by authors of textbooks and professional books, a sampling of the sales achieved by books in these areas suggests that on average these authors fare little better than those responding to the Authors Guild survey.

HOW PUBLISHERS FARE

It is tempting to conclude from the Authors Guild data that publishers grossly underpay authors not only with respect to the amount of work involved in writing books, but also considering the money made by publishing them. In reality, from a business point of view, most publishers lead a hand-to-mouth existence. This is true for all types of publishing, but it is especially true for trade publishers. Key members of a publishing house may be well paid, because the publisher must compete not only with other publishing houses, but also with other industries, in hiring and keeping staff. Although an editor-in-chief in a trade publishing house may be making a handsome salary, the house itself may be barely breaking even or even losing money.

Some understanding of the financial side of publishing may not increase your sympathy for publishers, but it may shed some light on their policies and procedures.

Figure 3-1

SIMPLIFIED PROFIT AND LOSS STATEMENT

Typical Adult Trade Title Selling (a) 15,000 Copies, and (b) 10,000 Copies at a List Price of $18.

	15,000 COPIES		10,000 COPIES	
Sales	Amount	% of Sales	Amount	% of Sales
Net Sales	151,000	100.0	100,800	100.0
Cost of Sales				
Prepress Costs[1]	$15,000	9.9	$15,000	14.9
Paper, Presswork, Binding	45,000	29.8	33,000	32.7
Royalties (at 10% of list)	27,000	17.9	18,000	17.9
Total Cost of Sales	87,000	57.5	66,000	65.5
Gross Profit from Sales	64,200	42.5	34,800	34.5
Subsidiary Rights Income	25,000	16.5	15,000	14.9
Total Operating Income	89,200	59.0	49,800	49.4
Operating Expenses[2]				
Editorial	9,000	6.0	9,000	8.9
Production	3,000	2.0	3,000	3.0
Marketing	25,500	16.8	20,000	19.8
Order Processing	12,100	8.0	8,100	8.0
Administrative Costs	15,100	10.0	15,100	15.0
Total Operating Expense	64,700	42.8	55,200	54.7
Net Operating Profit (Loss)	24,500	16.2	(5,300)	(5.3)

1. *Prepress costs, sometimes called plant costs, are the one-time costs of editing the manuscript, designing the book, jacket, and cover, typesetting, and so forth—all the direct costs of producing the book up to the printing of copies.*
2. *Most publishers charge operating expenses to a book as a percentage of the book's net sales. If sales are lower than expected, a proportionately smaller share of operating expenses is charged to the title. However, with the exception of order, processing costs, including shipping, and, to a lesser extent, marketing costs, these expenses are actually fixed costs per title that do not increase or decrease with sales volume. As a consequence of assigning expenses on a percentage basis, unsuccessful books do not look as unprofitable nor very successful books as profitable to publishers as they actually are. If operating expenses in the above example were assigned in this fashion, the ten thousand-copy sale would show a profit of $6,600 instead of a loss of $5,300.*

Profits and Losses

Figure 3-1 is a simplified profit and loss statement on a hypothetical, moderately successful trade book. Although the book in this example is priced at $18, publishers sell to bookstores and wholesalers at discounts from their list prices ranging from 20 to 48 percent. In this example, the average discount is 44 percent, and the publisher's net price per copy is $10.08. The first column shows how the publisher makes out on a sale of fifteen thousand copies, and the second column shows what happens if he only sells ten thousand copies, in each case after paying the author a royalty of 10 percent of the list price on all copies sold.

As stated earlier, the author's earnings are the royalties on the sale of copies, plus his or her share of subsidiary rights income. If we assume for simplicity a 50-50 split in the rights income, then the author's share of the rights income is the same as the publisher's, and a comparison of the author's and the publisher's earnings can be summarized as follows:

	15,000-COPY SALE	10,000-COPY SALE
Royalty on Copy Sales	$27,000	$18,000
Share of Rights Income	25,000	15,000
Author's Total Royalty Income		
Before Expenses and Taxes	52,000	33,000
Publisher's Pretax Income	24,000	(5,300)

Authors must pay their own expenses, such as the cost of permissions and illustrations, stationery and supplies, books and subscriptions, files, telephone calls, postage, and travel, out of their royalty income. These may reduce the author's net income substantially.

Since this data assumes a royalty of 10 percent on all copies sold, which is low, and a 50-50 split in rights income, which is minimal, a negotiated agreement that is more favorable to the author would increase the author's income and decrease the publisher's income in both cases.

Note that the publisher's profit is very sensitive to sales volume and that a publisher is therefore strongly motivated to market each book as effectively as possible. However, it is also possible for a publisher to over-market a book; that is, to spend money on advertising and promotion that does not create enough additional sales to cover the additional costs, in which event the publisher actually reduces his profit from the project. Publishers' expenditures on advertising and promotion are one of the main areas of contention between authors and publishers. Authors, believing that their publisher has not done enough, always urge more advertising and promotion, while the publisher, remembering how easy and how painful it is to overspend, resists in order to preserve the fragile profit.

Note also that in the data in figure 3-1, the publisher would show a loss without the subsidiary rights income even on the sale of fifteen thousand copies. This is a normal situation for a trade publisher and explains why the subsidiary rights on trade books are so critical to the publisher as well as to the author.

Authors should also understand that publishers acquire and produce each book in the expectation of selling it at a certain price and quantity that will produce an adequate profit. The estimated cost of producing copies and the marketing plan for selling it are both based on that estimated sales volume. If the book sells less well than expected, the publisher's profit quickly disappears because the publisher has spent to support a sales volume that did not materialize. Conversely, if a book sells better than the publisher expected, the publishing profit is substantially greater because the publisher has spent for a lower level of sales than actually occurred. This point is important in negotiating a publishing agreement, because it means that a publisher has very little latitude to negotiate a higher royalty rate at or below his own sales estimate for the work, but considerably more latitude on the upside of his sales estimate. This subject will be dealt with further in the chapter on negotiating.

RELATIVE PROFITABILITY OF TYPES OF PUBLISHING

Trade Books

The average after-tax profit of trade book publishers is between 3 and 4 percent of sales, with the individual results of publishers generally ranging from 10 percent of net sales to very substantial losses. The rate of profit in trade book publishing is low because of several factors:

1. Although higher prices would theoretically produce higher profits if the same quantities were sold, trade book buyers are relatively sensitive to price, making it difficult to price books higher without adversely affecting sales. Most are already being priced at levels that preclude a truly large sale.

2. Trade books are sold at larger discounts to bookstores than

are professional books and textbooks—on average about 45 percent off the list price—discounts that are necessary to keep bookstores in business. However, the larger the discount, the less money the publisher receives.

3. Many more trade books are published each year than retail stores can accommodate and effectively sell, and more perhaps than readers are willing to buy and read, even if all the titles were available in bookstores.

College Texts

College textbooks can be more profitable than trade books for a variety of reasons.

1. There is less price resistance, since instructors select the texts and students pay for them. Although the prices of competing books are a constraint, it is easier to price texts to yield an adequate profit. And although it is possible for students to share textbooks, it is certainly less convenient.

2. Marketing is more efficient since it is only necessary to "sell" the instructor in order to sell books for an entire class; and the text, once sold, usually will be used for more than one year.

3. Sales are somewhat easier to predict because enrollments by course can be determined.

4. Bookstore discounts on college texts are usually only 20 to 25 percent—much smaller than discounts on trade books. This is feasible because textbooks are actually sold by the publisher's representatives rather than by the college bookstores, which serve more as distributors than retailers. This discount advantage is offset in part by the cost of free materials that must be provided and the cost of sample copies.

5. The costs of filling orders are lower because most book orders are for class-size quantities, and these larger quantities cost less per copy to bill and ship than smaller quantities. Thus, a smaller portion of the sales dollars received by college textbook publishers is spent on manufacturing, marketing, and order processing, and a larger share remains for profit.

Although these advantages are offset somewhat by relatively insignificant subsidiary rights income, college textbook publishing on average generates a net operating profit after taxes of about 9 percent of net sales, with individual publishers showing profits as high as 18 percent. Big textbook publishers are more profitable than small and medium-sized ones, even though bigness does not seem to result in greater profit among trade and professional publishers.

Professional and Technical Books

These are typically more profitable than trade books but less profitable than college texts. As mentioned earlier, the cost of purchasing these books can usually be treated as a business expense for tax purposes, and the value of the information should well exceed the price of the book. As a result, there is much less resistance to high prices, and publishers can price them to achieve a satisfactory return. On the other hand, professional and technical books must be sold in part by direct mail to individual prospects, and this means high marketing and order processing expenses.

RETURN ON INVESTMENT

The profit and loss statement, however, is only part of the financial story. Equally important—perhaps more important—are the investments required in book publishing. A publisher must pay out large amounts of money on a book project long before getting any money back.

First, the publisher must pay the editor who receives and evaluates publishing proposals. If the author gets an advance against royalties, the publisher begins to pay out money on the project when the contract is signed, and additional advances may be paid while the manuscript is being written, as well as when it is completed and accepted for publication. Then the publisher begins paying for editorial and design work, typesetting, paper, presswork and binding, and then for a major portion of the marketing costs, all before publication.

Finally, if it is a trade book or a professional book, about forty-five days after the first copies of the book are shipped to bookstores, the publisher will receive his first payment for the book on which he has been paying out money for the preceding two or three years. It wll generally be at least a year after publication before the publisher has recovered the full amount of his investment—if he ever does. If it is a textbook published in April or earlier, as it should be, the publisher will not receive his first significant payment until the following October or November.

Taking as an example the book on which a profit and loss statement is shown in figure 3 - 1, the publisher would probably have $80,000 invested in that venture before beginning to receive any money back. If it does sell fifteen thousand copies, as the publisher hopes, the company will make $24,000, or a 30 percent return on its investment. But if the publisher's money has been tied up for two years, he will have earned approximately 15 percent a year. On the other hand, if the book only sells ten thousand copies, the publisher will fail to recover the full amount of his investment and have a loss of $5,300 to show for his efforts.

A publisher's overall profit is the sum of the profit and loss statements for each book published. Generally, only about half of the books published will earn back the investment made in them by the end of two years, and about a third never will. Therefore, a publisher's ability to pick books that are successful and turn down books that may not be is the largest single influence on profit.

The inability of most publishers consistently to identify and publish only books that will be successes reduces publishers' profitability, and their capacity to pay authors more. At the same time, that inability may actually contribute to our cultural diversity by making a broader range of books available than would otherwise be the case. If publishers were to conjure up an unfailing system for identifying successful works for each market, many fewer books would be published, but those books would have larger sales and their authors would receive larger royalty payments, while authors whose royalty incomes are now distressingly low would probably not be published at all.

To summarize, although there are exceptions, neither writing nor publishing books is the road to riches. Authors generally would earn more money doing something else—almost anything else—and most publishers would make out better by investing their money in a mutual fund. One must conclude, therefore, that authors and publishers alike exist not because of the financial rewards but because writing and publishing are what they most want to do.

Chapter 4

Developing Book Manuscripts

Before you attempt to sell a book idea to a publisher, your idea must be well enough developed so that a publisher can see its commercial potential. This means that you must have a clear picture of the market for which you are writing, the subject matter to be included, the approximate number of pages or words in the finished book, and how yours differs from existing books. Even for primarily literary, noncommercial works, it helps to have particular readers in mind and a clear idea of how to appeal to them.

WRITING BOOKS FOR MARKETS

Telling authors to write books for markets seems like telling dogs to chase cats, but one of the common failings of inexperienced authors is writing about a subject, rather than writing for a specific market. For the general nonfiction book, a definite market must almost always be demonstrated before the book can be sold.

First, though, what is meant by a market? For purposes of this discussion, it is a group of people with a common interest that can be identified and reached through some marketing technique. The more specific the interest, the smaller the group will be, but the easier it is to appeal to that group's interest.

For example, one can write a general book about dogs, and it will have some appeal to a large group of people who like dogs, but it will probably be too broad and unfocused to be of strong interest to anyone. It is much more likely to be successful if it is written for children about dogs, for dog owners about dogs, for veterinarians about dogs, or for hunters about hunting dogs, and these will all be very different books. Similarly, the book you are reading might have been written for editors instead of for authors, and covered many of the same topics, but from a different point of view and in different detail.

Each market group will have some preliminary knowledge of the subject, a reading vocabulary, and a limit to how much it wants to know. In writing for a market, you must keep the criteria for that market in mind, and write as though speaking to a member of that group in terms that the member will understand and find interesting and instructive.

Sometimes it is possible to write a book that combines two markets—such as dog owners and veterinarians. You then have the added challenge of satisfying the more sophisticated and knowledgeable readers, but in a language and style that is understandable and interesting to the general, nonprofessional audience.

Many trade and professional markets for nonfiction books can be identified through clubs or associations such as the Garden Club of America, the American Institute of Architects, or the Society of Appraisers. Frequently the markets for special-interest books can also be measured by studying the circulation of magazines serving these markets. *Writer's Market* lists magazine publishers and most magazines' circulation. Another useful guide is *Standard Rate & Data*, a directory for magazine advertisers, which can usually be found in larger libraries. *Standard Rate & Data*, which contains separate business and consumer volumes, is especially helpful, since it shows whether circulation is paid or controlled (free to people who qualify by virtue of their jobs or membership in organizations). Paid circulation is a more solid measure of a potential market, because the subscribers have indicated a willingness to pay for current information.

Unfortunately, only a small percentage of a special-interest group will buy a specific book and the size of that percentage will depend on many things. Books on business or professional subjects generally sell to a larger percentage of their markets than avocational books. Also important is the extent to which the book has a real payoff for buyers— for example, helping them make more money, improving their sex life, improving their golf game, or—to cite a famous example—telling them "How to Win Friends and Influence People." Depending on the market, price can also be an important factor. A high price on a book that is for a low income group—retirees, for example—will certainly decrease its sale to that group. And a publisher's skill in reaching a particular market is also a vital factor.

Except in the most unusual cases, authors cannot expect their books to sell to more than a 10 percent of their potential markets over a period of three to five years, and sales are usually below that amount. However, it is reasonable to expect some modest additional sales to libraries and into foreign markets that are not reflected in domestic circulation or membership data.

Most publishers of professional books are not interested in new titles unless they expect to sell at least 5,000 copies, and most trade publishers want to sell at least 7,500 copies of any book they publish. This means that, allowing for some sales to libraries and international markets, and something less than a 10 percent penetration of the market, a book needs a market of at least 50,000 to 100,000 persons in order to appeal to most publishers.

In determining markets and potential sales, the importance of other books written for the same audience can be tricky to evaluate. Publishers generally believe that if one book sells well, another book on the same subject for the same market will do equally well. The problem is that a really successful book frequently stimulates a rash of imitators. If an exercise book has an excellent sale, a year later there are twelve new exercise books competing in the same market. Unless your book has a different appeal and is better in some respect than the leader, it's better not to play the imitation game.

If you are writing for a market served by a successful magazine, the kinds of articles published and the styles of presentation can indicate what appeals to that market. Most magazines pay close attention to their readers, likes and dislikes, since this is critical to building and maintaining circulation.

For works of fiction, biographies, and memoirs, the same quantitative measure of markets do not exist, although there are "markets" in a very similar sense for these works. The only practical measure, however, is how similar works are known to have sold, and this is usually the guide used by publishers. For certain classes of works, such as mysteries, romances, science fiction, and so forth, there are fairly consistent markets, and sales predictions will be even more accurate for works by the same author or in the same series. Readers who have an enjoyable experience with a book usually want to repeat that experience. Even authors of general fiction will develop a following or market, so that one can predict with reasonable accuracy how a new work by an established author will sell. (And that, of course, is why the established author can command better publishing terms.)

College textbooks, more than any other works, must be written for markets, the markets being defined by specific courses in the college curriculum. However, a complication arises in that courses at various colleges and universities usually differ as to approach, length, degree of difficulty, major or nonmajor emphasis and so forth. And even at a single university, there may be as many as four first courses in physics all using different texts—separate courses for physics majors, for liberal arts students, for engineers, and for nurses.

Generally, textbook publishers tend to define the markets in terms of successful texts. And your objective as a textbook author is to write a better book than the ones being widely used. It may offer a different approach to the subject, or a clearer presentation of difficult material, or be better organized or contain more interesting examples, or better illustrations, or wholly new material, or some combination of these differences. The competition is severe, however. There may be as many as a dozen texts already competing for use in that course, and several new ones will be published each year. So unless your book is carefully targeted to the market and skillfully executed, it will not make a place for itself.

Publishers sometimes conduct surveys of instructors to get their opinion of the best sequence of topics, the emphasis to be given to certain subjects, and other suggestions to help the author in structuring a new book.

Textbooks must also reflect the most recent developments in the fields they cover. Each discovery—a new particle in physics, or fossil remains in some remote land—may affect course content in a minor or major way. Even historical events take on different meanings as lost documents are discovered and as our perspectives change. The incorporation of these changes in new and revised textbooks gives them a competitive edge over older works, and is the feature promoted aggressively by their publishers.

As noted earlier, a curious aspect of the college textbook market is that although the student buys and pays for the book, it is the course instructor who selects it. Authors write texts for the students' use, but with one eye on their fellow instructors who will do the actual selecting. This is good if it causes authors to set a higher standard of performance, but not so good when authors are motivated to show their peers how learned they are. The real market is the students, and in the long run the truly successful works will be those that communicate effectively with them.

Having defined the market for which you are writing, you must focus on that market as you develop your material. The content must be targeted to the needs and interests of your intended audience, the presentation must not be too elementary or too advanced, and the language and terminology must be appropriate. Some authors want to cover everything they know about a subject. This is normally much more than the audience wishes to know on some topics, and not enough on others, so you must distill your information where your fund of knowledge is extensive, and research those areas where your knowledge is thin.

BOOK SIZE

For other than textbook markets, the way in which a book is to be sold should be considered in planning its size. If a significant portion of a book's market must be reached by direct mail, then the book must be priced fairly high in order to cover the high cost of a direct mail campaign. For example, such a campaign will cost about $300 per thousand pieces mailed whether the book is priced at $5 or at $25. Although there will be some resistance to buying as the price of the book is increased, that resistance can be partially offset by the value that is delivered for the price. For example: all things being equal, a five hundred-page book priced at $25 will sell almost as well by mail as a hundred-page book priced at $5. But the $5 book will not generate enough income to cover the cost of mailing and editorial, production, and order processing. Following is a hypothetical comparison based on a mailing of 100,000 pieces, with a 3 percent response on the $5 book and a 2½ percent response on the $25 book.

FIVE-DOLLAR BOOK:

Net sales on 3,000 copies	$15,000
Manufacturing cost and royalties on books sold (at $1.10 ea.)	3,300
Margin	11,700
Cost of mailing (at $300 per 1000)	30,000
Administrative and order processing costs (20 percent)	3,000
Total operating cost	33,000
Loss	(21,300)

TWENTY-FIVE-DOLLAR BOOK:

Net sales on 2,500 copies	$62,500
Manufacturing cost and royalties on books sold (at $5.50 ea.)	13,750
Margin	48,750
Cost of mailing (at $300 per 1000)	30,000
Administrative and order processing costs (20 percent)	12,500
Total operating expense	42,500
Profit	6,250

At these hypothetical but typical rates of sale, a publisher cannot afford to run mail order campaigns on a $5 book, but he may do so profitably on a $25 book. Looked at another way, on the $5 book, the publisher would need to have 8.5 percent of the people who received the mailing buy the book, keep it, and pay for it, in order for it to be profitable. In actuality, the best that one can hope for is about a 4 percent response.

Because of the high fixed cost of direct mail selling, if you expect your book to be sold by mail, you must plan your book to be big enough and valuable enough to the buyer to justify a price of at least $15.

In contrast, books that are to be sold exclusively through bookstores and to libraries are not burdened by high fixed selling costs. Thus, a small $5 book can be sold quite profitably through bookstores and to libraries. In fact, selling low-priced books through bookstores and other outlets is the essence of paperback publishing.

This does not mean that a trade book must be small and low priced. Books priced at $16 to $22 abound on the current best-seller lists. However, trade publishers will normally set a limit on the size of each book they sign up, so that it can be priced reasonably for its audience.

Textbook prices and sizes are not subject to any special consideration, except that the book must be long enough to adequately cover the course material.

DEVELOPING AN OUTLINE

In writing any book, the essential first step is to prepare an outline or, in the case of fiction, a story plan or synopsis. To start writing without an outline or plan is like starting to drive a car without having decided where to go. And every hour spent in constructing the best outline for the project will save many hours later in reorganizing and rewriting the content.

In developing an outline, at issue are not only the topics to be included, but also the sequence in which they should be presented. There are many effective ways to structure a book. Some subjects lend themselves to a chronological approach. In other books, the subject matter is developed from the simple to the complex, i.e., one must read and understand one chapter before being able to read and understand the next. A book on investing, for example, would discuss the broad array of investments available, and how each serves the investor's objectives. It would then treat each type of investment in detail: stocks, bonds, mutual funds, savings tax shelters—in each case discussing risks and rewards, how to select the individual investment, how to make the purchases and sales. Although there is nothing about purchasing and selling stocks that would prohibit that from being presented first, it is not generally where the investor should begin.

It is extremely helpful to have the sequence of chapters firmly set before any material is written, because the content of each chapter will be determined in part by what has preceded it and what follows. To change that sequence at a later date frequently entails major surgery.

In determining the sequence of chapters, a rough listing of the topics and subtopics to be covered in each chapter should be made. This process will more firmly define the nature of each chapter, and sometimes influence their sequence. Ideally, this process should be continued until there is a detailed outline of a dozen or more pages. However, some writers find it difficult to structure their work that extensively, and are willing to risk some reorganizational work in exchange for getting on with the writing. Also, the structure and content of any work will inevitably change some during the writing process, so that some reworking is virtually inevitable. The less that is required, however, the easier the job for the author.

Although a detailed outline may not be needed in making an initial proposal to a publisher, it is an important tool for determining the nature of the book, its size, and its distinctive characteristics. In that way the outline contributes to a more salable publishing proposal.

Chapter 5

Selling Your Book Project to a Publisher

Selling a book idea to a publisher is an exercise in communications. Every publisher is anxious to find and publish books of merit that will sell marvelously and enrich the publisher and the author, and every author is eager to write those books and link up with a good publisher. It is your job as the author not only to produce the work, but also to convince publishers that it has merit and will sell successfully. The key component in your selling effort is a clear description of the work itself, the market for it, and your competence and qualifications.

There are a variety of ways of selling a book project, but it must be done with words on paper. The printed word is the medium of both author and editor, and few editors are interested in talking about a book project with a new author until after reading a written proposal.

TRADE BOOKS

Trade books by authors who have not previously been published are the most difficult to sell to publishers principally because many more manuscripts and proposals are written than the industry can handle. The ratio of unsolicited manuscripts and proposals to published trade books is extremely high—perhaps one thousand to one. As a result, even a truly promising unsolicited project runs a high risk of being lost in the morass of unpublishable manuscripts.

Thus, persistence is essential in trying to find a publisher. A project that ten editors do not like may appeal to the eleventh. It is not unusual for a very successful book to have been turned down by between ten and twenty publishers before finally being accepted. Anyone wanting to be a trade book author must accept this as a fact of life. Published authors find placing new manuscripts easier, but by no means a breeze.

Fiction

Generally, if you have not been previously published, you must submit a complete manuscript, since editors find it difficult to evaluate fiction without knowing how successfully you resolve the conflicts, how you handle character development, and the like.

If you have had a fiction work published, you should be able to get a publishing commitment based on a complete description of the plot, plus fifty or so pages of manuscript.

Nonfiction

If you are writing a nonfiction work, you may begin to sell your project on the basis of no more than an idea, by sending publishers a query letter. The letter should briefly describe the book you have in mind, its size and scope, the audience for which it is intended, and a brief statement about your qualifications, prior writing experience, articles published, and so forth. The query letter usually should not exceed one and a half to two pages, and should conclude by asking if the editor would be interested in such a work. Queries can be sent to a number of publishers at the same time.

If an editor is interested, he or she will ask you to develop a proposal, including a detailed outline and two or three sample chapters. The query letter is a good technique for getting a preliminary appraisal from a number of publishers before investing a lot of time and energy in developing a book idea more fully. Or you may want to have the proposal ready before sending the queries, so that if an editor expresses interest, you can submit it while he or she is still feeling positive about the idea.

There is always the possibility that a query letter will fail to arouse the interest in the project that a fuller book proposal might, and some authors skip the query and submit a proposal at the outset.

A book proposal describes the project in far greater detail, with a heavy emphasis on features that will make it a commercial success. Although there is no set formula that must be followed, the package may include a covering letter, a description of the book, its intended audience and your qualifications, an outline, and two or three sample chapters.

The cover letter should be individually typed and addressed to a specific editor at the publishing house to which it is being sent. *Literary Market Place* includes the names of editors at each house. The letter should be brief, since the enclosures will have all the pertinent data. It should include your address and phone number, since some editors prefer phoning to writing if they have questions.

The descriptive material should be headed "Book Proposal." Then list the title and your name, followed by a one or two sentence description of the book, similar to the blurb one might find on the front of a book jacket. This should be followed by an estimate of the number of words the manuscript is likely to contain, and the number and nature of any illustrations that are to be included.

Next, the descriptive material should include all the information you may be able to gather on the market for such a book: that is, who is likely to buy it and why. This is very important, because the editor's first question in considering a project is whether there is a market for it. For some book projects, you may include statistical data about the market. For example, for a book on battered wives, you should provide statistics on the reported cases of wife abuse and a projection of the size of the problem. The book's market would extend to social workers, family counselors, the clergy, psychologists, physicians, as well as some of the victims themselves who are seeking to understand the problem. Statistics on the size of each of of these groups would help identify the size of the market. If you know of any mailing lists or book clubs that consider books of this kind, that should also be mentioned. For example, Prentice-Hall has a book club called the Behavorial Books Institute, Macmillan has a Behavorial Science Book Service, and there is a Psychotherapy and Social Science Book Club, one or more of which might be interested in such a book. While the editor probably knows about these clubs, it is worthwhile to remind him or her of their existence when the project is first being considered.

Other nonfiction projects will not lend themselves to a statistical presentation of the market. For example, one would be hard-pressed to identify statistically the market for a book entitled *America's Ten Great Families*, except perhaps the lawyers for the family members who might be looking for a libel or invasion of privacy suit. Here, the editor will be primarily concerned with the content, and whether it is sufficiently new and interesting to create a market for itself, because, other than libraries, perhaps, it has no clear market. The only statistical guide to how such a book may sell is the sales records of similar books. If you have any of this information, it should be included, but the editor is more likely to know than you are.

Next, you should provide information about competing books,

and how the proposed book will differ from them in its approach and appeal. You should not go to great lengths to dig up obscure books that are marginally competitive, but rather concentrate on current works that have been distributed widely. The absence of competition may not be a good sign, since it may mean there is no market.

The next section of the description should present your qualifications. These would include occupational experience related to the subject of the book, writing experience, such as published articles and stories, and awards—in fact, any data that will help persuade the editor that you are capable of successfully executing the project. In addition, if you have experience as a speaker or entertainer that will make you attractive as a guest on TV or radio, that background should also be included.

The third part of the proposal is the book's outline. The purpose of the outline is to convey as accurately as possible the content of the work, and in that respect it resembles a table of contents. However, instead of just listing section headings within each chapter, it is more effective to write a paragraph describing the content of each chapter. The outline should be at least two pages long—long enough and detailed enough to persuade the editor that it will make a book, rather than an overblown magazine article.

The outline, by the way, is only a plan for the book and need not be followed slavishly if a better method of organizing the material is discovered while writing, or if it seems desirable to add or delete material as the project progresses. A final manuscript will rarely be rejected by an editor for not conforming to the outline in the proposal, so long as its content is essentially the same as the outline conveyed. It is a good idea, though, to check any major changes with the editor.

The fourth part of the proposal is two or three sample chapters. The chapters submitted should be representative of the main body of the work. If there are several chapters that are especially important, they should be the ones selected for inclusion.

You can send the project description and outline without sample chapters—preparing, in effect, a more elaborate query of interest—but if this is your first book, the publisher will almost certainly want to see sample chapters before making a commitment to publish it.

PROFESSIONAL AND TECHNICAL BOOKS

If you are writing a professional book, skip the query letter and develop a full book proposal at the outset. The reason? There are fewer publishers that are qualified to publish these projects well, and there is no point in risking a turndown because the information is too skimpy. In addition, most professional and technical pubishers will want to ask an adviser to review any proposal before giving encouragement for its development, and they are not likely to bother with this process for a query letter.

Your cover letter should be individually typed and addressed to the editor whom you would expect to handle your project. If an appropriate editor is not listed in *Literary Market Place*, phone the publisher and ask for the name of the editor who handles electrical engineering, or business books, or whatever your subject.

The proposal for a professional or technical book is essentially the same as for a nonfiction work. However, one difference is that the publisher will have a special interest in the changing technology and practice in the field served by the proposed book and the extent to which the project embodies the latest developments. Therefore, be sure to make clear that your material will not only be up to date but even represent the newest advancements in your profession. In addition, your qualifications assume far greater importance for a professional or technical book than for a nonfiction trade book. Be sure to mention if you give workshops, seminars, or courses in which your book can be used.

In discussing competitive material, include any government publications, loose-leaf services, data bases and journals that provide similar information, and describe the benefits to the user of having this information available in book form.

If you have had previous books or journal articles published, you may not need to submit sample chapters to get a publishing contract.

TEXTBOOKS

Book proposals for college textbooks, usually called prospectuses, are basically the same as those for professional books, with a cover letter, a description of the book, an outline, and two or more sample chapters. However, your prospectus needs to define the course for which your book is to be written—for example, a one-semester survey course in psychology for nonmajors, or a one-semester junior-senior level course in fluid mechanics in the aeronautical engineering curriculum. You should also discuss successful competing works, with a description of how the proposed book will differ from them, such as differences in the ordering of topics, and greater or lesser emphasis on specific subjects.

Also included should be ideas for supporting materials such as study guides, practice sets, and so forth, and any unusual or unique features of the work.

If you have an outstanding reputation, it may be possible to get a contract without submitting sample chapters, especially if more than one publisher is interested.

In all areas of book publishing, the proposal or prospectus is the critical vehicle for getting a book contract, and it should be prepared with all the care and attention to detail you can bring to the task. An editor must assume that an author submitting a poorly conceived or poorly written proposal will submit a manuscript of the same quality, and why should he think otherwise?

All elements should go through one or more drafts, and be put aside for several days before the final revisions are made, so that you can review them with a fresh eye. The final version should be typed neatly and proofread carefully before being mailed.

If you want your sample material returned, a self-addressed stamped envelope should be included with the submission.

Those expecting a quick response are likely to be disappointed. It may be a month, or three or four, before you receive a response, even if the response is only a printed rejection letter. Generally, professional and textbook publishers respond faster than trade book publishers, who are inundated with so many proposals and manuscripts that it is almost impossible to keep up with them. Such a small percentage of unsolicited trade book proposals result in book contracts that editors tend to treat them as junk mail, to be looked at briefly whenever time permits. However, a follow-up letter is appropriate if no response has been received within six weeks. A phone call is less likely to be productive; it may be difficult to reach a person familiar with your submittal, since no one may have looked at it yet.

In any event, because of such long delays, you may naturally wonder if your proposal was ever received. That nagging doubt can be eliminated by sending the material by certified mail so that you get a signed receipt.

All authors have the option of submitting proposals to a number of publishers at the same time, and whenever this is done it is customary to tell them that the project is being submitted to others.

There are several advantages to making multiple submissions: It can greatly reduce the time required to get a publishing commitment and, if more than one publisher expresses interest, you are in the happy position of being able to make a choice, and perhaps even get some competitive bidding going. However, there is the disadvantage that some editors are unwilling to invest their time in a project that may be taken by another publisher. Therefore if a publisher has the marketing capability and reputation that makes it clearly your first choice, then it may be worthwhile to say, "I am submitting this project to you first, because it is the kind of book that you handle so well."

Also, with single submissions, the reasons given for a rejection may suggest changes in the proposal or even in the project itself that will make it more salable. For example, if a rejection letter says that the market is already glutted with books on that subject, it may be a signal that the proposal does not highlight the ways in which this book will differ from and be superior to anything else available, or it may suggest that the project itself should be modified. If the proposal has already been sent to the five trade publishers who seem best qualified to handle the book, then the opportunity to modify the proposal for them has been lost. With professional and textbook publishers, there is generally more of an opportunity for dialog and modifying a project than with trade houses.

If you decide to submit material to one publisher at a time and have had no response in six weeks, you can write a follow-up letter saying that if you have no word in two weeks you will submit your project to another publisher. You are not obliged to tell your next choice that the material had been submitted elsewhere.

Generally speaking, multiple submissions make the most sense for trade books where the response to proposals are slowest, where you have no clear first choice, and where many submissions are normally required before getting a commitment.

If your proposal is rejected, be sure to check its physical condition before sending it out again, and replace any pages that show signs of being handled. A proposal that looks as though it has been making the rounds is likely to get less attention than a fresh looking one.

Chapter 6

Choosing a Publisher

Literary Market Place, published by R. R. Bowker Company, lists over 1,700 publishers who publish three or more titles annually. How should you proceed in choosing among them?

There are a number of stories that may be apocryphal about authors' methods of selecting publishers: One author approached them in alphabetical order; another approached them in order of their closeness to the hotel where he was staying. More commonly, an author sends material to a publisher because the sister of a friend works in the personnel department there, for example, and says they publish good books.

IMPORTANCE OF THE SELECTION DECISION

Because of the vital role the publisher plays in the success or failure of your book, the importance of selecting the best publisher for each project cannot be overstated. All publishers are not created equal. Their abilities to reach various markets differ greatly. They have differing philosophies or points of view about the publishing process and about their relationship with authors. They have varying degrees of general competence. They may be financially strong, or on the brink of bankruptcy.

The selection of a publisher is especially important because the contract between you and your publisher is binding for the life of your book. No matter how dissatisfied you may become with the length of time it takes for publication, with the quality of production and manufacture, or with the publisher's marketing program, you are inextricably bound to your publisher until your book is declared out of print.

Even if a publisher were willing to release your work, it is almost impossible to do after publication. All printed copies of the book carry the publisher's name. All catalogs, lists, directories, bibliographies, and library records identify the publisher as the source of the work. Finding another publisher willing to pick up the work under such adverse circumstances would be difficult indeed.

Picking the right publisher for your work at the outset is critical. There is no second chance.

The selection of a publisher entails two steps. First, develop a list of the publishers who appear to be well qualified to publish your project. (How to determine who is well qualified will be discussed later in this chapter.) If you carefully develop your initial list you will be well rewarded for your effort. The publishers who are most appropriate for your project are more likely to accept it for publication because they know how to make it a success.

Second, after receiving one or more offers to publish, it's wise to further evaluate the qualifications of the publishers on the basis of conversations or correspondence regarding key issues, including the terms being offered. If you are dissatisfied with what you learn about either the publishers or their terms you are faced with the difficult choice of turning down the offers and hoping to make a more satisfactory arrangement, or accepting one of the offers in hand. The choice is yours to make.

MARKETING STRENGTHS

Of all the factors to be considered in developing your intial list of publishers none is more important than the ability of the publisher to reach the book's market. Fortunately, a little research will reveal a publisher's strength or weakness in reaching specific markets.

Marketing Academic Books

Recall that textbooks are sold by publishers' representatives who deal directly with instructors giving the courses for which the books have been written. While it is possible at the college and university level to do some of this selling by mail and phone, it is a poor substitute for a face-to-face call. Therefore, the size of the publisher's sales force in relation to the number of titles it is currently selling is extremely important. A large sales force may sound impressive, but if it is representing a very large list of current titles, it may not be as effective as a smaller sales force representing a much smaller list.

An overextended sales force may have difficulty covering the large institutions thoroughly and even more difficulty reaching small institutions in remote locations.

The size of the publisher's program in the proposed book's discipline is also important. If it is small in relation to the publisher's other programs, then the representatives probably do not cover that market thoroughly. Imagine, for example, a college representative with a good selection of titles in sociology and psychology to sell, but only one title in mathematics. The representative can spend time most productively in the sociology and psychology departments. A call will be made on the mathematics department if time permits. But if the appropriate instructor is not available, the chances that the representative will take the time to make a second visit are remote.

Established programs are also important to authors of scholarly works considering publication by a university press. Although it is certainly convenient, there is no requirement that authors publish with their own university's press. A project is much more likely to be accepted for publication and sold effectively by a press that has a program of books in the same area. A press with a publishing program in African studies, for example, will know the journals that will be interested in reviewing books on Africa, the libraries that are most likely to add the work to their collection, and will probably have a list of persons who have bought other books on African studies to whom it can send mailings. In addition, that press will probably know the appropriate foreign publishers to approach regarding foreign language editions.

If you are an instructor, you are in an excellent position to judge the capabilities of both textbook and university press publishers. A look at your own bookshelves shows who is actively publishing in your field. Examine the books to determine how well they are designed and produced. You can visit publishers' exhibits at conventions, examine their books, and talk with representatives and editors there. You probably have publishers' catalogs on hand, showing backlist and forthcoming titles, and if not you can request them. Evaluate the representatives who call on you. Simply put, are they good salespersons? You can find out if they call on small colleges. Sales representatives are part of the rumor mill, and it is not uncommon for them to discuss what is going on at other colleges. If they don't know, they aren't calling there. You are also likely to know other authors whom you can ask about their experiences with publishers.

If you are writing a scholarly work you should be receiving catalogs and circulars from university presses publishing works in your specialty. The absence of promotion may not mean an absence of publications, but it certainly suggests a lack of aggressiveness in marketing.

Marketing Nonacademic Books

There are two basic means of marketing nonacademic books. First, retail bookstores are absolutely vital to the sale of books of general interest (novels, biographies, memoirs, current events, self-help, and so forth); they are the major marketplace where books and book buyers meet. (Retail stores are of less importance in marketing specialized books—books for professional and business people, engineers, scientists, technicians, and so forth—principally because these books sell more slowly, and many stores do not stock them, obliging publishers to sell them by other means.)

In order to sell books to retail stores, publishers must have a number of more or less routine policies and procedures. The publisher must have an acceptable discount schedule and a returns policy permitting unsold copies to be turned back for credit. The publisher must have some kind of cooperative advertising plan, so that the retail store can advertise selected titles locally and have the publisher pay a portion of the expense. The publisher must get copies into the retail stores before reviews appear, and before the author appears on television. Many are remiss in these areas.

Finally, the publisher must have a sales force calling on retail stores with jackets of forthcoming titles and a brief sales pitch as to why each title is going to be in demand. Generally large publishers of general interest books have a salaried sales force selling their titles to retail stores. Smaller publishers usually cannot afford to maintain their own sales force and either have another publisher's sales force represent them, or use independent sales representatives who work for a number of publishers on a commission basis. While these representatives are, for the most part, competent and hard working, publishers obviously have much less control over what stores they visit and what titles they promote most vigorously. The publisher with the salaried full-time sales force has the opportunity to do a better job of selling to retail stores, although there is no guarantee that he will take full advantage of that opportunity.

Talking to several retail bookstore managers can help you decide which publishers are doing the most effective marketing job, although authors must be careful that the crisis of the day has not destroyed a manager's objectivity.

The second basic approach to nonacademic markets—one vital to special-interest books—is direct-mail selling to mailing lists of prospective buyers, and space advertising with coupons in special-interest periodicals.

Mailing lists of all kinds of persons—from recent brides to atomic physicists—are available, and any publisher can rent them from list brokers or other publishers. In addition, any publisher can advertise in periodicals. However, some book publishers also publish periodicals or sell services to special-interest groups, and as a result, have access to mailing lists at cost or at reduced "house rates." Book publishers with such resources can make mailings and run advertising that other publishers cannot afford, because they can reach those potential buyers at dramatically lower costs. In choosing a publisher, authors—especially authors of special-interest books—should consider a publisher's in-house promotional resources for reaching potential buyers of their works.

These resources are not always obvious and some research may be needed to uncover them. For example, *Popular Mechanics* magazine is published by the Hearst Corporation. The Hearst Corporation also owns book publishers William Morrow & Company and Arbor House Publishing Company, as well as the mass paperback house, Avon Books. Therefore, Morrow or Arbor House would seem to be logical publishers for books that could be sold to *Popular Mechanics* subscribers, but the relationship between these companies is not readily visible. Another example is CBS, which publishes a large number of special interest magazines and is also the parent company of book publisher Holt, Rinehart and Winston, a logical publisher for books appealing to the same audiences as their magazines. The easiest way to uncover these invisible relationships is to start with a periodical in the same subject area as your book, and then determine if the same company publishes books under the same or a different name. A phone call to the company will provide the answer.

Also, keep in mind that in order to publish a special-interest book effectively, the publisher must have a program of books appealing to that same market. This applies not only to business and professional books but also to books on hobbies, recreation, travel, and so forth, for the following reasons:

In order to sell a book in volume by direct mail, a publisher must be able to go back to key mailing lists time and again, in order to reach potential buyers when they are ready to buy. However, after one or two mailings to the same list, the sales on a given book drop away to the point that it is no longer profitable to remail, although there are still good prospects on the list who have not yet purchased the book. However, if the publisher brings out another book appealing to the same audience, the new book can be sold profitably to the same list, and promotional material on the older book can be included in the same mailing at little extra cost. And if the publisher has an ongoing program of books, the older books will be promoted again and again to the same list of potential buyers, picking up additional sales each time.

In addition, in many hobby, recreational, and other special-interest fields, there are specialty retail outlets that will stock books that appeal to the interests of their clientele. Therefore, one can sell books on sports through sporting goods stores, books on pets through pet shops, books on boating through marine dealers, and so forth. However, a publisher cannot profitably sell a single title to a specialty shop market. For example, the cost of selling a single title on cat care to pet shops is prohibitive. However, if the publisher has a whole program of pet books that can be sold through pet shops, the publisher can reach that market profitably.

Another significant factor favoring programs of books is that retail stores who are already successfully selling several titles in a program of books will readily accept and stock a new title in that same program.

The publisher with a program is actually marketing a group of books at a cost that is not much greater than the cost of marketing a single title. Thus he has extra dollars to use in penetrating those markets.

If you are writing a special-interest book, it is clearly to your advantage to seek out publishers with programs in that field. Those publishers can reach the market for your book more effectively and sell more copies. A check of the subject-matter shelves of a large bookstore, or research in Bowker's *Subject Guide to Books in Print*, found in most libraries, will usually reveal the names of the publishers most actively publishing in a given subject area.

Book clubs are a special form of direct-mail selling, marketing both general interest and special-interest books. The book club operator offers books at a reduced price in return for the member's agreement to purchase a given number of books each year (an agreement that is rarely enforced). The book-club operator then buys "book-club rights" from the publishers on a royalty basis with a guaranteed minimum and down payment, and copies are printed specifically for the club, usually by the publisher's printer, but sometimes by the club's printer.

There are approximately two hundred book clubs listed in *Literary Market Place*, ranging from the Book-of-the-Month Club for books of broad general interest to the Organic Gardening Book Club and the Mechanical Engineer's Book Club for special-interest books. These clubs make it possible for publishers without mailing lists to reach special-interest audiences.

Although most book clubs are now owned by book publishers, they generally operate independently and make club selections from all publishers, based on the club's judgment of what will be most appealing to the club's membership. However, all other things being equal, a club will have a preference for "house" books because the company then makes both a publisher's profit and a book club profit on the same title.

Moreover, a publisher operating a special-interest book club is under some pressure to come up with new selections to offer members and is anxious to publish books that answer members' needs. Note, too, that this publisher is assured of some book income from the club, and for this reason can better afford to publish books that the club can use than other publishers would be. It follows that the publisher can also afford to pay larger advances for the club books. For these reasons, if you are writing a special-interest book, you should check the book-club section of *Literary Market Place* to determine if any publisher has a book club for which your book could be a selection. If so, that publisher should be placed near the top of your list.

There is a more subtle type of program or focus in trade publishing that has little impact on marketing, but that affects title selection. If a publisher has been successful with a certain type of book, he is likely to look for or be more receptive to other books of the same type. As a result, a publisher may turn out a number of biographies on rock stars, or baseball players, or historical novels set in medieval Europe or China, or inspirational books. To capitalize on this tendency, identify the eight or ten books published over the past two years that are most similar to yours, and see if any one publisher has published more than one of them. If not, then perhaps the publisher of the most successful of these books would be the most responsive to your proposal.

There are other marketing factors that should be considered in selecting a publisher, but they cannot be determined until the author is in a position to discuss publication with the publisher. These will be presented later in this chapter.

SMALL PUBLISHER VERSUS LARGE PUBLISHER

Most authors would prefer to have their work published by a large, well-known publisher, if for no other reason than it is more ego-satisfying. Who would not rather tell friends and associates that his or her book is to be published by Random House rather than by Paragon House? Yet it is only in textbook publishing that size is a very significant advantage.

All large publishers clearly have some advantages over small publishers. They can achieve economies in production and marketing that can result in more value for the same number of dollars spent. They can afford to have a salaried sales force, and hire specialists in each type of subsidiary rights sales or premium sales. However, these advantages can be offset by problems in communication and motivation. As a publishing house gets larger, there are increased specialization and additional levels of management that are responsible for coordinating the efforts of the specialists. In a small publishing house, for example, the director of marketing may personally oversee and coordinate the sales force, the mail order campaigns, the advertising, promotion, and publicity. In a large house publishing several hundred titles each year, there are likely to be separate managers responsible for each of these functions, each reporting to the director of marketing, each of whom must familiarize himself with several hundred titles. There can be breakdowns in communications among the marketing team. People may be less familiar with and care less about individual titles than is common in a small publishing house. Effective publishing requires orchestration, and orchestration becomes more difficult as the number of players increases. In a small house, since each title plays a larger role in the house's success, it is likely to be given more individual attention.

Much more important than size is the question of publishing programs. A non-textbook publishing house may be very small and have only a single program of first-rate books on gardening, or investing, or stamp collecting. All other things being equal (which they never are), that house will probably do a better marketing job than a large house with only a few books in one of those subjects.

MASS-MARKET PAPERBACK VERSUS HARD-COVER TRADE BOOK PUBLISHER

If you are writing a general interest book, you also need to decide whether to seek first publication by a mass-market paperback publisher, or go the more traditional route of finding a hard-cover trade book publisher.

There can be a significant economic difference to you. Generally, with a hard-cover house, you receive a full royalty on hard-cover sales and half the royalty on the sale of mass-market paperback rights. With a mass-market paperback house, you receive a full share of the paperback royalties and may even get a full share of the hard-cover royalties if the hard-cover edition is published by the mass-market paperback house, or only half the royalties if the rights are sold. The key to this decision, therefore, is the nature of the book. If it is a book which is likely to have a very large sale in its hard-cover edition, then you will do well to select a competent hard-cover house as publisher. On the other hand, if your book is likely to have a modest sale in hard cover but a big sale in its paperback edition, then arranging for publication directly with a paperback publisher will make the most sense, both strategically and economically. Remember, however, that if only a mass paperback edition is published, the book is unlikely to be reviewed by major media or purchased by many libraries.

These are difficult decisions for authors to make for themselves, and if you are considering publishing first with a paperback house, you should try to sign up with a literary agent first. An experienced agent not only can advise on this issue, but can help in approaching a paperback house if that is the course decided upon. This is important since mass-market paperback publishers are even less interested in unsolicited projects than hard-cover trade publishers.

OTHER CONSIDERATIONS

There are a number of other factors in selecting a publisher that cannot easily be evaluated prior to submitting material and receiving a favorable response. Only then can you question the publisher and decide if this is the company to which you wish to entrust your work. If you have more than one house express interest, of course, you are in a better position to evaluate these issues.

The Editor

For any author, the editor is the most important person in a publishing house, and nothing can make up for an incompetent or indifferent editor. The editor is the main liaison between you and the publishing house. He or she not only recommends the publication of your work to the company's management and guides it through the writing and editing processes, but also represents your interests and the interests of your work as it proceeds through the publishing process.

Because of the major role played by the editor, it is especially important that he or she continues to be responsible for the project after it is under contract. The editor who signs up your work not only knows the project well, but also has a commitment to it. Having persuaded management that your book will be successful, the editor, whose very job depends on publishing successful books, sees to it that everything reasonably possible is done to make it a success. If your editor leaves, or is transferred or promoted to a new position, and a new editor is given responsibility for the project, that in-depth knowledge of the project and that commitment to its success is lacking. Everything that needs to be done probably will be done, but that extra effort that often makes the difference between success and failure will be missing.

Of course, your original editor could be incompetent and the successor much more effective. But in most cases, you are better off not having to deal with more than one editor, especially during the period between the signing of the contract and the publication of the work.

You have no way of knowing of course how long you will be working with the same editor. For instance, some college publishers make it a practice to transfer staff between editorial and marketing positions every few years. While this is excellent training for the staff, it works a hardship on the authors. Then there are cases where the editor and publisher are simply not compatible, and are destined to part company, or the editor is promoted, or leaves to accept a better position with another company. These common situations are impossible to predict and you can do little more than hope that they don't occur.

Because there is always a risk of losing an editor at any publishing house, it is good when visiting the company to meet someone else there, such as the editor's boss, or the marketing director. A simple request, "I'd like to meet Mr.——— or Ms.——— while I am here if that can be arranged," can usually be accommodated, since publishing people are interested in meeting their authors if schedules permit. Although this may not help in a substantive way, there is some benefit in being more than a name to the publishing team, and it will partially allay your feeling of helplessness if there is editorial turnover.

International Sales

International sales can also be important to authors. Sales potential differs greatly from book to book, but, generally speaking, theoretical, high-level technical and professional books (except in law and accounting) often sell well throughout the world in their English language editions—sometimes as much as 50 percent of the total sale.

If your work seems to have a good international sales potential, consider the publisher's knowledge and coverage of that market. Usually, publishers of the kinds of books that have good international markets will have established the capability to reach those markets, which is one

more reason for choosing a publisher with programs of books similar to
your own. If in doubt, ask how many copies of the U.S. edition of your
book they expect to sell in foreign markets. If the publisher can provide
an estimate and a thoughtful rationale for that estimate rather than
vague generalities, then there is a good chance that an adequate job of
international marketing will be done.

Subsidiary Rights

The marketing of subsidiary rights and the income derived from their
sale is important to all books and their authors, but the amount of income generated by the sale of rights varies greatly, again depending on
the type of book and the subject matter.

As stated earlier, subsidiary rights are the rights to use the book
material in whole or in part in other media, markets, or formats, and include book club rights, translation rights, rights to paperback and other
reprint editions, serialization rights, dramatization in motion pictures,
television, radio or theatre, and other commercial rights in connection
with the promotion and sale of merchandise.

Book clubs have already been discussed. The chances of having a
book selected by a special-interest book club are quite good, but the selection of a general interest book by one of the major general interest
clubs such as Book-of-the-Month or the Literary Guild is less likely, simply because the number of books from which to choose is much greater.

Any title with a good potential for international sales will also
have a good potential for the sale of translation rights into three or more
languages, and some books end up in a dozen or more foreign language
editions. However, these sales do not come about spontaneously. They
must be sold by your publisher to foreign publishers at the time of publication.

Of all the subsidiary rights, the greatest source of income for
trade books is from the sale of mass-market paperback rights. Books of
broad general interest reach really large audiences only in these editions. These rights must be aggressively sold.

Dramatization rights continue to be a good source of additional
income for those works of fiction and biography that lend themselves to
dramatic presentation, but not nearly as large an income as in the past.

A publisher's experience and commitment to the sale of subsidiary rights is important to all authors, but especially important for books
of broad general interest. You should discuss subsidiary rights in detail
with your editor. Ask who is in charge of subsidiary rights, what experience that person has had, and ask for recent examples of successful

rights sales. If you are writing a trade book and you are not impressed by what you learn, you may want to consider another publisher.

Financial Soundness

Book publishing requires a sizable amount of working capital to pay author advances, editorial salaries, typographers, and printers for work on books that may not produce income for some months, and many publishers are undercapitalized. Such a publisher will not be an ideal partner with whom to work. The company may not be able to afford a decent advance. It may skimp on production costs, and on advertising and promotion. It may delay royalty payments. One or two mistakes, and the undercapitalized publisher may even go bankrupt owing royalties, or more likely, sell his business to another publisher who may cancel many of his publishing commitments.

Financial soundness has nothing to do with size. A publisher can be small and sound, or big and unsound. The issue is whether there is enough working capital to operate his kind and size publishing business. If a publisher's financial condition is such that the shortage of cash dominates his decisions, then he will not do a good publishing job.

Unfortunately, it is not easy for you to determine the financial soundness of a publisher. If the company is publicly owned, then you can ask for the publisher's most recent annual report and quarterly report to shareholders, and if you are not familiar with financial statements, ask an accountant to review the reports and advise you on the publisher's financial condition. The next best source of information is a Dun & Bradstreet report on the credit rating of the company. Although these reports are available only on an annual subscription basis, your banker may be a subscriber. You may ask for a copy of the publisher's balance sheet, but if it is a privately owned company, the publisher will probably decline to provide it. Finally, if you know one of the publisher's authors, you can ask if he pays his advances and royalty payments promptly. Lacking these sources, you are left to your own perceptions based on the publisher's reactions to money issues.

Publishing Terms

The most obvious part of any agreement for the publication of a book is the royalty rate that the publisher agrees to pay you on copies sold and on other income from subsidiary rights sales. If you are in the fortunate position of being able to choose from among several publishers, then the royalty rates and the share of subsidiary rights income offered must be taken into account. However, a word of caution is in order.

Most royalty terms are expressed as percentages of the list price or the net selling price of copies sold, and percentages of subsidiary rights income. But you are interested in dollars, not percentages, so the royalty terms must be considered together with your assessment of the publisher's marketing capability and probable performance. A sale of twenty thousand copies at a 10 percent royalty rate will yield considerably more dollars than ten thousand at 15 percent, assuming approximately the same pricing. Similarly, a smaller share of subsidiary rights income may yield more dollars for the author if the publisher has a really experienced and aggressive subsidiary rights program than a larger share from a less skilled, less aggressive publisher.

Making a meaningful comparison of the value of royalty terms offered by two publishers is also difficult because there are likely to be many different rates for different kinds of sales. One may be based on list price, the other on net price. One may provide for a lower royalty rate on copy sales but a higher percentage on the sale of certain subsidiary rights. To accurately assess the comparative value of two contracts, one must estimate the copies to be sold at each rate by each publisher, and the amount of income the publisher may collect for each of the subsidiary rights, an impossible task for an inexperienced author. The important point is not to be misled by a higher royalty rate on sales to bookstores only, or a higher rate on mail-order sales if the publisher does little or no mail-order selling. The whole package of rates and marketing ability must be considered in comparing terms.

However, in those relatively few cases in which there is competitive bidding among publishers for a manuscript with the potential to be a best seller, the advance against royalty earnings can become the key factor, because you keep the advance regardless of how few copies are sold. As the size of the advance approaches the reasonable expectation of what the book may earn in its lifetime, royalty rates, and other factors become of secondary importance. You can choose the publisher offering the largest advance and not worry quite so much about whether the publisher will effectively market your work. In fact you can feel assured that the publisher will make a real effort to sell enough copies at least to earn the advance, or otherwise almost certainly lose money.

Chapter 7

The Role of the Literary Agent

If you are writing a trade book, either fiction or nonfiction, you may find a literary agent useful in placing your book with a publisher and in getting a fair deal for its publication.

Although a few literary agents handle professional books and textbooks, most do not. There are a number of reasons for this. Authors of these works have less difficulty getting their works considered by publishers; the publishing agreement and the marketing processes are less complex, with subsidiary rights being a minor factor; and finally, most agents do not have the knowledge necessary to judge the merits and commercial possibilities of these types of books.

Although literary agents can be very helpful, they are not essential, and under certain circumstances may not even be desirable. In order to decide whether or not to seek an agent, you need to know what agents do, how the arrangement works, and what they cost.

First, some publishers will not consider a trade book project unless it is submitted by an agent. These publishers use agents to screen those projects with commercial possibilities from the many thousands of works that are written each year. To make matters even more difficult for new authors, many well-established agents will not handle the works of authors who have not previously been published, or failing that, who do not have at least an expression of strong interest in a project from a publisher. Agents must have a group of productive, successful authors in order to earn a good living. Newly established agents who are working to build a clientele are more likely to consider the works of unpublished authors, but being new, will usually have less developed skills and fewer contacts.

Most agents will not apply the criterion of prior publication to well-known persons writing in their special fields of expertise. It is doubtful, for example, if any agent would have asked Henry Kissinger if he had been previously published before agreeing to handle his memoirs.

A number of literary agents will read and advise unpublished authors on partial or complete manuscripts for a fee ranging from $50 to $300, depending on the agent and the amount of material submitted. If the agent decides to try to place the manuscript, the fee is usually cancelled. This may be helpful if you want more guidance than is provided by the traditional rejection letter.

In any event, if you have not been published, it is not merely a question of whether an agent is desirable, but also whether it is worth the effort to try to find one who is willing to handle your work. With the same amount of effort, you may be able to find an interested publisher directly.

WHAT AGENTS DO

Literary agents try to place manuscripts with publishers, and if successful, then manage the business relationship between author and publisher. They receive a percentage of the author's royalty income as compensation for their help. Following, in greater detail, is what they will normally do.

First, if they feel that your work, despite its merit, suffers from some significant defect that will put off publishers, they may recommend some changes. For example, if it starts off so slowly that an editor will quickly lose interest, they may recommend cutting back or revising much of that introductory material. Although a few agents with editorial experience will help authors with manuscripts prior to placement, most agents try to avoid editorial advice or help of a subjective sort that might conflict with the opinion of a publisher's editor.

Having in hand an apparently marketable project, agents begin the task of attempting to place the work with an editor, drawing heavily on their insight into the types of books each editor is looking for. Agents also consider the editorial and marketing skills and publishing terms of those who are likely to be interested in the project. If a manuscript needs a good deal of editorial work in order to be successful, editorial dedication and skill become important. If you need a large advance, the more generous publishers must be considered.

After weighing these and other relevant factors, the agent selects as his first choices the one, two, or three publishers who are best suited to the needs of the project. Usually, agents send material simultaneously to a small number of publishing houses for consideration. This not only speeds up the lengthy process of finding a publisher, but also stimulates competition. However, if a book seems especially appropriate for a specific publisher, and if a multiple submission might reduce the chances of its being carefully considered by that publisher, then the agent may first send it to that publisher.

Normally, the agent contacts the editors of the houses on his or her initial list to learn if they will consider the project, and sends copies along to those who express interest; or if the agent has a good continuing relationship with specific editors, he or she may send the material directly to them without a prior query. Usually editors want to take a look at anything recommended by an agent with whom they regularly work.

If this first round of editors is not interested in the project, the agent will try a second group, and so forth. If the agent has a deep conviction that the work is publishable, this process may be continued until as many as fifteen or twenty publishers have been approached before the agent gives up. On the other hand, the reactions of editors who have examined the material may cause the agent to give up much earlier. Since most reputable agents work solely on a commission basis and receive no compensation for their unsuccessful efforts, they have a right to stop when they wish to.

When an editor expresses an interest in a work, the agent begins the negotiation of contract terms between publisher and author. Prior experience gives agents a good sense of the terms that can be negotiated for a given project with a given publishing house, and based on that sense, the agent tries to get the best terms he or she can for you. However, as in any commercial negotiation, the agent's negotiating strength depends on the size of the market for the work and the income it can potentially generate for the publisher. If an editor considers a project to be publishable but risky, he or she is less likely to be flexible than if he or she thinks it is a good candidate for best-seller lists, book clubs, and a mass-market paperback edition.

In any event, the agent, acting on your behalf, deals with all the contract clauses and issues discussed elsewhere in this book, attempting to maximize the author's royalty income and minimize the author's risks and commitments. Although publishers have standard contract forms that cover all the publishing issues to their satisfaction, agents and editors who have negotiated with each other previously usually have an understanding about how that standard agreement can be modified. Most of the negotiating focuses on the bread-and-butter issues of royalties and advances against royalties on book sales and subsidiary rights.

It is unrealistic, however, to expect agents to devote much time to negotiating terms on the average project. Like real estate agents, literary agents are more interested in a deal than in the best possible deal. Unless a project has the potential to become a best seller, the difference in the income for an agent isn't worth the extra time and effort required to get it. However, most agents will not go along with anything they consider unsound or unfair to their authors.

There are two major differences in a publishing agreement when you are represented by an agent.

First, the agreement names your agent and stipulates that all royalty statements and monies due you under the agreement are to be paid to the agent on your behalf—it therefore becomes the agent's responsibility to audit the publisher's royalty statements and send along your share of the royalty income after deducting his commission.

Second, the agent generally retains on your behalf certain subsidiary rights which he will personally work to sell for you. These rights usually include first serial rights, dramatic rights (stage, motion picture, television), British Commonwealth English-language rights (except Canada), translation rights, and sometimes "other commercial rights" (the use of names or characters on products or for promotional purposes). These are generally referred to as the secondary subsidiary rights. The balance of the subsidiary rights—book club, mass-market paperback and other reprint rights—are normally granted to the publisher to sell, with earnings to be divided as the contract stipulates.

Publishers like to acquire all subsidiary rights since they then share in the income from their sale. Although an author without an agent may retain the secondary subsidiary rights (especially if the author has reason to think he or she can sell these rights directly), typically the publisher handles all rights if no agent is involved. Agents, however, believe they can do a better job of selling these selected rights than the average publisher. Some have offices on the West Coast to negotiate television and motion picture sales, or work with West Coast agents and split the commissions. Similarly, some agents have London offices or work with English agents to sell rights to British Commonwealth editions. In reality, who can do the better job depends on the agent and the publisher handling the project. As a rule, the more experienced agent or publisher will do a better job in selling subsidiary rights.

One of the less obvious advantages of having an agent handle dramatic and translation rights is that your share of the income from the sale of these rights is payable immediately to you. On the other hand, if they are sold by the publisher, your share will be credited to your royalty advance rather than paid out to you. Even if the advance has already been recovered by the publisher, the money will normally be held until the time the next royalty payment is due. And if the royalty advance, which does not need to be repaid, is never fully recovered by the publisher, the income from the sale of dramatic and translation rights by the agent in excess of the unearned royalty advance is all extra income for you. For example, you have a $10,000 nonreturnable advance against royalties, but the royalties earned by the publisher's sales of books and rights amount to only $8,000, and the agent's sale of dramatic and translation rights generates $5,000 for you, you will have made $15,000 in total from the book. However, if the publisher had sold the dramatic and translation rights for the same amount, you would have received only $13,000, because $2,000 of that rights income would have been kept by the publisher to pay off the outstanding advance. One would think that the amount that a publisher is willing to advance against earned royalties would be less if the publisher did not acquire dramatic and translation rights, but that does not usually appear to be the case—testimony, perhaps, to the lower potential they see in the exercise of these rights, or an unwillingness to gamble on their potential.

Although the publishing contract is negotiated by your agent, the contract is between you and the publisher. Your agent is not bound by or liable for anything in the contract. Generally, authors accept what their agents negotiate for them. However, it is important that you read and understand everything that the contract contains, and if you are unhappy or troubled by any of the publishing terms, you should feel at liberty not to agree to them. Your financial and even emotional well-being can be affected by that contract for several years—perhaps many years—and it is vital that it not be entered into lightly. The chapters in this book on publishing terms should help in evaluating an agent's recommendation.

After the publishing contract is signed by you and the publisher, your agent rarely becomes involved in the author-editor relationship as work proceeds on the manuscript, unless one or the other asks the agent to intervene to help resolve some problem. Then, sometime after the publisher accepts the completed manuscript, your agent proceeds with efforts to sell those subsidiary rights that he or she has retained, by sending either copies of the final manuscript, or page proofs, or bound copies of the book when available, to the agent's offices or to cooperating agents on the West Coast and in England, and to foreign publishers for consideration of foreign language editions.

In addition, the agent, who has a stake in the book's success, informally monitors the publisher's performance in selling subsidiary rights and in marketing the book to see that nothing is done or left un-done that is contrary to your interests. This includes a review of the publisher's periodic royalty statements to be sure (to the extent that the data permits) that the author's earnings are being properly computed and reported. It's wise, however, to double-check all royalty statements you receive, since agents are not infallible.

WHAT AGENTS CHARGE

As stated earlier, agents are compensated by receiving a percentage of their authors' royalties as a commission, and so have a financial interest as well as an obligation to see that their authors' works are handled and sold effectively.

Not all agents charge the same rates. Most charge a basic commission of 10 percent of the author's royalty income from the U.S. publisher. Some have increased their rate to 15 percent, and some charge 15 to 20 percent for handling the work of authors who have not been previously published. There is no evidence that agents charging the higher commission actually do more for their clients. On the sale of subsidiary rights, they usually charge 10 percent of the author's income from the sale of dramatic rights, 15 to 20 percent on the sale of British rights, 20 to 25 percent on the sale of translation rights, and 10 to 15 percent on the sale of first serial rights—usually the same percentage as on income from the U.S. publisher.

In addition, most agents charge authors for incidental expenses incurred in promoting the sale of their works, such as making copies of manuscripts, long distance phone calls, messenger service, postal charges for air mailing copies of the manuscript or bound books, and so forth.

All royalty statements and royalty payments made by the publisher or by firms who have purchased subsidiary rights from the agent are sent to the agent and all checks are payable to him or her. The agent audits the royalty statements, takes his or her commission from the payments, and pays the balance to the author. Most reputable agents maintain a separate account for the author's share in order to avoid operating their businesses on the authors' funds and jeopardizing their ability to pay their authors promptly.

As a result of this payment system, agents always take their commissions at the time payments are made by publishers as provided for in the publishing contract. If you receive an advance against royalties, your agent takes a commission on that advance. If you choose to receive deferred payments, your agent usually must wait for those deferred payments to be made before taking his or her commission. Because of this, there can be a conflict between what is best for you and what is best for your agent. An agent short of money may be anxious for you to get a large advance on signing the publishing agreement, but you may be better off for tax reasons with a smaller advance on signing the agreement and a larger advance on acceptance of the final manuscript. Although you should certainly consider your agent's recommendations regarding the timing of payments, you should also talk to your accountant, and recognize that on this issue, your agent's interests may not be identical with your own.

Clauses giving the publisher an option on your subsequent work is another area where there is a potental conflict of interest. It is not generally in your interest to sign a contract containing an option clause, for reasons discussed in detail in the separate chapter on options. However, if there is an option clause in the contract, most agents extend their representation and their share of the royalties to include the subsequent work, if taken by the publisher, on the grounds that it is part of the package they negotiated. Thus, the option clause, although not in your interest, assures the agent revenue from the optioned work, even if you are dissatisfied with the agent's performance on the first one. Most agents strike the option clause from publisher's contracts. If yours doesn't, you should understand that your agent is also acquiring the right to represent your next work.

The extent to which agents formalize their relationship with authors varies a good deal. Some prepare and sign a contract with the author; some send a letter that states briefly what the agent will do and what the commission arrangement will be; others are even more informal. While an informal approach may suggest that your agent has great confidence in your integrity, your agent really doesn't need the protection of a contract as much as you do. Because the publishing agreement makes your agent the payee of all royalty income, he or she is never faced with the problem of collecting money from you. On the contrary, it is you who needs protection regarding the amount your agent will withhold, and when he or she will pay out your share. Therefore, you should obtain from your agent a written agreement specifying the percent of commission payable on each of the sources of publishing income, the expenses that are to be charged to your account, and how soon after receiving payments your agent will pay out your share of the earnings.

The written agreement should also specify the rights of both parties in the event that you decide to change agents. These things happen, and it is better to provide for them in advance rather than attempt to ne-

gotiate them later when there may be hard feelings. In the event of termination, your agent is entitled to continuing commissions on all deals
that have been negotiated, even if they have not actually been formally
signed. However, when a subsidiary rights deal negotiated by your
agent expires, those rights should revert to you. If your agent
has not concluded a deal with a U.S. publisher, those rights should be
recovered by you immediately. On the sale of subsidiary rights, your
agent should be given at least thirty days in which to complete any
agreement that may be in the works. Another approach on the sale of
rights is to limit to two years the period of time your agent has to sell
dramatic, British, and translation rights. This enables you to reassign
those rights to a publisher or to another agent, and in effect to terminate
the arrangement, if you believe your agent has not done a good job of
promoting the sale of those rights.

ARE AGENTS NECESSARY?

Under what circumstances should you try to get an agent? It depends
largely on your nature and the nature of the project.

   If it is a practical book on golf, or how to become a millionaire, or
collecting antique automobiles rather than a work of fiction, or a biography, or your memoirs, an agent is less important. The task of identifying
a publisher who might be interested is easier, and if you have creden-
tials to back up a well-prepared proposal, it will be less difficult to get a
publisher to consider the project than would be the case for a literary
work.

   But more important is your personality. If you like to get into the
nuts and bolts of daily living and study and resolve problems, and, above
all, if you like the give and take of negotiating, you will probably be hap-
pier working directly with a publisher. Because of inexperience, you
may not negotiate as favorable a set of terms as an agent would, but this
will be offset, at least in part, by not having to pay an agent's commission. On the other hand, if you want to devote all your time and energy
to writing, and to be relieved of the business details, a good agent can be
a godsend, and worth every penny of the commission paid.

SELECTING AN AGENT

How should you go about picking an agent? Carefully. Like authors, editors, and publishers, literary agents come in all shapes and sizes, de-

grees of intelligence, experience, diligence, and integrity. Kitty Kelly, author of *Elizabeth Taylor: The Last Star*, was unable to get a full financial report from her literary agent, and brought suit for breach of contract, breach of fiduciary duty, and fraud. The jury awarded Miss Kelly $60,000 in royalties and $640 in punitive damages. However, poor performance by agents is more likely to involve neglect or sloppiness than fraud or deception.

 Literary Market Place, the annual directory of the book publishing industry that can be found in most libraries, lists about three hundred agents or agencies, coded to indicate if they are literary or dramatic agents, or both. Some entries note the agent's specialty (books for juveniles, adult fiction, how-to, and so forth), which helps somewhat, but there are still many options. The entries are also coded to show if the agent is a member of the Society of Authors Representatives or the Independent Literary Agents Association. The Society of Authors Representatives has a code of ethics or professional guidelines for its members, but an agent who is not a member of SAR can be equally or even more scrupulous in fulfilling his or her obligations to authors.

 Another useful source is *Literary Agents of North America*, an annual directory compiled by Author Aid Associates, 340 East 52nd Street, New York, NY 10022, which is also a literary agency. Information on over 450 U.S. and Canadian agencies is based on responses to questionnaires, and includes whether the agency reads unsolicited queries, or unsolicited manuscripts, whether they will represent new authors, the kinds of books they handle, and in some cases the commission rate they charge.

 The best way to select an agent is the way you select a doctor or lawyer—by getting recommendations from people they serve. Furthermore, if a client will recommend you to his or her agent, your chances are greatly improved. If you know someone working in a trade publishing house (or have a friend of a friend at a trade publishing house), it may be possible to get a recommendation from that source. Failing this, you are on your own and must determine for yourself, as you must sometimes in selecting lawyers and doctors, the competence and integrity of agents based on their responses to your proposals and questions.

 Seeking an agent is similar to seeking a publisher. Many agents will not read unsolicited manuscripts, but will read query letters. Such a letter should describe your project and the audience for which it is to be written, and should also include any information about yourself that may encourage the agent to believe you will be a productive client. The letter should indicate the amount of manuscript that is available and the estimated length of the finished manuscript. If it is a work of fiction or a non-fiction work of general interest, the letter should describe the plot or other content in sufficient detail so the agent will understand the nature of the work. If it is a special-interest project, the letter should explain the market for which it is written, including the size of the market if you can estimate it, other books that are available, and how this project differs from them. On projects of this type, it may help to enclose an outline. Above all, the query on a special-interest project should describe your qualifications for writing a sound and successful book. If you want material to be returned, be sure to enclose a self-addressed, stamped envelope.

Since most unpublished authors can expect to be turned down by a number of agents, the process can be speeded up by sending queries to four or five simultaneously. If more than one expresses interest in seeing some material, you may pick one, or even submit material to more than one for consideration, although agents prefer that authors not make multiple submissions.

As soon as an agent agrees to represent your work, be sure to get a written agreement specifying the agent's terms. If the agent is successful in placing the work, it is really too late then to find out that his or her terms are unreasonable.

Although it may be useful to be in touch with more than one agent while seeking one to represent you, once you make your decision, you must notify any others to whom you have submitted material that an agent has been selected. Even if there were no agreement to the contrary, it would be chaotic to have more than one agent seeking a publisher for your project.

You may postpone the selection of an agent until after you have found an interested publisher. In fact, some editors will urge authors who do not have an agent to get one. The editor is then spared explaining the details of the business to you and coping with unreasonable requests, as well as avoiding the risk of spoiling a good editorial relationship by hard feelings that might develop while negotiating directly with you.

There are advantages in delaying the selection of an agent. With an interested publisher already located, it is easier to get a well-qualified agent. An editor will usually be willing to recommend several agents. It is unlikely, however, that the editor will recommend an agent who will be exceptionally aggressive on your behalf.

If you find your own publisher and then seek an agent, you will normally be expected to pay the agent's full commission rates, even though you have performed the agent's first task. However, you will be able to acquire the services of an experienced agent, one who probably would not have been willing to represent you earlier, and the chances are that the agent will get you a better deal with your publisher.

Finally, there is a small but increasing number of lawyers who are serving as authors' agents. They obviously bring a different expertise to the relationship; they're normally stronger on the legal implications of an agreement than on its publishing implications. If you are interested in estate planning involving literary properties, then the skills of a lawyer who also knows publishing will be especially useful. Some authors use the services of both a literary agent and a lawyer, but this is expensive and seems worthwhile only in more complex situations involving a good deal of money. Lawyers generally work on a fee basis, but there is nothing to prevent their working for a percentage of royalty earnings if they are functioning as literary agents.

Chapter 8

How Publishing Decisions Are Made

You may well wonder why it takes weeks, even months, to learn whether a publisher is interested in your work. Sometimes, frankly, it is because the publishing proposal is sitting in a pile with others, waiting for the editor to get to it. Sometimes it is because of the decision-making process.

In order to make a publishing decision on any book, trade or text, professional or scholarly, the editor needs answers to four basic questions:

1. *Does it fit into our publishing program?*
2. *Is the quality of the sample material good?*
3. *What will it cost to publish?*
4. *Will it sell enough copies at a price to recover those costs and make an adequate profit?*

Editors can usually make a negative decision in a matter of minutes, and the more experienced the editor, the more projects he or she can dispose of quickly. But for potential candidates for publication, answering the basic questions can require some work.

Does it fit our program?

A publisher ordinarily does not just publish every good book that he or she can get, because this would result in a miscellaneous array of books, expensive to market, and with no identity in the marketplace. Therefore, most publishers have programs that are in effect definitions of the kinds of books they want to publish for a given market or markets. A trade publisher may establish a nonfiction program in sports, a textbook publisher may establish a program in advanced physical sciences, a scholarly publisher may have a program in Renaissance literature, and so on. Most publishers have a number of programs, and a large publisher has dozens. If the book proposed for publication does not fit within these established programs, then it is likely to be rejected, unless it is outstanding. As suggested earlier, it is also in your interest to have your book in a program, since the publisher will be able to do a more effective job of marketing it.

Is the quality of the sample material good?

Will it interest the market for which it is written? If it is nonfiction, is it factually accurate? Is it well organized and well written? As noted above, editors can quickly recognize and reject obviously poor material. However, projects that look promising on the surface need a more thorough review. If the proposal is for a trade book, the editor will usually do the more thorough review personally. If it is not a trade book, one or more outside advisors will evaluate the material. The editor will not proceed with this outside review, however, unless the project seems able to clear the other hurdles regarding costs, sales, and profits.

What will it cost to publish?

There are several elements in a publisher's costs: the cost of physically producing the books; royalties for the author; and the marketing, order processing, and other operating costs. There are guidelines for figuring most of these costs, although estimating production costs is sometimes tricky. If the book is straight text, as in most novels, the editor can usually estimate its cost from schedules provided by the production manager. If it is a technical book with tables, or equations, or many illustrations, the editor will have cost estimates made by the publisher's production manager. Again, however, the editor will not do this unless it appears on the surface that the project is publishable.

    An important element in the cost of making books is the size of the print run. The more copies that are printed at one time, the lower the cost per copy will be. However, the more copies printed, the longer it takes to sell them, and the lower costs are offset by the cost of having money tied up for a longer period of time, the cost of storing copies, and the increased chance that they will not be sold. In trade publishing, the quantity printed is limited to the number of copies the publisher is confi-

dent of selling, and because of the uncertainty of trade sales, these tend
to be small quantities, perhaps five thousand to ten thousand copies. On
a successful trade book, it is not uncommon for the publisher to make
three or four such printings and sometimes as many as a dozen small
printings in the first year, not knowing how well it will continue to sell.
On the other hand, the first printing on books by well-known authors
with established track records, such as James Michener or Sidney
Sheldon, may be as large as 250,000 copies.

On textbooks and professional books, publishers try to print no
more copies than they believe they can sell in a year. Publishers of scholarly books frequently print a three-year supply, because a printing for a
one-year sale—perhaps only eight hundred to one thousand copies—
would be prohibitively expensive.

Deciding the size of the first printing, which in turn is determined by initial sales estimates, is always difficult. If the estimated sale
and proposed first printing are conservative, high costs may make it impossible to publish the book. On the other hand, if the sales estimate and
proposed print run are too optimistic, the publisher will proceed, only to
lose money because it will not be possible to sell all the copies printed.

This leads to the next and related question.

Will it sell enough copies at a price to recover costs and make an adequate profit?

This is the critical issue, and for the answer the editor must rely less on
facts and more on intuition. First, there is the question of price. Every
experienced editor has a good perception of the price that can reasonably be set on books in his or her programs, based on the length of the
book, the market for which it is written, and the price of other books already available. Second is the question of how many copies of the proposed book can be sold at that price over a period of time. The time
frame used depends on the expected life of the book. On front-list trade
books, the life span will often be a year or less. A college textbook for a
course in which books need to be revised every four years would obviously have a life span of four years. Advanced professional books and
scholarly books, provided they are not on a fast-changing subject, generally sell over five years or longer.

Editors normally base sales estimates on several criteria, such as
how comparable books have sold in the past, if there are competing
books already on the market and the number and quality of those books,
how large a potential market exists, the publisher's ability to reach that
market effectively, and the relative importance of the book to its poten-

tial market. Editors frequently consult with their sales managers and sometimes subsidiary rights managers to get their opinion of a project's probable sale. If it requires an unusually large investment or represents a significant departure from the house's usual offerings, the editor may even undertake some kind of survey of the market for it.

With an estimated cost, price, and sale, the editor can put together a simplified profit study on the project showing whether it can be published profitably. Because production costs affect price, price affects sales, sales determine print quantities, and print quantities determine costs, there is frequently a lot of recasting and recycling of the numbers before coming up with a satisfactory profit study. For example, if the project seems sound but too costly to be priced competitively, the editor may explore the possibility of reducing the size of the book or the number of illustrations, or modifying the specifications, or reducing the royalty rate. Alternatively, the editor may try a higher price on the premise that a superior book will support a higher price.

When the editor is satisfied that the proposed project can be published profitably, the next step is to obtain the necessary approvals to proceed. Since one of the key items to be approved is the royalty terms to be offered the author, the editor may want to discuss royalty rates, advances, and any other critical terms with the author prior to seeking approval. The editor will usually know the maximum he or she can offer based on the book, its costs, and prospects. However, the editor may offer less than the maximum acceptable amount, unless he or she knows this will be totally unacceptable to the author.

The procedures for approving projects differ from house to house, but in almost all cases entail getting the approval of the "publisher," that is, the person who has overall responsibility for the publishing operation for the company or for a division of the company. This approval may be sought directly, or more often, the project is presented to an editorial committee, which the publisher chairs, consisting of other editors as well as marketing, subsidiary rights, and publicity people. The editor normally makes a brief presentation of the project, including information on the estimated number of copies that will be sold, the list price, and the profit it will generate. This information is usually summarized in a document that becomes the company record of the reasoning behind the publishing decision. Frequently the profit study is worked out in great detail, showing, for example, a profit of 16.3 percent after all expenses. Since all of this is usually based only on sample material for a project that probably will not be published until two or three years later in a fast changing world, and which may actually sell only 70 percent of the amount estimated, the detailed arithmetic sometimes required for the approval of a project is little more than a security blanket for the editor and the publisher.

Although the members of the editorial committee will ask questions or possibly make comments about a project, it is the publisher who approves or turns down a project. New editors have more difficulty getting their projects approved because their judgment has not yet been proven. Occasionally editors will be asked to get additional information about projects or to rework their figures based on a different estimate or a different price and to resubmit the project at a later meeting. This may require the editor to reexamine the size of the project, or the number of illustrations, or even to change the book's approach somewhat in order to enlarge its potential market, subject, of course, to the author's agreement. Some flexibility on the part of the author is essential for the publication of many projects.

Authors are often dismayed by the two or three months or longer it takes to get a firm commitment from a publisher. It is not the decision, usually, that takes the time, but the process of gathering information. Many people can be involved in providing the information, including outside advisers, production people, marketing and sub-rights people. The process is complicated by the frequent need to modify the proposal, get new cost estimates, recheck sales estimates, and so forth. In addition, the editor may be working on as many as twenty or thirty other projects at the same time, all in various stages of development, and the need to juggle many projects adds to the time required. The best thing that can be said is that the quick decisions are usually negative. The affirmative decisions take longer.

Chapter 9

The Publishing Contract: an Overview

The publishing contract is both a beginning and an end. It is the end of an often long and frustrating search for a satisfactory publisher and the negotiation of publishing terms, and the beginning of a formal, structured relationship. Although the type of book, the individual publisher, and the nature of the work itself will determine the specific details of the contract, the topics covered in all contracts are essentially the same, except that trade book contracts include some matters not usually included in contracts for other types of books.

The topics generally found in publishing agreements will be explained briefly in this chapter. The most important of them will be dealt with in greater detail in subsequent chapters. (Also see Appendix.)

THE AUTHOR'S COMMITMENT

● The author agrees to deliver a finished manuscript and agreed-upon illustrations by a specified date, and this material must be satisfactory to the publisher. This is one of the more critical issues between authors and publishers since the wording of most contracts makes the publisher sole judge of what is satisfactory. As a result, this clause can be used to cancel a commitment that the publisher, for whatever reason, no longer wishes to honor. He can also cancel the agreement if the manuscript is not delivered on time. This clause will be discussed more fully in Chapter 10. The potential problems in providing illustrations are treated separately in Chapter 17.

● The author agrees to obtain written permission for the use of any copyrighted material that is to be included in the work. Permissions are discussed in Chapter 12.

● The author agrees to read and make necessary corrections in proofs of the work. Further, if the author makes changes in proofs that are not corrections of publisher's or typographer's errors, the author agrees to pay for the cost of any such changes that exceed a specified percentage (usually between 10 and 20 percent) of the cost of composition. This is to protect the publisher from an author who may be inclined to rewrite major portions of a book after it has been set in type. Proofreading and corrections are discussed in Chapter 21.

● Unless it is a fictional work, the author agrees to prepare an index. This is discussed in Chapter 21.

● The author guarantees that the work is original (except for copyrighted material for which permission will be obtained and for material in the public domain) and that there is no other publishing agreement or other legal obstacle, such as a court injunction, to prevent the author from entering into the agreement. The author also guarantees that the work contains no libelous, obscene, or dangerous material and assumes some financial liability for any legal actions arising out of any violation of the guarantee. The extent of the author's financial liability is an important issue, especially on works where the risk of a libel action is high, such as in novels based on factual events, memoirs, biographies, and so forth. This topic is discussed in Chapter 15.

● In many trade book contracts, the author is asked to grant the publisher an option or the right of first refusal on the author's next work. This is also a critical issue and is discussed in Chapter 14.

● The author grants the publisher the right to publish the work and to sell the rights for other editions and uses (paperback, book club, and foreign language editions, magazine serialization, dramatizations, and so forth). The contract should also stipulate that in the event of the publisher's bankruptcy (a rare event), all rights revert to the author.

● The author agrees not to write, edit, or produce a competing work, that is, a work that a person might reasonably buy instead of the work covered by the contract.

● The author agrees to prepare a revision of the work if requested by the publisher, or if the author is unable or unwilling to do so, to permit the publisher to arrange for a revised edition to be prepared by another party and to deduct the cost of the revision from the author's royalties to be earned from that revision. This clause will not normally be included in a contract for a novel or biography, or any other work that the publisher is not likely to want revised. Revisions are discussed further in Chapter 18.

● If the author has a literary agent, the agent is authorized to act on the author's behalf in any matters pertaining to the publication of the work, and to receive all royalty statements and payment provided for in the contract. This subject was dealt with more fully in Chapter 7 on the role of agents.

● The author gives the publisher the right to discontinue publication of the work if, in the publisher's judgment, the level of sales does not justify keeping it in print. Termination of the agreement is discussed in Chapter 19.

THE PUBLISHER'S COMMITMENT

● The publisher agrees to publish the work, usually within twelve months after the final manuscript has been accepted. This protects the author against the publisher losing interest in the manuscript and shelving it indefinitely. However, the commitment to publish within twelve months is common only in trade book contracts.

● The publisher agrees to copyright the work either in the author's name or the publisher's name as agreed. This matter is dealt with separately in Chapter 12 on copyrights and permissions.

● The publisher agrees to pay the author a royalty on all copies sold and on all subsidiary rights sold. The publisher also agrees to provide royalty statements and make payments on a specified schedule. The royalty percentage paid customarily varies both by the number of copies sold and the nature of the sale. The publisher may also agree to give the author an advance against those royalties. The royalty arrangements are the financial guts of the agreement for both parties and are the issues over which much of the negotiating is done. Royalties are treated at length in Chapter 11 as well as in Chapter 20 on negotiating a book contract.

● The publisher agrees to give a certain number of copies of the work to the author, usually less than twenty, and to sell additional copies to the author at a discount from the list price. However, publishers may be flexible in the number of free copies to be provided, and if the author will need to give copies to people who helped in preparing the book, or in exchange for permissions granted, or to friends and associates, he should be sure to ask that the number of free copies be increased.

ISSUES AFFECTING BOTH PARTIES

● The contract may not be transferred by either party without the consent of the other.

● The contract stipulates the state whose laws are to apply to the agreement, which is usually the state in which the publisher is located. New York is actually the best state in this regard, since the heavy concentration of publishing there has resulted in a larger body of law and precedents than elsewhere.

● The agreement is binding on the heirs, representatives, and successors of both parties.

WORK MADE FOR HIRE

Sometimes an author will be asked to prepare material on a "work made for hire" basis, that is, to write a piece of material which the contracting publisher or individual will own outright, and for which he may pay either a fixed fee or a royalty. This arrangement is common when the project is large and requires many contributors, such as an encyclopedia or other large reference work. A fixed fee is usually paid for such contributions because the division of a normal royalty among many contributors would be difficult to do equitably, and the number of small royalty checks to be distributed semi-annually would be burdensome to manage as well. Work made for hire arrangements will also be used sometimes, however, when the publisher plays the major role in defining the nature of the project and in creating the content.

In work made for hire agreements, the commitments made by both parties are generally similar to those in a standard book contract, but topics relating to any continuing interest or rights of the author in the work are omitted.

The subject of works made for hire is discussed more fully in Chapter 13.

Chapter 10

Delivering the Manuscript

If you have signed a contract based on sample chapters, you are probably elated at having cleared this significant hurdle, but there is a still larger hurdle ahead. The manuscript must be written and delivered by a specific date, together with any agreed-upon illustrations, and it must be satisfactory to the publisher in all respects—in content, in writing style, and in physical form. That is what the contracts usually say.

Although these may seem to be tough and perhaps arbitrary conditions, it is easy to see from a publisher's point of view why they must be set.

DELIVERY DATES

A delivery date is important for two reasons. First, a book is accepted for publication based on an evaluation of a market for it at a given time, and the size of that market will change with changing interests, new events, and, in some cases, new technology. The importance of the delivery date and the subsequent publication date differs greatly from project to project based on the subject matter and the circumstances. A year or two may not be critical to a novel, whereas one month can be vital to a book about a political candidate, or the Olympics, or a new income tax code.

Delivery dates can be especially important on textbooks because sales are highly seasonal. For example, a textbook for a college course that is usually given in the fall of the year should be published not later than the preceding April, so that it can be presented to instructors who must make a selection in June. To meet the April date, the completed manuscript must be submitted, at the latest, the preceding spring. Otherwise, the book may appear too late to be effectively marketed (a fate from which it can be difficult to recover) or the publisher may postpone publication for a year. The author's royalty income is thus delayed, and the book is likely to be slightly out of date on publication.

Lateness irritates publishers for another reason, too. The publisher will only begin to recover the author's advance after the book is published. The longer that money is tied up in the project, the less is available for other expenses (including advances to other authors). The larger the advance, the more concerned the publisher is likely to be about significant delays in the completion of the manuscript.

Normally, unless timing is really critical, publishers are fairly understanding about delays of a few months in the delivery of the manuscript, and if there is no significant advance outstanding and no evidence that the book's market is diminishing, a delay of a year or more may be tolerated. However, keep in mind that failure to deliver your manuscript on schedule can be cause for your publisher to cancel the contract and demand the repayment of the advance. It is important, therefore, that you allow a reasonable amount of time for the completion of your work, including time for some rewriting. One approach is to develop a weekly production schedule that takes into account other commitments, and then add 50 percent more time to accommodate unforeseeable problems. It is reasonable to set tough performance goals for yourself, but they should be set privately, not in the contract with your publisher.

If you see that it will be difficult to meet a delivery date, the best course of action is to notify your publisher immediately and ask for an extension. In the unlikely event that the publisher is unwilling to grant an extension, you still have time to do something about it, such as cancelling other commitments, taking a leave of absence, or finding a collaborator to help.

THE SATISFACTORY MANUSCRIPT

It is easy to understand why publishers reserve the right to reject a completed manuscript; it may turn out to be rubbish, despite a promising beginning, or the author may have unconsciously drifted away from the original concept while writing. Therefore, the publisher must have the right to return the manuscript for further work, or to reject it if the author is unable or unwilling to revise it so that it conforms to the project that was originally envisioned.

In addition, most publishing contracts state that if an acceptable manuscript is not submitted for publication, then any outstanding advances against royalties are to be returned to the publisher, not an unreasonable requirement if the author fails to perform.

Faced with an unsatisfactory manuscript, some college textbook publishers, subject to the author's agreement, will bring in a professional writer to get the work into publishable form, and charge the cost to the author's royalties.

There are many cases in which manuscripts have been rejected and reasonable arbiters would agree that the manuscripts indeed were not publishable. Unfortunately, however, there are also many cases in which the publisher has simply changed his mind about wanting to publish the project and rejected it as unsatisfactory.

Why might a publisher do this? There are a variety of reasons that have nothing to do with the author or the quality of the book.

● The project may have been assigned by an editor who has since been fired for poor editorial judgment, and to minimize the damage, the editor's projects have been reevaluated, and many rejected.

● The publisher may decide to discontinue a whole program of books of which the author's is a part. Or the publisher may be overcommitted, and have more projects due for publication than he can finance. As a consequence, the company may be rejecting those projects that seem to have a slower, or uncertain payback.

● Another publisher may have just published a book that effectively preempts the market that was seen to exist for the project. Or marketplace interest in the project may have evaporated for reasons that could not, or at least were not, foreseen.

● Finally, there is the gray area where, despite possibly extensive communications between author and publisher, including an outline and sample material, the two parties have had quite different perceptions of what the completed project would be like. The more communication there is between you and your publisher as the writing proceeds, including submitting parts of the manuscript as they're completed, the less likely the final manuscript will be rejected or need a complete overhaul.

Some contracts are more lenient regarding the advance, stating that if a manuscript is rejected as unsatisfactory, you must repay the advance from any monies you may earn if the book is accepted by another publisher. Or the contract may specify that you may keep half the advance if the final manuscript is not accepted. These are reasonable solutions if you truly have not prepared a publishable manuscript. They fall short of being fair if the publisher has simply changed his mind.

As one might expect, a number of cases involving rejected manuscripts have ended up in court. Most frequently, the judgment has been in favor of the publisher, because under the contract, the publisher is the sole arbiter of what constitutes a satisfactory manuscript. However, this was not the outcome of a suit and countersuit involving Senator Barry Goldwater and Harcourt Brace Jovanovich. Goldwater signed a contract with Harcourt in 1977 for the publication of his political memoirs, and at the time received an advance against royalties of $65,000, with an additional $135,000 to be paid when the final manuscript was accepted for publication. However, the final manuscript was rejected as being badly organized and uninteresting, and Harcourt demanded the return of the $65,000 advance. Goldwater brought a countersuit for the $135,000 additional advance, claiming that he had requested editorial help from Harcourt, but that none had been forthcoming. Judge Thomas P. Griesa decided in favor of Goldwater. The judge found that Harcourt had an implied obligation to provide some editorial guidance to the author and that this had not been given. Supporting or perhaps contributing to the judgment was the fact that in the meantime, William Morrow and Company had published the work in a somewhat revised form and the book had been quite successful.

A more recent case by the same U.S. district court tends to reinforce the Goldwater ruling. Dell Publishing Company sued Julia Whedon for the return of a $14,000 advance paid for a manuscript that Dell later rejected. Judge J. Edward Lombard decided in favor of Whedon, arguing that "Dell was under a good-faith obligation to give Whedon an opportunity to revise the manuscript to Dell's satisfaction," and that Dell had failed to fulfill that obligation. Curiously, Doubleday & Company, the parent company of Dell, accepted the book for publication one month after it was rejected by Dell, and even more curiously paid an additional advance of $15,000 to Whedon, apparently unaware of Dell's action.

Every author writing a book under contract runs the risk, however small, that the final manuscript will not be accepted for reasons well beyond the author's control and that he or she may be obliged to return the royalty advance.

The Authors Guild has wrestled with this problem at considerable length and recommends that contracts include the following four points:

● That the author shall deliver a manuscript that is "professionally competent and fit for publication."

● That the manuscript will be considered accepted unless the publisher provides a written statement of the specific nature of its shortcomings, and that the author has sixty days in which to submit a revised manuscript in response.

● If the revised manuscript still is not acceptable, the publisher may cancel the contract within sixty days of its receipt, or if no revised manuscript is submitted, within ninety days of having given written notice of the manuscript's shortcomings.

● In the event the contract is terminated, the author is permitted to retain a stated portion of the authorized advance, with any balance to be repaid only from any receipts resulting from the publication of the manuscript by another publisher.

While these are sound provisions from the point of view of the author, it is doubtful if many publishers will accept the "professionally competent and fit for publication" clause, since it is easy to envision a manuscript that is professionally competent and technically fit for publication but which is wide of the mark in terms of its appeal to its market.

Some publishers also object to allowing the author to keep some portion of the advance if the contract is cancelled, since it leaves the publisher vulnerable to the author who fails to produce a good manuscript. While this is true, it would seem a reasonable balance to the risk the author takes in preparing a manuscript in the expectation of receiving royalty income.

In any event, it is certainly desirable for both parties to do whatever they can to reduce the risk of manuscripts being rejected. One step is to have a written description of the project that can be made a part of the publishing contract. If you reread that description periodically, and adhere to it while writing your publisher will find it more difficult to claim that you have not fulfilled your commitment. Furthermore, if you find that the project is changing from the original concept, then you should ask the publisher's approval of the change immediately.

Some contracts require the author to submit portions of the manuscript in order to qualify for advances in increments that can be kept by the author, even if the completed work is rejected. For example, if the total advance is to be $10,000, the publisher can give the author $2,000 on signing the agreement. When the author submits the first quarter of the manuscript and it is found acceptable, the publisher can advance the second $2,000 and release the author from any obligation to return the first $4,000. When the second quarter of the manuscript is submitted and found acceptable, the third $2,000 can be advanced on a nonreturnable basis, and so forth. This procedure requires added discipline on both sides. The author must polish each segment being submitted, and the publisher must in effect reconfirm his interest in the project based on these submissions. This procedure is least workable for fiction, since fiction can seldom be prepared in neat parts, but if it had been followed on the Goldwater book, for instance, it would have saved both parties a lot of grief.

Unless you are an established author with a performance record that makes you a good risk, you will not find it easy to get your publisher to change the "satisfactory to the publisher" clause. However, if you and your publisher follow the procedure suggested above, the risk of rejection can be reduced to a minimum.

Royalties

The royalty terms in any book contract are the money terms, and, other factors being equal, determine how much you make on your books. Although authors may occasionally work for a flat fee, in the vast majority of cases they are compensated by royalty payments based on the publisher's two sources of income from the work:

  1) The sale of copies by the publisher, and

  2) The sale of rights to others to produce and sell copies, or to produce and sell the work in other media (broadcast, recordings, stage, and so forth).

PAYMENTS BASED ON COPY SALES

Royalty payments on copy sales may be a percentage either of the publisher's suggested list price of the book, or of the net selling price (or "net receipts"). The suggested list price is the price in the publisher's catalog and on the jacket or cover of a trade book, and the price at which the publisher sells the book directly to individuals by mail. The net selling price paid by bookstores or wholesalers.

Generally, royalty rates for hard-cover books are between 10 percent and 15 percent of the list price, or if based on the lower net selling price, sometimes a somewhat higher percent. Usually, the rates will step up from 10 percent to 12½ percent to 15 percent as specific sale objectives are achieved, so that a contract might set the royalty rate as 10 percent of the first five thousand copies sold, 12½ percent on the next five thousand copies sold, and 15 percent on all copies sold thereafter. The quantities at which the royalty rates increase may be lower, for example, at twenty-five hundred copies, or higher at ten thousand copies or in some cases the rate may not escalate at all.

The royalty arrangement in any given contract depends on many factors, including the type of book (trade, text, professional, or scholar ly), the flexibility the publisher has in pricing the book, the estimated production cost, the publisher's estimate of the book's potential, the performance of the author's earlier works, and the extent to which there is competition among publishers for the work. The rates discussed in this chapter for various types of publishing are the most common, but if you are writing a trade book and have not been published before, you may have to accept less in order to get your work published.

Trade Books

The Authors Guild conducts surveys of the royalty terms on hard-cover adult trade books published each year. The data below is a summary of survey results over the last eleven years.

ROYALTY RATE	NO. OF CONTRACTS	PERCENT
10% of list price on first 5,000 copies sold; 12½% on next 5,000 copies sold; 15% on all copies sold thereafter	1,032	57.0
10% of list price on first 5,000 copies sold; 12½ on next 2,500 copies sold; 15% on all copies sold thereafter	141	7.8
Straight 15% of list price	216	11.9
All other royalty rates based on list price	383	21.2
All royalty rates based on net receipts	34	1.9
All other arrangements (such as fixed fees)	3	.2
Total	**1,809**	**100.0**

Despite the many different publishers in the survey and the diverse nature of the books, the first three sets of terms, all in the range of 10 to 15 percent of list price, account for 76.7 percent of the arrangements, and a few of the "all other royalty rates based on list price" fall within that range as well. However, about 90 percent of the responses are from the six thousand members of the Authors Guild who tend to be established, successful trade authors who can command higher royalties. A response from all published trade authors would undoubtedly show a higher percent of contracts at lower rates, and more contracts based on net receipts.

The Authors Guild has also done several surveys of royalty terms on contracts for children's books. These surveys show that for the highly illustrated books for the preschool to eight-year-old group, most authors and illustrators each receive a royalty of 5 percent of the list price. If the authors provide both text and illustrations, most receive either a straight 10 percent of list price, or 10 percent stepping up to 12½ percent or 15 percent at specified levels of total sales. On books for children eight years old and older (books in which illustrations play a lesser role) most authors receive either a flat 10 percent of list price, or 10 percent stepping up to 12½ or 15 percent at specified levels of total sales, and in most cases the authors provide whatever illustrations are needed. If the publisher provides the illustrations, their cost will usually be deducted from the author's royalty.

Royalty rates on trade paperbacks usually begin at 6 percent of list price for the first ten thousand to twenty thousand copies and increase to 7½ to 8 percent thereafter. Sometimes the rate is increased to 10 percent when sales reach greater amounts, such as fifty thousand copies. Royalty rates on mass-market paperback editions are similar, but with increases at much higher levels of sales. For example, a royalty rate of 6 percent of the list price is usually paid on the first 150,000 copies, increasing to 8 percent on the next 150,000 copies, and possibly increasing to 10 percent thereafter. If the mass-market or trade paperback rights are sold to another publisher, then the original publisher keeps half of the royalty income and pays the other half to the author. If the original publisher also publishes the paperback editions, the author normally gets the full royalty.

Since almost all trade books are sold at discounts ranging from 40 to 50 percent of the list price, net receipts average about 55 percent of the publisher's list price, and a given royalty rate based on net receipts produces proportionately lower royalty payments.

It is not altogether clear why trade book royalties are usually based on list price and textbooks based on net. Perhaps it is largely tradition, for the early trade publishers in the U.S. were often both book printers and bookstore proprietors, selling their own books at retail, so that there were no discounted sales in the picture. Also, agents find royalties on list prices easier to explain and audit than on net sales at various discounts. Nevertheless, some publishers prefer to pay royalties on net sales, not only because it is easier to sell an author a higher rate on a lower net amount than a lower rate on list price, but also because net sales income is all that the publisher actually receives.

Professional Books

The royalty terms on domestic trade sales of professional books normally range between 10 and 15 percent of the net selling price (or net receipts). Many contracts provide for the royalty rate to increase as certain sales levels are reached, such as 10 percent on the first twenty-five hundred copies sold, 12½ percent on the second, and 15 percent thereafter. Sometimes the royalty rate increases at five-thousand-copy intervals. A few contracts are written at a 10 percent rate on all sales, and a few at 15 percent. If the market for a book tends to resist high prices, the publisher will want to keep the royalty rate down so that he can keep the price down. If the market tends to be less sensitive to high prices, then the publisher can afford a higher royalty rate. If the book contains complex graphs, charts, or illustrations that result in high initial production costs, the publisher may want only a 10 percent royalty for, say, the first five thousand copies, aiming to recover his costs on those sales, but be willing to pay a higher royalty on sales beyond that point.

The discounts at which professional books are sold to bookstores range from a trade discount schedule of 40 to 46 percent (depending on the size of the order) for books of very broad appeal all the way down to a 20 percent discount on medical and other highly technical books. In order to estimate your royalties on bookstore sales, ask your publisher for not only the probable list price to be set on your book, but also the discount at which it will be sold to bookstores and wholesalers, so you can estimate what the net selling price will be.

College Textbooks

Most college textbook royalties are based on net selling price (or net receipts) rather than the publisher's suggested list price. Since most college texts sell to bookstores at a 20 percent discount, or in a few cases at 23 or 25 percent, royalty payments at the net selling price are 75 to 80 percent of royalties at list price.

Royalty rates paid on college textbooks vary considerably, depending in part on the size of the market for the book, its nature and quality, and the number of publishers interested in it. Typically, the college textbook author will receive a royalty of 10 percent, 12½ percent and 15 percent of the net selling price, with the royalties stepping up at intervals of anywhere between twenty-five hundred and fifteen thousand copies. If the textbook is a book of readings or a study guide, the royalty is often 10 percent of the net selling price, since publishers need to keep down prices of supplementary materials. Also preparing readings requires less work (mostly getting permissions and paying fees) on the part of the author, and a study guide tends to enhance the sale of the text that it supplements. Authors of textbooks with unusual promise for success may receive a flat royalty of 15 percent of net, or even as high as

18¾ percent of net if several publishers are bidding. At a 20 percent discount, this is equivalent to 15 percent of list price.

In competitive situations, some college textbook publishers occasionally offer royalty rates that step up retroactively if the book achieves a given copy sale in a given period of time. For example, the basic royalty may be 15 percent of the net selling price with a provision that if the book sells fifty thousand copies in its first two years, then the author will receive an additional 3 percent of net sales on those first fifty thousand copies, as well as on all sales thereafter. While this type of arrangement has a lot of initial appeal to the author, it may cause problems if the book just falls short of achieving the qualifying sale. For example, if the book sells 49,600 copies in its first two years, is it possible that the publisher slackened his marketing effort as the fifty thousandth sale became imminent? Is it possible there were unprocessed orders for four hundred copies in the publisher's distribution facility when the two years were up? Or if the book was out of stock for two weeks during the critical second-year selling period, should the author be deprived of the extra royalty income, which could amount to $25,000, because the publisher didn't keep the book in stock? This type of arrangement is such fertile ground for the seeds of suspicion and ill will that it should be avoided by both parties.

School Textbooks

These royalties are also usually based on the net selling price, or gross receipts. Sales are normally made at a discount of 25 percent to bookstores and schools, but some publishers set only a net selling price, rather than a suggested list price that is discounted to their accounts. Royalty rates on school textbooks can range from 3 to 10 percent, depending on the size of the author's contribution as compared to work done by the publisher. For example, it is not uncommon for schoolbook publishers to do a large share of the research and writing, as well as the preparation of illustrations, and these contributions by the publisher are reflected in the royalties paid to authors. However, even at 3 percent, the earnings on a sale of several hundred thousand copies a year can produce a good supplement to one's income.

Scholarly Books

On scholarly monographs, university presses usually pay no royalty at all on the sale of a specified number of copies, such as on the first one thousand or two thousand copies, and then pay 10 percent of the net selling price on all copies sold thereafter. The royalty rate may step up to 12½ and 15 percent when higher levels of sales are achieved. On sales to bookstores, the discount is likely to be 40 percent with an even higher discount to wholesalers, so that a royalty of 10 percent of net is likely to be less than a 6 percent royalty based on list price. However, these terms are not surprising when one considers that scholarly books are rarely profitable, and usually require a subsidy either from the press or from an outside source.

When a university press publishes a more traditional trade book or a textbook, the royalty terms will usually be similar to the terms offered by a trade or textbook publisher.

Royalties on Other Sales and Special Situations

Almost all contracts for trade, professional, text, and scholarly books provide that a lower royalty rate will be paid on foreign sales, usually half the amount payable on domestic trade sales, and for copies sold to consumers by direct mail, a 5 percent royalty is normal. These lower rates are paid because of the higher costs of selling, shipping, billing and collecting on sales to these markets. Also, because of the high cost of making very small printings, most also state that if the book is selling less than five hundred copies a year, for example, and a reprint must be made to keep the work in print, then a reduced royalty rate will be paid, usually half the rate otherwise applicable on sales. (This clause disturbs authors, because a publisher could reduce an author's royalty rate by suppressing sales, but it is unlikely that this is ever done.)

Trade book publishers in particular have a number of clauses that specify smaller royalty rates under certain circumstances. For example, if royalties are on list price, most specify that on sales at discounts of 48 percent or greater, the royalty rate will be lower by one or two percent. At these larger discounts, publishers can't afford to pay a full royalty on list. For the same reason, most also provide that if a large quantity sale is made at a specially negotiated low price for premium or promotional use rather than for resale, the author will receive a royalty on the publisher's net receipts.

A number of trade book publishers have instituted a "freight-pass-through" plan in order to provide bookstores with some relief from high postal costs for the delivery of books to their stores. Under this plan, the publisher sets two prices on each book, an invoice price which is the price from which the bookstore's net price is computed, and a jacket price which may be about 50 cents higher than the invoice price, which becomes the publisher's suggested list price. In other words, under this plan, publishers have added a small amount on to the suggested list price of the book which the bookstores pocket to help them pay their delivery costs, without publishers changing their own costs of doing business. Publishers who are employing some form of this plan state in their contracts that royalty payments are to be based on the invoice list price rather than on the jacket list price. As a result, instead of a 10 percent royalty, for example, you receive a royalty of between 9.5 percent and 9.8 percent of the actual price that the bookstore's customer pays for the book, the percentage depending on the price of the book and the nature of the publisher's plan.

Participation in a "freight-pass-through" plan is hardly critical in selecting a publisher, but you should know that these plans exist and understand their impact on royalty earnings. Furthermore, in such cases, you should require your contract to state that the jacket list price on your book be no more than 50 cents higher than the invoice list price in order to prevent any greater decrease in your royalty payments.

Caveats Regarding Royalties on Copy Sales

On all contracts with royalties that increase as specific sales targets are reached, be sure to understand what sales are to be counted toward the higher royalty rates. Some contracts will specifically exclude certain classes of sales from the count, such as premium sales, direct mail sales, or even international sales.

Royalties based on the net selling price or net receipts may create problems for you if your publisher has subsidiary or affiliated companies in book publishing or book sales, such as bookstores, book clubs, and international subsidiaries. A publisher selling either books or rights to its own subsidiaries or affiliated companies is free to establish any discount schedule or price it wishes in dealing within its corporate structure; thus, royalties based on that net price can be substantially less than they ought to be. For example, if a publisher with a chain of bookstores sells its own books to its chain at a discount of 55 percent instead of the more usual 45 percent, perhaps in return for its chain stocking all the publisher's titles, and if your book had a list price of $10, your royalty at 10 percent of net sales would be 45 cents per copy sold through that chain instead of 55 cents. You can protect yourself against this in your contract by having an appropriate royalty rate applied to the list price of the book instead of the net price on sales to its subsidiaries. In the example given, a royalty of 5.5 percent of list price would give you your proper return on the sale. Similarly, the royalties on selections by the publisher's own book clubs should be based on the price to members, rather than on the net price the publisher charges its own club for the books—which can be any price it chooses.

Copy Distributions on Which No Royalties Are Paid

Most contracts, and all trade book contracts, specify that no royalty will be paid on copies that are destroyed or copies that are sold at or below the cost of manufacture as "remainders." Remainders are copies that the publisher has printed but has been unable to sell over time through normal distribution channels at normal discounts. Instead they are sold in bulk at a price usually below cost to distributors specializing in remainders. The distributors in turn sell them to retail outlets who sell them to the public at a fraction of the publisher's suggested list price.

Since remainders may occasionally be sold above the manufacturing cost, your contract should be specific that royalties will continue to be paid unless books are sold "at or below manufacturing cost." Sometimes publishers remainder a portion of their stock and retain a portion for continuing sales. For example, if they have ten thousand copies on hand, and the book is selling one thousand copies a year, they may remainder seven thousand copies. However, this practice angers booksellers who are trying to sell the book at its list price in competition with the low-priced remainders. As a result of remaindering, authors provide many readers with material for which they receive no compensation—material that competes in the marketplace with other books on which authors receive royalties.

If a trade book is unsuccessful from the outset, it may be remaindered as early as six months after publication. On the other hand, a book may do very well for two or three years before sales drop off, leaving the publisher with copies to be remaindered. Authors often wish they could prohibit publishers from early remaindering, but publishers are no more eager to remainder books that might continue to sell than their authors, so there is little point in requiring them to postpone the inevitable. However, authors should insist on being given the right to purchase copies at the remainder price if they wish to do so.

Textbooks and professional books are not normally remaindered, because there is no organized market for them. Copies that publishers cannot sell may be donated to organizations who distribute them in third-world countries, or they may be destroyed. Publishers also destroy copies that are defective or damaged and not in salable condition.

Most contracts state that the publisher will pay no royalty on free copies distributed to promote the sale of the work. Most of this free-copy distribution is to various media for review or for some other type of publicity, or to instructors so they may consider the work for use in courses of instruction. This kind of distribution should certainly be encouraged, since it is usually the best promotion a book can have. In some cases, in order to increase the number of copies stocked by bookstores at the time of publication, trade book publishers will make a prepublication offer to bookstores of one free copy for every ten ordered. The publisher's only cost is the manufacturing cost of that copy. The bookseller gets eleven copies for the price of ten, which is equivalent to an additional 9 percent discount. But when the extra copy is sold—and it is usually considered the first copy sold—the author makes nothing. One could argue that authors should receive a royalty on those extra copies. However, publishers are not making any money on these copies either, and if they had to pay royalties, they would probably give up this practice, one which can be effective in boosting prepublication orders. You should understand, however, that you are contributing your royalty income on the free copies distributed in these offers.

ROYALTIES BASED ON THE SALE OF RIGHTS

If you do not have an agent, your publisher normally will acquire all rights to your work. Your publisher may then exercise some of those rights himself by publishing a hard-cover or paperback edition of the work, and may sell other rights, such as book club rights or dramatization rights, to others. Publishers usually retain some flexibility as to whether they will exercise certain rights themselves or sell them. In particular, they usually want to be able either to publish a paperback edition themselves or to sell the paperback rights to another publisher. If they operate one or more book clubs, they may want to use the author's work in their own clubs, but also sell book club rights to others. On all publishing rights exercised by the publisher, the author normally receives a royalty on copy sales as specified earlier. On the sale of rights, the author receives a share—most often 50 percent or better.

Earnings from the sale of subsidiary rights in textbooks, scholarly books, and technical and professional books are relatively modest, since rights sales are generally limited to foreign language editions and small, special interest book clubs. Contracts for these books normally specify a single royalty arrangement for all subsidiary rights sales, usually a 50-50 split between the author and the publisher.

On trade books, however, income from the sale of subsidiary rights can dwarf the income from copy sales, and the contractual arrangements may be complex. Following is a brief description of the full array of rights that may be sold by the publisher, and how the income is normally shared with the author.

• First Serial Rights. This is the right to publish the work, or an abridgement or selection from the work, in a magazine or newspaper prior to the publication of the book itself. This is usually granted as an exclusive right. Although it might appear that serialization of the work prior to publication would hurt book sales, in practice it is valuable publicity. The author is usually paid 90 percent of the publisher's receipts.

• Second Serial Rights. These are the rights to publish abridgements or selections in magazines and newspapers after the publication of the book, and are normally not exclusive. The author is usually paid 50 percent of receipts.

• Mass-Market Reprint Rights. Typically, this is the most lucrative of the subsidiary rights. The publisher tries to solicit bids from mass-market publishers when interest in the book is at its peak. The mass-market publishers bid in terms of the royalty they will pay, usually between 6 and 10 percent of the paperback list price, and an advance against those royalties, which can be anywhere from $2,500 to several million dollars. Since the advance does not need to be repaid even if sales do not cover it, this is a guaranteed minimum royalty. The reprint publisher receives a license for the paperback edition usually for a period of five to seven years. Since the publication of the mass-market paperback reduces the sale of the hard-cover edition, the original publisher sets the earliest date on which the paperback edition may be published, usually at one year after publication of the hard-cover edition. The author is usually paid 50 percent of the publisher's receipts from the sale of these rights.

If the publisher operates or is part of a corporation that owns a mass-market paperback house, then the company may choose to exercise those rights rather than sell them, and the contract will probably provide for royalties of between 5 and 10 percent of the list price to be paid on all sales of the mass-market paperback sold. In this event, authors get the full 5 to 10 percent, whereas if the rights are sold, the authors only get half of royalties paid by the mass-market paperback publisher. Authors usually receive no separate advance for the paperback edition if it is published by the original publisher, but the original advance may be larger.

• Other Reprint Rights. These are the rights to publish other editions of the work, such as a trade paperback edition or even a hard-cover reprint. It is not uncommon for several editions of the work to be in print at the same time, each appealing to different segments of the market. Frequently, trade publishers will publish their own trade paperback edition and pay the author a royalty on copy sales. However, they may sell the rights to another publisher if this seems a more attractive alternative. As noted elsewhere, university presses sometimes pick up reprint rights to works that the original publisher no longer wishes to keep in print. On the sale of all reprint rights, the author is usually paid 50 percent of receipts.

• Book Club Rights. If one of the large book clubs, such as Book-of-the-Month or Literary Guild, selects an author's work, the additional income to the publisher and the author is quite attractive. Such a club normally pays a royalty to the publisher of 10 percent of the club price for all copies sold, and the advance against the royalties for a main selection will be around $100,000. The royalty split between publisher and author is normally 50-50. Some publishers deduct the cost of providing the club with reproduction materials before dividing the advance with the author.

Given the number of candidates and the limited number of books selected by these clubs, the average author's chance of having a work selected is only slightly better than their chance of being struck by lightning. The chances are far better that a work will be selected by one of the smaller, special-interest book clubs. These also usually pay the publisher 10 percent of the club price for all copies sold as well as an advance, but the total amount paid is almost always much less.

If the publisher operates a book club or is affiliated with a company operating a book club, then the contract should provide for a royalty payment on the sale of copies through the club. In such cases, most contracts provide for a royalty of 5 percent of the price at which the book is sold to members; the contract should also provide for a royalty of 5 percent of the club price on copies used as premiums or dividends in the club.

There is some royalty advantage in having club offerings delayed until after a book has been on the market for six months to year. Some club members may buy the book from a store in this period, and an author receives a larger royalty on such sales. On the other hand, the word-of-mouth impact of a club selection, linked with reviews and other promotion at the time of publication, can stimulate sales dramatically.

• Dramatization Rights. These involve adaptations of a book for live theatre, motion pictures, television, and radio. The greatest potential source of income is the sale of rights to a Hollywood studio, a TV network, or an independent producer of motion pictures for theaters or TV.

Normally, publishers grant authors 90 percent of the income received from dramatization rights. Usually producers begin by purchasing an option on the work for a period of time for a relatively modest amount; this is shared with the author on the same terms as the income from the sale of the rights themselves. Many options are never exercised.

● Translations. Foreign language editions are another source of income for trade books, texts, and professional books as well. Publishers solicit the sale of translation rights by sending copies of works to foreign publishers for their consideration. Usually there is only one deal per language, so that the sale of Spanish language rights to a Colombian publisher, for example, gives him the right to sell the work in the Spanish language throughout the world. The foreign language publisher, who must pay to have the work translated, pays the U.S. publisher a royalty of between 5 and 7½ percent of the list price of the foreign language edition, and an advance against those royalties. Although the royalty earnings on each deal tend to be small, usually not more than a few thousand dollars, if there are a number of them, they can add up to a worthwhile total. If the foreign publisher fails to publish the translation within a specified time, the translation license is cancelled, but the publisher and the author keep their shares of the advance. On trade books, publishers usually pay authors 75 percent of the income received for translation rights. On textbooks and professional books, publishers usually split the income 50-50 with their authors.

If a publisher operates a foreign subsidiary, the publisher should not claim that it is "selling" translation rights to that subsidiary; the company already has those rights, and is merely assigning them within the company. Any so-called "sale" is likely to be on low, noncompetitive terms. Instead, the contract should provide for royalty payments to the author of between 5 and 7½ percent of the translation's list price, preferably stepping up from 5 to 7½ percent at a specified level of sales.

● British Commonwealth English-Language Rights. U.S. publishers normally sell their own editions of textbooks and professional books to the entire English-speaking world. But trade book publisher often sell rights to British and sometimes Australian publishers to sell editions in their own countries and other specified English speaking areas such as South Africa and New Zealand. These foreign publishers ordinarily buy printed sheets from the U.S. publisher, but they may print their own copies if they can do so more economically. If the U.S. publisher sells sheets, the author usually receives 10 percent of the publisher's receipts from the sale. If the U.S. publisher sells the rights, the authors usually receives 75 to 80 percent of the publisher's receipts. U.S. publishers usually retain the rights to the Canadian market, and sell copies of the U.S. edition through Canadian distributors or Canadian publishers acting as distributors.

● Audiovisual Rights. Licenses may also be granted for microfilming the work, or making filmstrips or overhead transparencies, or sound recordings. Authors usually receive 50 percent of the publisher's net receipts.

● Other Commercial Rights. At times, a work will take on a life of its own, and its characters may be used to endorse products, may appear on T-shirts, be made into dolls, or be used in new toys and games. The publisher normally pays the author 50 percent of receipts from such sales. These rights are usually sought by the buyer rather than marketed by the publisher, since it is difficult to identify potential buyers.

Authors with literary agents usually hold back selected subsidiary rights, typically first serial rights, dramatic rights, British Commonwealth English language rights, and translation rights. The agent will then try to sell these rights for a commission of between 10 and 25 percent, which is comparable to the share of the income that is normally retained by a publisher handling their sale.

Whenever a publisher can make internal deals with subsidiaries or affiliated companies for the sale of either books or rights, either the terms for such deals should be spelled out in the contract, or the contract should state that the terms for any such arrangements are subject to the author's approval in writing. In such cases, authors must be sure that their share of the income is at least equal to what they would receive through an arm's-length negotiation between separate organizations.

WHEN ROYALTIES ARE PAID

Publishers make royalty payments periodically, and payments are usually accompanied by a statement that should spell out in detail the quantities sold at each royalty rate specified in the contract.

All publishing contracts should state the frequency and timing of royalty statements and payments. Most publishers pay royalties semiannually, a specified amount of time after the close of the calendar half year. A typical contract reads: "Royalty payments shall be made semiannually in March and September for royalties due for the preceding half year." However, some publishers have fiscal years that differ from the calendar year, and customarily pay royalties based on the end of the fiscal year. Some contracts provide for paying royalties as long as 120 days after the close of the royalty period in question.

There are both a financial and an operational reason that publishers do not pay royalties more promptly.

First, publishers can use this money to pay bills, an important consideration to a publisher who is undercapitalized. A chronic problem in publishing is that booksellers are very slow to pay for the books they buy from publishers because bookstores are almost always undercapitalized; as a result, publishers must wait on average about ninety days for the money due from bookstores. Meanwhile, they have printers to pay, a payroll to meet each week, and all the many other operational expenses of doing business.

The second reason to delay paying royalties is the complexity of determining the amount owed to the author. In this day of advanced computer systems, one would expect publishers to be able to get their royalty statements quickly. In practice, however, the nature and variety of the royalty terms negotiated with authors is such that publishers frequently need to make manual adjustments in the statements, and they all need to be checked to be sure, as far as possible, that they are complete and correct. As a result, it is no easy job to get royalty statements and checks to authors within ninety days from the end of a royalty period. And, even so, many contain errors.

Normally, publishers' contracts are worded so that royalties and advances against royalties resulting from the sale of subsidiary rights are paid on the same schedule as royalties on copy sales. However, there is little justification for the publisher holding the author's share until the next regular royalty payment is due. Therefore, you should ask that your contract provide for payment of your share of such income within two weeks of receipt by your publisher, after deducting any royalty advances that are still outstanding.

RESERVE FOR RETURNS

One of the most perplexing problems in book publishing is the large quantities of books that are purchased by bookstores and wholesalers only to be returned to the publisher at a later date, usually for full credit.

Books that are returned unsold are deducted from gross sales to arrive at the net sales figure—either copies or dollars—used to compute royalties. Returns are especially troublesome in the areas of fiction, biography, memoirs, and current affairs. Typically, these books, if successful, sell briskly for an unpredictable period of time—perhaps four to eight months—and then sales diminish rather suddenly, and both retail stores and wholesalers return most of their unsold copies. If the strong selling activity occurs during one royalty period and the returns arrive in the next royalty period, the publisher will have paid the author a royalty on sales in the first period and the author will owe the publisher money on the returns in the second.

In order to avoid this situation, most trade book contracts permit the publisher to withhold up to 15 per cent of the amount earned by the author during the first two or three royalty periods as a reserve against later returns.

However, there are many cases in which such a reserve is not needed. Some books, by their nature, are "backlist" titles that will continue to sell steadily for a number of years. Royalties from these continuing sales would cover any short-term indebtedness resulting from a surge in returns. In addition, for many titles, subsidiary-rights sales would offset any money due on returns. Finally, the returns may well be received in the same royalty period as heavy sales, and so no problem will arise. Because of these factors, the general application of a reserve for returns is unreasonable.

A publisher wishing to establish a reserve for returns should be required to document the need. For example, the contract can state that if the publisher can demonstrate, based on reasonable estimates of sales, subsidiary rights income, and returns, that the author will owe the publisher monies in the subsequent royalty period, then the publisher may withhold up to 15 percent of the royalties payable on sales during the prior period. You may find your publisher reluctant to make this change because it will require extra work to get the reserve.

ROYALTY STATEMENTS

Royalty statements are customarily sent out semiannually and accompany any royalty payments that are due. These statements are intended to show how the royalty earnings have been determined. As discussed previously, most contracts provide for differing royalty rates to be applied to different types of sales (bookstore, foreign, mail order, and so forth), and in order to understand how the total royalty payment is arrived at, the number of copies sold and the rate applied need to be shown, as well as information on each source of subsidiary rights income. Also, during the royalty period the sales volume may have triggered a rise in the royalty rate (say, from 12½ to 15 percent); conversely, returns can reduce total sales below the point at which a higher royalty rate has applied.

Thus, preparing detailed, understandable royalty statements is no easy task, and it is frequently not done well. Many publishers do not provide the detail authors need to audit the statements, and the inability to audit gives rise to the suspicion that one is being cheated. Although it would be reckless to state categorically that no publisher has ever intentionally cheated its authors, there is little evidence to suggest that it is a common occurrence. Aside from the ethical considerations, a publisher with a reputation for cheating his authors would be severely handicapped in attracting and keeping good ones. However, honest mistakes are made from time to time, even by the best of publishers; and authors should be given enough information so that they can protect themselves against mistakes when they are made.

The Authors Guild advocates that publishers' royalty statements include the total number of copies printed and the total copies on hand at the end of the royalty period, in order to help authors audit their payments. In theory, these figures should, by simple subtraction, demonstrate the number of copies sold. However, there are too many ways in which copies are disposed of for it to be that simple. There are review and promotional copies that are given away; copies that are damaged in transit to or at the warehouse, or in the mails, and then destroyed; there are copies lost in the mails and subsequently replaced free of charge by the publisher. Thus, unless a statement explained the fate of each copy, knowing the quantity printed would only reveal an error if more copies were reported sold than were printed, and no author spends much time worrying about that. Moreover, any publisher systematically cheating authors by underreporting sales could as easily underreport the quantities printed as well.

Authors should know the number of copies of their works that have been printed, but that information may not be much help when trying to interpret a royalty statement.

Literary agent Richard Curtis goes one step further and urges publishers to pay a simple royalty rate based on the list price of the total copies printed. The rate would be perhaps as low as one half a normal royalty rate. Payment would be made or credited to the author's account within a few weeks of the delivery of the printing. Rights sales would continue to be accrued or paid as is presently done. It might appear that this system would create a serious cash flow problem for publishers, but because of outstanding advances, a major portion of the earlier "payments" would simply be credits against the author's royalty advance. Although this plan certainly has the virtue of simplicity, it also increases the uncertainty of the profit on each book published. Profits would be better on the books on which the printings are sold out, but losses would be worse when copies had to be remaindered or destroyed. In any event, there seems to be no rush on the part of the industry to embrace this plan.

If you cannot interpret a royalty statement, you should insist on a detailed explanation of how the amount of royalties earned is arrived at, even if this ultimately requires letters to several persons, including the head of the house. (Continued pressure of this sort may make the design of more useful royalty statements an attractive alternative for publishers.)

You should also insist that your contract gives you the right to audit, or have someone audit for you, your publisher's records. Although the cost of such an audit will keep most authors from exercising this option, the opportunity should always exist, and this should help authors get the accurate information they need without recourse to actual audits. Certainly no publisher wants to be caught with his hand in the author's cookie jar.

ROYALTY ADVANCES AND DEFERRALS

One of the major disadvantages to authors of the royalty system of compensation is the enormous length of time between the actual work of writing and the payment. It usually takes at least a year to write a book, a year to get it into print, and on average another six months before any royalty payment is made. Hence, two to three years can easily pass between the beginning of the writing effort and the first regular royalty payment. While this may be tolerable for authors whose main source of income comes from teaching or business or professional practice, it is terrible for authors who live on their writing. For these authors, advances against future royalty earnings can be essential for survival.

Generally, advances to authors of textbooks and reference books are modest because the authors usually have other sources of income. Advances for such works are usually intended to cover the author's out-of-pocket expenses for producing the manuscript. Occasionally, however, if the book promises to have a very large sale and if the author is willing to take a sabbatical to complete the work quickly, then a much larger advance may be forthcoming.

University presses give advances infrequently, and never on

scholarly works on which the author forgoes royalties on some initial sales.

On books of general interest, the advance can be anywhere from a modest $1,000 to a substantial $1 million. However, advances rarely exceed the amount the publisher expects the book to earn back in one year, that is, the number of copies the publisher expects to sell in the first year, multipled by the estimated royalty per copy. Of course, the publisher would prefer not to pay any advance at all, but publishers recognize that advances are one of the costs of being in the publishing business—especially the trade book business—and that they will not be able to attract and hold good authors unless they are reasonably competitive in the advances they offer.

Usually half the advance is paid when the author signs the publishing contract and half when the final manuscript is submitted and accepted for publication. Occasionally, progress payments are made as the author completes and submits portions of the manuscript. For example, on a $10,000 advance, the first $2,500 may be paid when the contract is signed, the second $2,500 when the first third of the manuscript is completed and submitted, the third $2,500 when the second third of the manuscript is submitted, and the final $2,500 when the final manuscript is accepted for publication. Progress payments give authors short-term incentives and a more even flow of income. However, they also require an author to develop chunks of manuscript systematically, which may not be the way he or she likes to work. From the publisher's point of view, progress payments reduce the amount of advances outstanding and the risk of large advances to nonproducing authors. Furthermore, they give the editor a chance to review the material and work with the author if it seems to have gotten off course. As a result, it reduces the risk for author and publisher of a completed manuscript being rejected as unsatisfactory.

If you fail to complete the project, or if it is not accepted by your publisher as "satisfactory," then the contract normally requires you to pay back the advance. This can be difficult to do if you have been using the advance to feed and clothe your family. This problem is dealt with at greater length in Chapter 10. However, if the book is accepted for publication, you are normally under no obligation to pay back any advance in excess of the royalties earned. Your contract should explicitly state that the advance is not to be repaid if the author has fulfilled all his or her obligations set forth in the contract.

If you are under contract to publish several works with a company, the contract or contracts frequently provide for a joint accounting for the advances. That is, although there may be separate advances for each of the projects, royalty earnings from any of the projects can be credited by the publisher to any outstanding advances before additional royalty earnings are paid out to you. You are clearly better off if each project is accounted for separately, since you can keep all the advances even if one or more of the projects do poorly. On the other hand, publishers are generally willing to give larger advances if they are jointly accounted.

Sometimes authors need money before the next royalty payment is due. If the publisher is not short of cash, he may be willing to give you an advance against earned royalties, that is, some portion of the amount your book has earned as of the date of the request. However, this will rarely be provided for in the contract, and certainly should not be counted on.

Keep in mind that you must pay income taxes on royalties and advances against royalties in the year in which the money is received. Since many authors have incomes that fluctuate widely from year to year, it is prudent to negotiate and contract for the payment of advances to fall in years of otherwise low incomes. For example, if you are anticipating a relatively high level of income in the current year, you may ask that the contract specify that the first payment of the advance is to be made in the following year rather than in the current year.

You may also have your royalty payments deferred in order to smooth out earnings over several years and avoid the tax burden of a large income in one year. A typical arrangement is for the payments in any given calendar year not to exceed a given amount, such as $10,000, and royalties earned in excess of that amount accrued and paid out in the following year or years. However, beware of such arrangements. First, there is always the possibility, however remote, that the publisher will go bankrupt. Second, you should not expect the publisher to agree to an earlier payout than the contract specifies, even if the author urgently needs the money for unforseen medical or other catastrophic expenses.

Finally, the book may be enormously more successful than there is any reason to expect, and a limited payout in any calendar year might not allow you to get your full royalty for many, many years. An author can guard against such a situation by having a clause in the contract state that if the amount accrued and owed the author at the end of the calendar year is a specified multiple of the annual limit (five times, for example) then the annual limit is to be increased to a specified amount.

It is also possible to have the so-called advance payments deferred, especially if it is a work on which a very large advance can be negotiated. For example, if you negotiate an advance of $500,000, it can be stipulated that $100,000 is to be paid to you each year for five years, and that any royalties earned in excess of that advance are to be paid out in the years following the last advance payment, but not to exceed $100,000 a year. In such an arrangement, the publisher should be willing to increase the size of the total advance or the royalty rate, since he will have the use of that money until the deferred payments have all been made.

The point is that there are a number of ways in which the timing of royalty payments can be scheduled in order to minimize your tax burden. However, consult your accountant about such arrangements to be sure that the desired objectives will be achieved. Care must be taken to avoid a ruling by tax authorities that you actually had access to the income earlier, a situation called "constructive receipt," and that the income is therefore taxable and at a higher rate.

When large advances are made to authors, publishers sometimes take out life insurance policies on them. Some authors are offended by this practice, taking this to mean that the publisher thinks they are on their last legs. No offense is intended. The publisher is merely protecting his investment against unforeseeable events that can befall the robust as well as the frail.

How negotiable are advances? About as negotiable as the other publishing terms. There is usually an amount beyond which the publisher is not willing to go on each project, but an author has no way knowing what that amount is without negotiating. The maximum amount possible will be determined by the expected sale of the book, but smaller amounts may be dictated by the publisher's policy, or by what the publisher can afford.

GRANTS

Occasionally publishers will make outright grants of money to authors, either in place of or in addition to advances. Grants are most commonly made in highly competitive situations for textbooks, ostensibly to help defray the cost of preparing illustrations, or for some other specific purpose. In really, they are usually used as an incentive to get the author to sign up with the publisher offering the grant. Grants are also given on trade and professional book projects, but usually under special conditions, such as the author's preparation of final artwork or undertaking of other design or production work normally performed by the publisher. Occasionally, if a trade publisher wants a book badly, he may be willing to pay a share of the research or travel expenses needed to write it. This is better than an advance, since it is additional money for the author.

Chapter 12

Copyrights and Permissions

Copyright is of enormous importance to authors. It protects their proprietary rights in their material, making it possible for them to earn a living by writing. Copyright law also deals with the rights of authors to use in their own works limited amounts of material originated by others.

This chapter deals almost exclusively with the provisions of the Copyright Act of 1976, which took effect on January 1, 1978, and is applicable to all works written on or after that date. The new law addresses a broad array of copyrightable materials, including music, dramatic and choreographic works, motion pictures, sound recordings, and even sculptural works; however, here the focus is on what most book authors need to know about copyrights. If you need more detailed information, most libraries have a copy of the law, and, of course, if you are to be seriously affected by a copyright issue, you should consult a lawyer who is knowledgeable about copyright matters. In simplest terms, the copyright law states that, subject to certain exceptions, the originator of any written work is the exclusive owner of that material and has the exclusive right to reproduce and distribute copies of the work and to make derivative versions of the work (adaptations, translations, screen plays, and so forth), or to authorize or license others to do any of the above. It is, of course, the exceptions that make for the complexity.

Limitations

The law explicitly states that copyright protection does not extend to ideas, procedures, processes, systems, methods of operation, concepts, principles, or discoveries that are included in an original work of authorship; that is, the verbal or graphic presentation of such material, if original, is protected by copyright, but not the ideas or concepts themselves.

In addition, works created by employees of the U.S. government as part of their duties are not protected by copyright.

OWNERSHIP AND TERM OF COPYRIGHT PROTECTION

If you are the author of an original work, you are its owner when it is created, and the work is protected by copyright from that moment until fifty years after your death. During that period, you or your heirs may publish and distribute it, or while still retaining the copyright, license other parties to publish and distribute it; you may transfer the copyright to another party, in which case the party to which the copyright is transferred owns all the rights; or you may transfer separately any of the exclusive rights provided by the copyright. If you intend to grant certain rights to a publisher, and grant certain other rights directly or through an agent to another publisher or a producer, then you must retain the copyright.

Generally, authors of trade books retain the copyright and by contract license others to exercise some or all of the rights, primarily because they intend to assign certain subsidiary rights to literary agents. On the other hand, authors of textbooks and reference books usually transfer their copyrights to their publishers because they normally assign all rights to them. In practice, if all rights are granted to the publisher, it makes no difference which party owns the copyright so long as the contract satisfactorily spells out the rights of each party and, if the copyright is transferred to the publisher, provides for the reassignment of the copyright to the author upon termination of the agreement.

If you either transfer the copyright or license another party to publish the work, you have the right to terminate that transfer or license forty years after the date of the transaction or thirty-five years after the date of publication. After you die, the termination interest is owned and may be exercised by your surviving spouse, and by your children and grandchildren, all of whom have an equal interest. Since the termination interest may be divided among a number of persons, more than half of the author's interest must favor termination in order to exercise that right.

If you write an original work as part of your job as a company employee, or if it is commissioned as a contribution to a collective work, or as a translation, or as supplementary material to another work, or as a textbook, and if you expressly agree to this in writing, then the work is considered a "work made for hire," and the copyright is owned by the person or organization for which you prepared it. In such cases, the material is protected by copyright for a period of seventy-five years from the date of publication or 100 years from its creation, whichever occurs first. This same period of protection applies to works of unknown authorship, since the date of the death of the author cannot be determined.

"Work made for hire" is a controversial issue discussed more fully in Chapter 13.

Collective works may also be prepared and published in which the author (or other owner or licensee) of each segment retains the copyright and in which the overall copyright for the work only pertains to prefatory material, introductory statements, indexes, and so forth.

COPYRIGHT NOTICES, DEPOSITS, AND REGISTRATION

Whenever a work protected by copyright is published, it must carry a copyright notice that contains the copyright symbol ©, or the word "copyright," the year of first publication, and the name of the owner of the copyright. Use of the symbol © provides some added protection under the Universal Copyright Convention. The notice is usally printed with both the word "copyright" and the symbol as, for example:

Copyright © 1983 by John Doe

Publishers normally add the expression "All rights reserved," since this provides some protection in countries that are not signatories of the Universal Copyright Convention.

The notice must be printed in the work in a position that will give reasonable notice to the reader that the work is protected by copyright. The customary position for such notices is on the reverse side of the title page.

Whenever a work consists "preponderantly" of material prepared by the U.S. government and which is therefore not subject to copyright protection, the copyright notice must include a statement identifying those portions of the work that are protected by the copyright notice versus those that are not.

In the case of collective works in which the copyrights in each of the contributions are held by different persons or organizations, it is best that each such piece carry its own notice of copyright, in addition to the notice for the work as a whole, in order to reduce the chance of inadvertent infringement.

When a work protected by copyright is published, within three months of its publication, either the owner of that copyright or the licensee is required to deposit two copies of the work with the Copyright Office for the use of the Library of Congress.

It is not necessary to register a copyright with the Copyright Office in order for it to be valid. However, in the event of copyright infringement, the copyright must be registered prior to any judicial proceedings, and no award of statutory damages or attorney's fees will be made if the copyright was not registered within three months of first publication. Therefore, registration is generally considered desirable for any major work.

Registration entails completing the Copyright Office's application form and sending it, together with two copies of the work and a check for the $10 fee, to the Copyright Office. The two copies to be transmitted for registration will also satisfy the deposit requirement mentioned above.

The copyright on an unpublished work may also be registered with the Copyright Office, and in such cases only one copy of the work needs to be deposited, but a copyright notice and registration of an unpublished work seem an unnecessary precaution unless the work is to be circulated and is highly susceptible to infringement.

MANUFACTURING REQUIREMENT

The "manufacturing clause," as it is known, is an anomalous piece of legislation embedded in the copyright act to protect the printing and binding industries in the United States from foreign competition. It has survived despite bitter attacks by both publishers and authors, and despite the fact that printers and binders need the protection far less than most other industries in the United States today.

This section of the act states that a literary work in the English language written by a citizen or a person domiciled in the United States may not be imported unless it has been printed and bound in the United States or Canada. But of course there are exceptions, including the following:

- Upon the request of the copyright owner, the Copyright Office will issue a permit for the importation of two thousand copies or less.

- Single copies may be imported for an individual's use, and copies may be imported as part of a person's baggage.

- Copies may be imported for the libraries of educational, scholarly, or religious organizations.
- The manufacturing requirement does not apply if the author is a U.S. citizen who has been domiciled in a foreign country for a full year prior to the work's importation.

Although you may be affected in some ways by the manufacturing requirement, it is primarily a restriction on where U.S. publishers have their books printed and bound. Because of the special problems in communicating, scheduling, and controlling quality when printing and binding books abroad, U.S. publishers would have most of their books manufactured in the U.S. even if this restriction did not exist.

FAIR USE

The copyright law provides that the reproduction of material for certain uses without the permission of the copyright owner is not an infringement. The law cites, as examples, reproductions made for purposes of criticism, comment, news reporting, teaching, scholarship, or research. The law also states that in determining if such use can be considered "fair use," the following factors are to be considered:

- The purpose and nature of the use, including whether or not it is for profit.
- The nature of the work reproduced.
- The amount of the work used in relation to the length of the original.
- The effect of the use on the commercial value of the work from which the material is taken.

With these criteria as a guide, authors, publishers, lawyers, and ultimately the courts, are left to decide in each circumstance what constitutes fair use.

This is, of course, quite troublesome to authors, since virtually every author upon occasion wants to quote anything from a few lines to a few pages of material from some copyrighted work, and would dearly love to have a yardstick by which to determine if the material can be used without getting permission from the copyright owner. Although it is sometimes suggested that three hundred words from a book, or up to 5 percent of a work can be used without permission, there is no legal or practical basis for such criteria.

One must be especially careful with poetry and musical lyrics because they are relatively short and polished works. Therefore, anything in excess of one or two lines of poetry may not be considered fair use, and it is best to ask permission for the use of any lyrics. In addition, there is no "fair use" of copyrighted illustrations, and permission for their use must always be obtained.

One helpful approach is to put yourself in the place of the other author, and ask yourself if you would consider the use as fair, or as stealing. If in doubt, it is usually best to ask for permission. Even if the author is confident that the planned use qualifies as "fair use," credit should be given to the original work and author to avoid a charge of plagiarism. More about permissions and plagiarism later.

Photocopying by Libraries

Another exception to the exclusive rights of the copyright owner is granted by the law to libraries, which are permitted to make single copies of copyrighted works for noncommercial use, so long as the libraries are not engaged in the systematic reproduction of materials instead of purchasing commercially available copies.

PERMISSIONS

In seeking permission to use copyrighted materials, you should write to the original publishers of the material, who either have the right to grant permission, or will seek the permission of the copyright owner. The permission should be requested for all rights that the author is granting his or her publisher, so that it is not necessary to make a second request for one or more of the subsidiary rights.

Permission requests will be handled more expeditiously if the requests provide all the information needed for a decision, including:

- A brief description of the work in which the material is to be used and the nature of its distribution. Is it a textbook, trade book, scholarly book? Will it be handed out free at a conference, published commercially, distributed free to a class of students? Also give the approximate size of the first printing as indicated by the book's editor.

- The precise material that the author wishes to use by reference to the pages and paragraphs of material in the published source, including the date or volume number if it is from a periodical.

An example of a permissions letter is shown below. However, the format of the request is not important so long as all necessary information is provided.

February 15, 1986

Permissions Department
Warner Books, Inc.
666 Fifth Avenue
New York, New York 10103

I am writing a trade book entitled "How the Computer is Changing our Society," to be published by Armageddon Press. It will consist of approximately 250 pages, and be priced at approximately $18, and I understand that the first printing will be approximately 7,500 copies.

Identified below is material from one of your publications that I would like permission to include in my work, including any paperback, book club, braille, large type, and foreign language editions or recordings of the work that may be made throughout the world.

A duplicate copy of this letter and a self-addressed, stamped envelope is enclosed for your convenience in replying. If permission is granted, please sign and return one copy of the letter, indicating on it how you would like the credit line to read.

Sincerely yours

MATERIAL TO BE USED

From MEGATRENDS by John Naisbitt, text beginning in the middle of page 35 and ending at the bottom of page 35, (hard-cover edition), "Many observers are betting . . . later rejoining the office staff for awhile."

PERMISSION GRANTED BY _____ Date _____

Requested Credit Line _____

The publisher, responding on his own behalf or on behalf of the author, will either grant permission, requiring a credit line, or if the amount of material is substantial and intended for commercial use, the publisher may charge a fee. The fee, which should be in proportion to the amount of material to be used, becomes subsidiary rights income that the publisher shares with the author of the source work. The publisher's share of these fees, though, is rarely enough to cover the cost of handling permissions.

In some cases, even if the publisher owns the copyright, he may check with the author of the source work about the permission and the size of the fee, if any. For example, if the material is to be used in such a way that it appears to be an endorsement of a product or service, the author may have serious objections.

It is your responsibility to pay whatever fees are charged for the use of copyrighted material. If a fee seems unreasonable, you have the option of either leaving the material out, or paraphrasing it and crediting the source author with the ideas. Before doing so, however, it is a good idea to check with your editor, since he or she may be able to help by contacting the publisher of the original material. Also, it is wise not to pay any fees until publication, as there is the chance the quoted material may be cut from your work in its final version.

Checking permissions can take time, especially if the author's permission is needed or the source work was published some years earlier. It is almost always necessary for the permissions person to examine the work to determine if the copyright on the material in question is actually held by another party. It may also be necessary to check the contract file to determine if the contract has been terminated and the copyright reassigned, or if there are any other restrictions on the use of the material.

Because of the work and time involved in checking permissions requests, you should not expect an immediate response. It is a good idea to write at least two months before you plan to send in your final manuscript, and even earlier if the material you want to use is critical to your work.

MATERIAL IN THE PUBLIC DOMAIN

Material that is not subject to copyright protection is in the public domain, available for unrestricted use, with no permission required. This includes material prepared by agencies of the U.S. government (although government publications may contain copyrighted material), or material on which copyright protection has not been provided, or material on which the term of copyright protection has expired.

The absence of copyright notice on a work published in 1978 or later is no guarantee that the work is in the public domain. Because material is occasionally inadvertently published without a notice, the new copyright law permits the owner to obtain protection by recording the copyright and by attempting to notify all persons who have received a copy without notice. Although the courts will not hold a person using such material liable for damages, they may prohibit the continuation of the use without an appropriate fee to the owner. Therefore, before freely using material published without notice in 1978 or later, it is a good idea to check with the copyright office to be sure that it is not being protected under this provision of the new copyright law.

The term of copyright protection depends primarily on when the work was first published. On works published since 1978, the term is for the author's life plus fifty years. On works published prior to 1978 when the old law was in force, works are protected for an initial term of twenty-eight years with the option of renewal prior to expiration for an additional term of forty-seven years, for a total of seventy-five years from the date of publication.

The table that follows shows the publication dates of books that enter the public domain sometime during the years shown in the left-hand column.

Publication Dates of Books Entering Public Domain in Year Shown in First Column

Year	Copyright Renewed	Copyright not Renewed
1985	1910	1957
1986	1911	1958
1987	1912	1959
1988	1913	1960
1989	1914	1961
1990	1915	1962

The chart demonstrates that in 1986, for example, books published in 1911 whose copyrights were renewed as well as books published in 1958 whose copyrights were not renewed enter the public domain.

PLAGIARISM

From time to time in cases of alleged copyright infringement, reference is made to plagiarism as well, as though the terms were interchangeable. They are not.

Plagiarism is the taking of another person's words, thoughts, ideas, or plots and using them as one's own. It is an ethical rather than a legal concept. While there is a considerable body of copyright law, including numerous court decisions, there is no such body of law pertaining to plagiarism.

If the plagiarism involves the publication of material protected by copyright, then it is copyright infringement as well. However, if one were to republish as one's own an obscure short story by Charles Dickens, there would be plagiarism but no copyright infringement, since the work would be in the public domain. And finally, if one were to publish material protected by copyright without permission (and not considered "fair use") but with credit to the original author and work, then it would be copyright infringement, but not plagiarism.

A certain amount of plagiarism occurs inadvertently. Authors read material, take notes, and sometime later incorporate their notes into their writing without being conscious of their source; plots can be duplicated without the author realizing it. However, intentionally copying another's work and claiming it as one's own is unethical and, when discovered, very embarrassing for the guilty party.

In order to avoid charges of plagiarism, even where the borrowing is relatively minor, it is best to credit the original author, even if from the copyright standpoint it would seem to qualify as "fair use," or if the term of copyright protection has expired.

Chapter 13

Work Made for Hire

Books written and published as works made for hire involve a different relationship between author and publisher, a relationship that is not well understood by many writers.

The concept of work made for hire has existed for some time, but it has been formalized by the 1976 Copyright Act, which specifies two types of situations, touched on earlier, in which the original copyright in a work need not be held by the creator of the work.

First, if you prepare a work as part of your job as a salaried employee of an individual or organization, the original copyright is held by your employer, unless there is a written agreement to the contrary.

Second, if the work is commissioned by an individual or organization, the original copyright is held by that individual or organization, provided there is a written agreement between the parties that it is a work made for hire, and provided that the work is one of the following types:

An instructional text (i.e., a textbook)

A contribution to a collective work

A translation

A compilation

An atlas

A supplementary work (including pictorial illustrations in a work)

A test, or answer material for a test

A part of a motion picture or other audiovisual work

For all other commissioned works, the creator owns the material and holds the original copyright.

Although the 1976 Copyright Act defines what can be copyrighted as a work made for hire, the Copyright Office has no enforcement capability, since it has no way of knowing if a work actually qualifies for that treatment. As a result, a publisher can register the copyright claim to a work in his own name as a work made for hire, even though it is not the work of an employee and is not a commissioned work that qualifies. Such a claim would presumably not be upheld in the courts.

Writers of commissioned works made for hire are frequently paid a fixed fee for their work rather than a royalty, at least in part because in many cases it would be difficult or impractical to come up with an efficient or fair system of royalty compensation. For example, as mentioned earlier, encyclopedias are usually written by hundreds of writers who are paid a fee for their contributions. As a result, many authors and perhaps some publishers believe that if a work is made for hire, authors must accept only a fixed fee for the work, and cannot reap any additional benefits from unforeseen large sales or from the sales of subsidiary rights. This is simply not true. The question of who owns the original copyright and how the writer is compensated are two entirely separate issues. There is no reason why the writer of a work made for hire cannot be paid a royalty on the sale of copies and on the sale of subsidiary rights if that is what the two parties agree to. In fact, authors of textbooks written as works made for hire usually receive royalties just as other authors do. Conversely, there is no reason why an author holding the original copyright in a work cannot sell some or all of the publication rights for a fixed fee instead of for a royalty if that is the arrangement the parties negotiate.

For the writer, there are only three basic differences between a normal contract and a work made for hire arrangement:

1. If it is a work made for hire, the copyright is in force for a period of seventy-five years from the date of publication or 100 years after its creation (whichever is less) rather than for the author's life plus fifty years.

2. The person or organization for whom the work made for hire has been prepared owns the material and can modify it or use it in any way without the writer's approval. (If your name is to be on the work, however, you should insist that the work made for hire agreement specify that no changes in the material can be made without your approval.)

3. Under the copyright law, authors have the right to terminate

their agreements with the proprietors or publishers of their works thirty-five years after publication, but a writer of a work made for hire does not have that right. Since most works have little or no value thirty-five years after first publication, the issue of terminating agreements is important only to a select few authors and their estates.

In summary, work made for hire arrangements by themselves have relatively little impact on your rights as a writer, and need not affect your earnings, since the way you are paid and the amount you are paid has nothing to do with those arrangements.

Illustrations commissioned by authors or by publishers are also works made for hire, and are subject to the same rules and principles as textual material. Chapter 17 covers these and other issues relating to the acquisition of illustrations.

Chapter 14

The Option Clause

Most trade book contracts contain an option clause which grants the publisher the right of first refusal on your next work. A typical option clause reads as follows:

> *The Author agrees to submit to the Publisher his next book-length work before submitting it to any other publisher. The Publisher shall be entitled to a period of six weeks after the submission of the completed manuscript in which to notify the Author of its decision, but this period shall not commence until at least one month after the publication of the work covered by this agreement. If within that time the Publisher notifies the Author of its desire to publish the manuscript, it shall then negotiate with him regarding the terms of such publication. If within thirty days thereafter the parties are unable to arrive at a mutually satisfactory agreement for its publication, the Author may submit his manuscript elsewhere, provided, however, that he shall not enter into a contract for the publication of such manuscript with any other publisher upon terms less favorable than those offered by the Publisher.*

Why an option clause? Publishers defend it by pointing out that they invest heavily in developing a market for an author's work through advertising, promotion, and publicity, and the option clause gives them an opportunity to recoup that investment through the publication of future works, rather than permitting another publisher to reap the benefits of that investment. (The same argument could be applied to employees trained by one company only to be lured away by another, yet companies are not permitted to hold employees in bondage because they have invested in their training.)

Option clauses work a real hardship on authors, and should be eliminated from contracts whenever possible. Following are some of the problems they present.

First, many option clauses, as in the sample given, require you to submit a completed manuscript. Most authors want to be able to get a publishing contract and an advance based on sample material, in order to avoid writing on speculation. On a nonfiction work, a publisher should be willing to make a commitment on the basis of a detailed outline and sample material, especially since the publisher will have a completed first project in hand as a measure of the author's competence. With fiction, a better case can be made for needing a completed manuscript.

Second, most option clauses require you to wait until after the first work is published and the publisher has had a reaction from the marketplace before he is willing to make a commitment on your second. But what if you are prolific and your publisher is slow in getting the first work published, so that the second manuscript is complete several months before the first work is on the market? The option clause requires you to wait for a publishing decision, whereas in the absence of an option clause your publisher would either need to make a decision quickly or risk losing the work to another publisher.

Finally, and perhaps most importantly, you may be dissatisfied with how your publisher handled your first work—and the possible reasons for dissatisfaction are legion. As a matter of equity, why should you be locked into a situation where your publisher can accept or reject your next project, but where you cannot accept or reject the publisher? Furthermore, if you have an agent, the option clause creates another potential problem, since the same agent will automatically represent the second work, no matter how dissatisfied you may be with your agent's performance. (This situation is also discussed in Chapter 7 on the role of the literary agent.)

Option clauses deal with the royalty terms for the second work in a variety of ways.

Some state that the terms shall be the same as those for the initial work covered by the agreement. These terms may seem adequate to you at the time, but after the publication of the first work, especially if it is very successful, you are likely to have a different view of what those terms should be.

Some specify that the terms of the agreement for the second work are to be negotiated, and further, that if those negotiations fail and you find another publisher for the work, the first publisher will be given an opportunity to take the work on the same terms offered by the second. This discourages the second publisher from considering the project, since he faces the possibility of the original publisher matching the terms and taking it. And from your point of view, it sets up a procedure whereby you may have to go through three negotiations in order to get your second work published.

Some option clauses state that if you and your publisher fail to reach a mutually satisfactory agreement, you may seek another publisher, but the work cannot be published by another on terms that are less favorable than those offered by the publisher of your first work. This is probably the least objectionable arrangement, since it permits you to seek better terms without having to go back to your first publisher. In addition, because of the array of royalty terms in most contracts, it could be difficult to establish that the second publisher's contract was less favorable. For example, if the second publisher offered a lower rate on copy sales, but a larger share of the subsidiary rights income, only time would tell which terms were more favorable.

There are ways in which you can attempt to get out of an option commitment. For example, you can dust off an old unpublishable manuscript and submit it, but it may be challenged as not being your "next work," especially if there are tell-tale clues to its age. Or you can write some new material that will be unacceptable, but that will involve work for which you will never be paid. The only good solution is to reject the option clause and be free of the problem.

There is no question that a continuing relationship between author and publisher can be good for both parties, as each learns to work more effectively and efficiently with the other. However, notwithstanding its benefits, a continuing relationship should be voluntary, based on confidence and mutual respect, and on publishing terms negotiated to be competitive in the marketplace, rather than dictated by an option clause on an earlier contract.

Many publishers are willing to strike the option clauses from their contracts. However, if a publisher is adamant about it, then you must decide whether to look for another publisher, or settle for negotiating an option clause that provides as much flexibility as possible. For example, be sure the clause for a nonfiction work reads that the publisher will make his decision on an outline and sample chapters and not require a complete manuscript; and strike the clause that permits him to delay his decision until after the first work is published. Finally, the royalty terms should be mutually agreeable, and failing agreement, you should be permitted to publish elsewhere on better terms without giving him the opportunity to match them.

Chapter 15

Authors' Warranty and Indemnity Clauses

All book contracts contain clauses in which authors make certain warranties about their manuscripts and agree to protect publishers from any costs resulting from breaches of those warranties. These clauses tend to be treated casually by editors and authors, as a formality with no consequences. In reality, they create a serious financial risk for authors.

A typical clause reads as follows:

> *The author represents and warrants that the work is original and that he or she is the sole author; that the work has not been previously published in whole or in part; that the author has the right to enter into this agreement and grant the rights that are granted herein; that the work contains no libelous or obscene material or dangerous formulations; that the work does not infringe any copyright, trademark or trade name; and that it does not violate or invade any right of privacy, or any other statutory or common law right. The author agrees to indemnify and hold harmless the publisher from any liabilities, damages, costs, charges and expenses, including rea, sonable attorneys' fees, arising out of the publication of this work or the exercise of the rights granted the publisher by this agreement.*

Such warranty clauses make authors accountable and financially responsible for their books. This is not unreasonable, since in many cases it is only the author who can know if he or she is committing libel, or invading an individual's privacy, or using previously copyrighted material. On the other hand, the penalty for a lapse in judgment or an oversight can be so great that it is an unreasonable risk for authors to run.

LIBEL AND INVASION OF PRIVACY

Few issues in publishing are more perplexing to both authors and publishers than libel and invasion of privacy. In 1980, the Authors Guild surveyed its members, and the respondents indicated that 3.8 percent of their books had been subject to claims of libel or invasion of privacy. While the incidence of problems is relatively low, the stakes in legal fees, court costs, and awards are high. In addition, suits without merit sometimes seem to be initiated for the publicity, or to imply that the plaintiff has been falsely defamed, or in the expectation of an attractive out-of-court settlement. And to make matters worse, the legal benchmarks are not always clear cut. As a result of this somewhat perilous environment, any material that might be construed as libelous or an invasion of privacy is best avoided unless it is absolutely necessary, in which case it should be included only with the advice of a lawyer experienced in such issues.

Definitions

Although each of the fifty states has different laws on libel and invasion of privacy, the basic principles are the same.

Libel is the publication of defamatory, untruthful material about a living person. However, even if the facts presented are true, it is possible for a plaintiff to mount a successful libel action, since the truth can frequently be difficult to prove.

In order not to constrain the press from freely discussing issues of public concern, a more permissive standard is applied to public figures than to private persons. In order for libel suits to be brought successfully by public figures, it must be shown that the defendants acted with malice, either knowing that the libelous statement was false, or with reckless disregard for whether it was true or not.

Invasion of privacy is a much broader concept, encompassing any act that intrudes upon the privacy of a private individual, including the use of an individual's name or likeness without his or her consent, the publication of false or misleading information, or even true but embarrassing information about a private individual. Special care must be taken in the use of photographs showing recognizable people.

The Problem for Authors of Fiction

In factual works describing real events and people, the risks are obvious and the potential libels and invasions of privacy are usually visible and, with the aid of a lawyer experienced in these matters, can usually be handled in a way to minimize risk. In the case of fiction, however, the risk is more insidious. Authors usually base fiction on their own experiences—events they have participated in or read about and people they have known or read about. Therefore real people, wholly or in part, find their way into works of fiction in guises meant to render them unrecognizable. While these guises may make them unrecognizable to the publisher and his lawyer, subjects can sometimes spot themselves in such works, or imagine that they do. Therefore, most lawyers counsel authors whose fictional characters are developed from living individuals to change everything possible about the character—name, physical characteristics, and so forth, but this is not always easy for authors to do.

One of the more interesting libel cases involving a fictional work in recent years is *Bindrin v. Mitchell*. Gwen Davis Mitchell attended a nude encounter session in southern California given by Paul Bindrin, a clinical psychologist. Prior to the session, Mitchell signed an agreement that she would not disclose what was to occur at the session. Some months later, Mitchell submitted a novel to Doubleday, which was published under the title *Touching*. Prior to publication, Doubleday discussed the libel issue with Mitchell and was assured by her that her characters were entirely fictitious.

In the novel, one of the characters attends a nude encounter session in southern California given by a Dr. Simon Herford. Shortly after the work was published, Bindrin wrote Doubleday and Mitchell claiming that he was the Simon Herford depicted in the work and threatening to sue for libel. Doubleday again talked with Mitchell and was again assured that all the characters were fictional. Paperback rights had been previously sold, and, because of Mitchell's assurances, Doubleday took no action to halt the publication of the paperback edition. Bindrin brought suit against Mitchell and Doubleday.

During the trial, Bindrin played a tape he had recorded at the very session Mitchell attended, and it was established that the account of the session in the book closely followed the actual session as it was taped. Although the physical description of Herford given in the book was totally different from the physical appearance of Bindrin, Bindrin argued that anyone familiar with encounter sessions in southern California would know that he was Herford. The jury found Mitchell guilty and awarded Bindrin $75,000 in compensatory and punitive damages. The jury found Doubleday not guilty in the original publication of the work, but guilty of having allowed the paperback edition to be published after notice from Bindrin had been received. The decision was upheld by the United States Supreme Court on appeal. Doubleday held Mitchell accountable for Doubleday's share of the damages, feeling that Mitchell had been less than forthright regarding the relationship between Bindrin and the fictional Herford.

This is a curious case in that the character of Herford is actually fictional, but performs a nonfiction role that identifies him with the plaintiff, and whose fictional statements and acts are construed to libel the plaintiff. It demonstrates how careful authors must be in transferring real events and characters into the world of fiction so as to avoid charges of libel.

Another similar case, *Springer v. Tine*, eventually had the opposite outcome. In a novel by Robert Tine entitled *The State of Grace*, published by Viking Penguin, there is a prostitute named Lisa Blake. Lisa Springer, Tine's former girlfriend, brought suit, claiming that Lisa Blake was a defamatory portrayal of her. Indeed there were similarities between Lisa Blake and Lisa Springer, but there were also differences. The lower court awarded damages to Lisa Springer. The Appellate Division of the New York Supreme Court overturned that decision, stating that " . . . for a defamatory statement or statements made about a character in a fictional work to be actionable the description of the fictional character must be so closely akin to the real person claiming to be defamed that a reader of the book, knowing the real person, would have no difficulty linking the two. . . ." In a dissenting opinion, Judge Theodore R. Kupferman wrote, "There can be no question but that the portrayal in the book is defamatory, and the only issue is identification. The dissimilarities which the court stresses, 'both in manner of living and in outlook,' are the very basis for the allegations of defamation. To accept them as leading to the conclusion that there is no connection is the essence of a bootstrap operation."

Would the outcome of these two cases have been the same if they had both been reviewed by the same court? Or if Springer had been a male clinical psychologist? We'll never know the answers, but it is clear that in order to avoid the risk of a libel action when fictionalizing characters and events, every effort should be made to eliminate any means of identifying real people who may or may not have been the models for those characters.

OTHER WARRANTIES

Authors warrant that their materials are original and violate no copyright. The issues of copyright and plagiarism are covered in Chapter 12 on copyrights and permissions. The best course to follow is to obtain permission for the use of all copyrighted material that may exceed the hazy criteria for "fair use" in the Copyright Act, and to be sure to credit source material when necessary. Special attention should be paid to keeping careful records of sources during the stages of research and writing, so that permissions and proper credits are not lost sight of along the way. Publishers usually want copies of the letters authorizing the use of copyrighted material.

Authors also warrant that their works are not obscene. In 1973, the United States Supreme Court, in *Miller v. California,* established three criteria to be taken together for determining what constitutes obscenity: "(a) whether the average person, applying contemporary community standards, would find that the work, taken as a whole, appeals to the prurient interest; (b) whether the work depicts or describes, in a patently offensive way, sexual conduct specifically defined by the applicable state law; and (c) whether the work, taken as a whole, lacks serious literary, artistic, political or scientific value." As a result of this decision, only an author who is intentionally writing offensively obscene material runs any risk of legal action on the grounds of obscenity. Such an author would be well advised to strike obscenity from the warranty since, unlike the other warranties, the publisher is in a better position to judge the risk of some legal action.

Authors also warrant that there are no dangerous formulations or instructions in their work. Although there have been several legal actions in this area over the past ten years, few awards have been made. However, in these litigious times, it pays to be careful. Particularly at risk are books on health, diets, drugs and medication, and laboratory manuals for students. Care should also be taken to avoid any ambiguity in instructions that might lead to the injury of a reader. Above all, don't count on the publisher catching errors that could result in injury. That is the author's responsibility.

OTHER INDEMNITY ISSUES

There are general problems with some indemnity clauses. Suppose that in a suit brought against the author and the publisher, the publisher wants an out-of-court settlement even though the author believes the plaintiff's case has no merit. Should the author be obliged to accept a settlement that implies he or she is in the wrong? Should the author have to pay the entire cost of the settlement? Should the author be required to pay all the legal expenses if the action is successfully defended?

Some contracts state that the publisher will not make an out-of-court settlement without the author's written consent, and a few contracts provide for the cost of the settlement to be shared equally by the author and the publisher. Some say that if the action is successfully defended, the costs of that defense will be divided equally between author and publisher.

Some contracts give the publisher the right to defend the action with attorneys of his choice, as he sees fit. Some specify that the defense shall be controlled jointly by the author and the publisher.

In recent years, a number of trade publishers, led by Viking Penguin, have extended their own liability insurance for a small additional premium to protect their authors from losses caused by suits charging libel, invasion of privacy, slander, plagiarism, injurious formulations, and copyright infringement. Under Viking Penguin's policy, for example, the first $25,000 of loss is deductible. The publisher shares the first $2,000 of loss with the author, but the publisher assumes all of the remaining $23,000 of the deductible amount. The insurance company covers the balance of any loss up to $3 million.

Most of the plans include a deductible amount, a portion of which is shared with the author, and a balance that is covered by the insurance carrier up to a specified maximum, but the dollar amounts for the share to be borne by the author and the maximums tend to differ. These plans reduce an author's risk to a manageable size.

RECOMMENDATIONS

If you are writing a book that could generate a claim of libel or invasion of privacy, the areas of greatest risk for an author, it is certainly desirable, all other things being equal, to select a publisher who provides liability insurance.

If not, then the wording of the indemnity clause becomes critical. Try to get it changed so that your approval is needed for an out-of-court settlement, and so that if a claim is successfully defended, or if it is settled out of court, you will only be liable for half the costs. Also try to have it stipulated that you and your publisher will jointly control the defense against any claims or actions.

For both fiction and nonfiction work, it's wise to bring to your publisher's attention every instance where there might be a problem. One publisher requires authors to complete a form for the purpose of identifying areas of risk, which among other questions, asks if the author knows anyone depicted in the work, and if so, if the author has any strong personal dislikes regarding them. If your work contains photographs of identifiable people, either obtain a release from them stating they have no objection to the use of the photograph, or alter the photograph so they cannot be identified.

Avoid copyright infringement problems by seeking permission for the use of material if there is any question in your mind that it might not be considered fair use by the copyright owner, and avoid charges of plagiarism by giving credit generously not only for copyrighted material, but for all sources drawn upon.

In providing instructions for physical activities, or for foods and drugs, or for experiments of any sort, or engineering data for the design of structures and equipment, be extra careful that the information given is correct and clear, and does not put anyone's welfare at risk.

Above all, even if you are covered by your publisher's liability insurance, exercise the same precautions as though you were not. You will still be responsible for some portion of the deductible amount, and months of your life could be taken up by your legal defense if an action is brought against you.

Chapter 16

Joint Authorship Arrangements

$\mathbf{M}$any times, two or more persons will find it desirable to write a book together. For trade books, the most common arrangement is for a person with a story or a specialized skill to work with an experienced writer to create the book. The writer may be a "ghost" whose name does not appear on the book, or may be credited under the line "as told to," or may be shown as coauthor. Often, the publisher brings the parties together in order to get a book that otherwise might not be written.

Professional books and college textbooks are frequently coauthored. If a text is for one of the large introductory courses, the publisher may encourage the author to work with a professional writer. In other cases, several authors—sometimes as many as four—write a text or professional book together.

There are a number of advantages to a joint authorship. It can reduce the workload for each author, and each usually brings a different experience, expertise, and point of view to the project. The old adage that "two heads are better than one" usually applies.

Working with more than one author on a project creates no significant problems for the publisher, provided the authors work together cooperatively. Obviously, a publisher does not want to serve as middleman between two authors no longer speaking to one another.

Authors don't want to find themselves in that position either, so they must choose their coauthors carefully, recognizing that differences of opinion may arise, and hard feelings develop. Each author needs to have a good understanding of the other's technical and professional competence, writing ability, and commitment to the project. One author does not want to work long hours to meet an agreed upon schedule, only to find that a coauthor has gone on a vacation that sabotages that schedule. Coauthorship requires cooperation over a long period of time, so you can't be too careful in your selection.

Planning is especially important. In order to minimize problems, work out in advance who is to do what in the way of research, writing and rewriting, the supplying of illustrations, typing of the final manuscript, and so forth. When possible, it's also essential to work out in advance how the royalties are to be divided.

The most common arrangement is for an equal division of both workload and royalties. However, this is by no means necessary. The royalties can be split one-third and two-thirds, or any other way that makes sense to the authors. One author can even pay the other author a fixed fee plus a small share of the royalty, or no share of the royalty at all. Whatever the arrangement, it should be spelled out in a letter of agreement between the parties. If the authors feel they cannot predict how the workload will fall, they may postpone the decision on how to divide the royalties. However, they should at least agree at the outset on the method of arriving at a fair split (such as a count of the pages written), and this should be part of their written agreement so that the method itself does not become an issue.

It is also useful to agree in advance on the sequence in which the authors' names are to appear on the work. If there are clearly a senior and a junior author, then it is customary for the senior author's name to appear first. If they are professional equals, but one is contributing more material to the work, then logic would suggest that the name of the larger contributor should be first. If one author is well known, there may be a publicity advantage in putting that name first. If these criteria don't help, flip a coin. This decision does not have to be made too early, but must be rendered by the time the final manuscript is submitted, so that the publisher's original listings and announcements of the work are correct.

If a project has more than one author, the arrangements for advances or deferrals for each author can be made separately and independently of the other, depending on the needs of each. In effect, each author has an account with the publisher, into which royalty earnings will be deposited and from which advances, earnings, or deferred income will be paid. However, the publisher will normally limit the size of any one author's advance to that author's proportionate share of the total advance the publisher would be willing to pay on the project. For example, if the publisher is willing to advance no more than $10,000 on a project with two authors who are to share equally in the royalties, he will not advance more than $5,000 to one of the authors, even if the other does not want an advance, since he risks not recovering the additional amount from one author.

If two or more authors jointly prepare an original work with the intention of merging their contributions into an inseparable whole, then they are co-owners of the copyright in the total work and therefore, must all cooperate in arranging for publication or in licensing any of the rights protected by the copyright. The term of copyright protection and the termination right are the same for joint authorship as for a single author, except that the copyright endures for the life of the last surviving author plus fifty years. Authors may also retain their individual copyrights in their contributions to a joint work. For example, if two authors want to combine their work into a single book, but one wishes to retain periodical rights and sell his or her contribution as a series of magazine articles, then they would each maintain their separate copyrights.

It is also possible to arrange for another person to contribute chapters or do rewriting as a "work made for hire," either for a fee or a share of the royalty income. In either case, you are the sole owner of the work; however, you must have a written agreement that it is a work made for hire, or your contributor can claim to be a coauthor and co-owner of the work.

In coauthorship arrangements, each author must sign the contract with the publisher and each is jointly responsible for fulfilling the commitment to deliver a satisfactory manuscript by a prescribed date, to indemnify the publisher against losses resulting from a libel action, and so forth. However, the publisher may reserve the right to take action against individual coauthors who do not fulfill their contractual obligations. For example, if only one coauthor receives an advance, and the manuscript is never completed, the publisher may sue that coauthor individually for recovery of the advance. Nevertheless, because you are jointly responsible, you must be careful that your coauthor does not commit libel, or violate a copyright, or include any injurious formulations in the final manuscript, or you may have to share in paying for your coauthor's mistake. On the other hand, if a portion of the work is done for you as a work made for hire, then you are the sole author to sign the publisher's contract, and you alone are responsible for any errors committed by your contributor.

Despite the potential problems inherent in joint authorship, many books have been written successfully by coauthors, and it may be a good solution for your project.

Chapter 17

Illustrations

Illustrations have been an important part of books for as long as books have been is existence. The oldest example of an illustrated work is an Egyptian papyrus dating back to about 1980 B.C., but it is likely that combining illustrations and text in documents had its origin in even earlier times.

Illustrations continue to play an important role in books today, although they are perhaps more utilitarian and less decorative than they have been in the past. Thus, because of cost considerations, it is no longer customary to illustrate works of adult fiction, but in most other types of books—textbooks, reference works, juvenile, recreational, and hobby books—there is an abundance of charts, graphs, line drawings, renderings, and photographs.

For certain types of books, words alone are inadequate. For example, books on architecture, sports, wildflowers, woodworking and other handicrafts would be useless without illustrations. And for communicating information, a complex electrical wiring diagram is worth far more than the proverbial one thousand words. In other cases, illustrations help to support the text, set the mood and break up the formidable appearance of page after page of solid type.

Finally, in books of cartoons, art, and photoessays, the illustrations are the dominant medium of communication.

SELECTING ILLUSTRATIONS

Many authors are word oriented and do not naturally think of their material in terms of illustrations. If you are like this, review your material especially carefully, looking for places where illustrations will help the reader to understand the message. Other books on the same or similar subjects may help give a sense of how best to use illustrations effectively. There is certainly a wide variety of media, techniques, and styles to choose from, including photographs, line drawings, sketches, paintings, charts, and graphs, and many ways in which to use them.

Illustrations can be a sizable expense, and it is best not to proceed with acquiring or producing more than a few samples of art until after a publisher for the work has been found. The editor probably will want to have a hand in determining the type and number of illustrations. The editor may also be able to provide some advice on sources. On the other hand, you need to know the cost of obtaining illustrations before signing a contract, since that may affect the size of the advance needed to complete the work, or whether the project is feasible.

Your contract will probably spell out, for example, that the final manuscript is to contain fifty photographs and 100 line drawings. Some contracts state that the author is to supply camera-ready artwork; some say that the author is to provide rough sketches drawn to scale from which the publisher will prepare final line drawings; some textbook publishers have photo researchers who get necessary illustrations and charge their cost either to the author's royalty account or to the cost of the book. These details can impact your costs significantly, and need to be resolved before you sign a contract.

A warning about photographs: Authors tend to favor photographs because they feel they can take them themselves, or because they already have them on hand. As a result, many photographs of inferior quality are used, resulting in unattractive and less effective books. In taking or selecting photographs, it is important to keep in mind what each photograph is intended to show, and to be sure the photograph conveys that information clearly. If the intent is to show, for example, what a particular joint in furniture making looks like, does the photograph clearly show the three-dimensional shape of the pieces making up that joint, or do the lights and shadows obscure the detail? Does the photograph tend to be too black and white, so that the detail in the light and dark areas is lost, or is it too flat and gray overall? While it is possible for the printer to correct some deficiencies in photographs, it usually requires special work which will only be done in those unusual cases where the publisher requests it and is prepared to pay for it. For best results, photographs should be taken by a professional photographer, or at least by an experienced amateur.

Because of the nature of the reproduction process, you must assume that there will be some loss in clarity when photographs are published. The printer begins by taking photographs of the photographs submitted and some quality is lost immediately. In addition, he uses a fine screen to convert the negative images into groups of very fine dots. He then photographically transfers those dot images to a printing plate. When the plate is on press, ink is applied to it, and the ink is then transferred to the surface of a sheet of paper. Therefore, the photograph appearing in the book is actually four steps removed from the photograph that was submitted, with a slight loss of sharpness in each step. Considering the process employed, the results are remarkably good, but realistically, one must expect some loss in quality. Therefore, unless the photographs submitted are of the highest quality, the results will be disappointing. For best results, 8x10 glossy prints should be provided. In order not to mar the glossy surface of the print, paper clips should not be used, and any identification on the back should be made with a soft-tipped marker or grease pencil. If color photographs are being used, original transparencies should be provided.

Finally, in order to avoid offending any segment of the market for which a book is prepared, the illustrations must be free of any bias with respect to race, creed, or sex. For example, authors should avoid showing women and minorities in subservient roles. Care should also be taken to avoid material that becomes quickly dated. With luck, the book may still be selling ten years after its publication, and photographs of women dressed in the style of the day can look very much out of date ten years later.

Line drawings are frequently much more effective than photographs in communicating information, since they can omit extraneous detail or look inside a piece of equipment or the human body to show how it works, something a photograph can't easily do. Line drawings can also be used as thematic decoration to make the book more inviting or interesting.

Line drawings should be produced using India ink, and should be made twice the size they are to be in the book. The printer will then reduce them by 50 percent, and as a result, the illustrations will have finer detail than would be possible if they had first been drawn to size.

As a general rule, you should assume that color is too costly to be practical in your book. Color photographs require the use of a four-color press, with four separate printing plates. Not only are the presses and the extra plates expensive, but also paper spoilage is considerably greater. Therefore, producing books with four-color illustrations is usually prohibitively expensive.

There are obviously exceptions, however. A book using four colors throughout that can be printed in quantities of 100,000 copies or more at a time may well be economically feasible, since a major part of the added cost is spread over enough copies so that it is not prohibitive. Therefore, because of the size of the press runs, four-color presses are used to produce many elementary and secondary school textbooks and many books that are sold by mass mail-order campaigns whose sales are expected to exceed one hundred thousand copies. There is a trap, however. If sales are disappointing, although adequate to sell out the first printing, it will be prohibitively expensive to go back to press for, say, twenty thousand more copies, and frequently the only solution is to let the book go out of print.

There are also books in which the use of four-color photographs is essential, even though sales are not expected to approach the quantities that would permit the use of four colors throughout. This is true of many art and medical books. The solution is to print all the color work as a unit on a four-color press, and the balance of the book on a one-color press. The pages of four-color illustrations can either be put in one section of the book or divided into smaller units of four or eight pages and placed in a number of locations in the book.

Some books are printed in two colors, with the second color used to print selected headings or subheadings, or screened to a lighter shade for graphs and charts, or occasionally to overlay blocks of text and make the book more attractive. This is done quite often in college textbooks and how-to trade books. It should be emphasized, however, that this is done only when substantial continuing sales are expected. As with four-color books, the cost of small reprints can be prohibitive. Because of this, the use of two colors in college textbooks is usually limited to later editions of books that have proved successful in their first editions.

OBTAINING ILLUSTRATIONS

If you have the ability to do your own illustrations or take your own photographs, you are in a good position with respect to cost and control of the project. However, most authors do not have the necessary skills, and must go to some trouble to obtain and pay for illustrations.

The copyright law applies to all illustrations in much the same way it applies to text. Thus, the creator of the illustration is the owner and holds the initial copyright in the work from the moment it is created, unless it is commissioned as a work made for hire and there is a written agreement to that effect. Remember, however, that there is no "fair use" of illustrations.

For authors who want art prepared for them, *Literary Market Place* lists photographers and illustrators who undertake such assignments. The American Society of Magazine Photographers, 60 East 42nd

Street, New York, NY 10017, provides the names of professional photographers. And editors often know good sources. Students taking illustration or photography courses at a local university may be able to provide artwork at reasonable rates.

Several types of payment arrangements can be made. An author may commission a photographer or illustrator to prepare the material as a work made for hire for a fixed fee, in which case the author owns the illustrations and all rights regarding their use. Alternatively, an author may commission the work, but acquire from the photographer or illustrator for a lesser fee only the nonexclusive rights to use the material in all editions of the book, including its promotion and publicity, and permitting the photographer or illustrator to retain all other rights. A third alternative, appropriate when the illustrations are a major part of the work, is to make the photographer or illustrator a coauthor, sharing in the royalty income from the project.

If you want to use illustrations that already exist, you must assume that someone owns them and holds the copyright on them, or a license to reproduce them. You must track down the individual or organization that owns the rights by writing the organization that published or displayed them, and probably pay a fee for their use. A word of warning is needed here. The new copyright law makes a distinction between the physical ownership of artwork and the ownership of the copyright or rights of reproduction. For example, an illustrator may sell a piece of art to a collector, but retain the copyright. Anyone wishing to reproduce that artwork must obtain a license for its reproduction from the illustrator. Therefore, one must be sure that the owner of an illustration also has the right to license its reproduction. If you purchase existing illustrations (as distinct from commissioning their preparation), don't forget that you must also obtain a written assignment of the copyright, or a license for their reproduction from the photographer or illustrator.

The fees for using illustrations in books are usually based on the extent of the book's distribution. The following categories are often used:

- North American English language rights
- Worldwide English language rights
- Worldwide rights (all languages)

Fees are generally higher for four-color photographs and for art used as frontispieces, chapter openings, book jackets or covers, or in advertising. However, it is the publisher's responsibility to pay the cost of illustrations for jackets, covers, and advertising.

It is usually best to obtain worldwide rights, even though the fee may be signficantly more than for North American English language rights, since most books will have some worldwide sales and one or more foreign language editions. However, if your book will have no appeal outside of North America (for example, a book on the wildflowers of North Carolina), then it may not make sense to pay the higher fee for worldwide rights. However, before making that decision, discuss the issue with your editor, who ought to know where the company expects to sell the work.

Major sources of illustrations are the various archives and other organizations that maintain collections of illustrations and license their use. *Literary Market Place* lists ninety such organizations, including their names and addresses, and the nature of their collection. *PICTURE SOURCES 3*, published by the Special Libraries Association, is also a good guide to collections that may be drawn upon. Many large libraries have picture collections. Among the largest archives are:

Life Picture Service, Time-Life Building, Rockefeller Center, Room 2858, New York, New York, Telephone 212-841-4800. As the name suggests, this collection is made up primarily of photographs that appeared in *Life* magazine over a period of thirty-six years, and contains approximately eighteen million photographs on over ten thousand subjects. A fee of $50 an hour is charged to research requested photographs, but individuals can research copies of *Life* magazine to save research time and cost. It is necessary to make an appointment to visit the collection.

Bettmann Archive, Inc., 136 East 57th Street, New York, NY 10022. Telephone 212-758-0362. This is a collection of about five million pictorial artifacts. A flat fee of $35 is charged for research. The archive will mail copies of art for consideration, and if they are the illustrations wanted, prints for reproduction will be sent in exchange for the fee for their use. A book called the BETTMANN PORTABLE ARCHIVE containing 3,500 pictorial examples can be found in major libraries.

The Still Picture Section, National Archive, Washington, D.C. Telephone 202-523-3236. This archive containing five million items is the depository for all photographs and illustrations created by or for government agencies, plus a number of donations. The Still Picture Section provides limited research for up to five items, and will send photostats for consideration. They also provide guidance to persons undertaking their own research, or employing a researcher. Since the photographs and illustrations are in the public domain, there is no charge for the right to use them, only the small cost of the prints themselves.

Prints & Photographs Division, Reference Section, Library of Congress, Washington, D.C. 20540. Telephone 202-287-6394. This collection contains approximately ten million items that have been donated to the Library of Congress, plus a number of purchases and exchanges. The collection includes the archives of *Look* magazine. Research must be done by the client or someone on the client's behalf. There is no charge for the rights, but users must pay for the prints. The Library of Congress also has a list of persons in the Washington area who are available to do research.

The absence of any fee for the use of illustrations from the National Archive and the Library of Congress make these sources extremely attractive, especially if a large number of illustrations are needed. A print from these sources costs less than $10, whereas the fee for a print from other sources may be $400, or even more.

There are also many free sources of illustrations. Companies are usually willing to provide illustrations of their products or even their facilities. Chambers of commerce may be willing to provide illustrations of their communities. Any organization that is interested in publicity is a potential source.

CAVEATS

Although it is always tempting to settle for free or homemade illustrations, the temptation should be resisted unless they are of high professional quality and generally fit the tone of the book. A few poor illustrations mar the whole appearance of a book and damage its sales appeal.

Before signing a contract with a publisher, if you plan to use illustrations in your work, you need to do some preliminary research. If the illustrations are going to be purchased, commissioned, or licensed, it is important to find out in advance what they will cost. If they cost $200 each, and 100 are needed, you are facing an out-of-pocket expense of $20,000. This may make the project impractical unless your publisher is willing to pick up part of that cost, or at least provide a sufficient advance to cover it. On the other hand, if you are going to take the photographs or prepare the illustrations yourself, then show representative samples to the publisher to be sure they will reproduce well.

Providing illustrations can be a pitfall for the unwary author. Therefore, it is highly desirable to uncover all the problems before, rather than after, signing a contract.

Chapter 18

Revised Editions

Y ou may not be ready to think about a revised edition of your book before the first edition is even signed, but most publishing contracts deal with revisions, so it is not an issue that can be postponed.

Between 15 and 20 percent of the books published each year are revised editions, that is, books that have been substantially rewritten and republished as though they were new books.

Sometimes books are changed only in a minor way, with a few statistics updated and a few new developments added, and are said to be revised. But a true revision is essentially republished—reset and given a new jacket and new advertising and promotion.

Literary and scholarly works are rarely revised. On the other hand, successful special-interest trade books, professional books, and textbooks are all candidates for revisions.

There are two main reasons for publishing revised editions. The obvious reason is to bring the material in the book up to date and add new material that improves it. The second reason is that it permits the publisher to repromote the book and strengthen its position competitively in its market. If a book is not revised, its sales will gradually diminish until it is no longer feasible to keep it in print. If it is revised periodically, its life may be extended for decades.

TIMING OF REVISIONS

The frequency with which a book is revised depends in part on the content and part on the market for which it is written. Some special-interest trade books, such as travel guides, tax guides and directories, are revised annually. On the other hand, many special-interest books on fishing, woodworking, knitting, and sports become out of date much more slowly, and revisions every eight or ten years may be adequate.

Similar differences occur among professional books. Books in the fast-moving fields of semiconductors and microprocessors become out of date rapidly, while books on structural design and electric power generation need revision much less often.

The timing of college textbook revisions depends more on the size and competitiveness of the secondhand market than on changes in the field. New books and new editions sell best in the first two years after publication, and then sales diminish in the following years as more and more books enter the secondhand market. The publication of a new edition wipes out the secondhand market, because all assignments are tied to the content and pagination of the new editon. Textbooks for large enrollment freshman and sophomore courses are usually revised every four years. Texts for more advanced courses, in which more students keep their texts, and where smaller classes mean it will take publishers longer to recover their investments, are more likely to be revised every six to eight years.

Because revisions can extend the life of some books for many years, contracts for all books, with the exception of most literary works, commit the author to preparing revisions at the publisher's request, or if the author is unwilling or unable, allow the publisher to arrange for a revision and deduct the cost of its preparation from the author's royalties.

PREPARING A REVISION

Although revisions can be a chore, most authors are willing to undertake the job unless their health or other personal circumstances make it impractical. Sometimes, because of an author's age or because he is no longer active in the field in which he originally wrote, his publisher may want a new person to take over against the author's wishes. This is a delicate situation which may be handled by having the publisher persuade the author to take on a collaborator to help with the next edition, and then take over preparing all editions after that. If the publisher is unable to sell this approach, however, it may be necessary to postpone any further editions until the author dies or is willing to admit that it is time for someone else to do the revising.

Should the author be willing or even eager to have someone else prepare the revision, the question of reasonable compensation for the new author can be difficult to resolve. Normally, the new author is given a share of the royalties on the new edition, and a larger share on subsequent editions, until ultimately he or she is receiving all the royalties.

Although contracts usually give the publisher the right to determine the royalty split, it is customary for the publisher to negotiate the split with the two parties. In theory, the split should be determined by the amount of material that needs to be rewritten, the existing reputation of the work, and perhaps the reputation of the reviser, but in practice it may also be affected in part by how determined the original author is to keep a large share of the royalty and by the willingness of the reviser to settle for a lesser share because of the long-term benefits. A more or less standard arrangement grants the new author one-third of the royalty income on the first revision, two-thirds on the second revision, and the entire royalty on any revisions made thereafter, but any split that both parties agree to will be satisfactory to the publisher, provided the new author receives enough to be motivated to do the work.

If the revision is made by the original author, no new contract is needed, since the terms of the original contract cover revised editions. In most cases, contracts state that the provisions of the contract are to apply to the revision as though it were a new work. Among other things, this means that if the original contract provides for a royalty that starts at 10 percent and increases to 15 percent when ten thousand copies are sold, the royalty rate on the revision will go back to 10 percent, and increase to 15 percent when the revision has sold 10,000 copies. The reason given by publishers for this return to a lower royalty rate is that the publisher has all the same expenses on a revision that he had on the first edition. The counter argument, however, is that a publisher has a much lower risk on a revision than on a new work, and lower investment risks normally yield lower rewards. In any event, minor revisions in ongoing editions should not cause the royalty rates to return to their original levels, and to be safe, your contract should refer to revised editions "to be republished as if a new work." Furthermore, if you think you will need an advance against royalties for preparing revisions, the amount of the advance should also be stated in the contract.

Editors usually need to go through the same steps on revised editions as on new books—estimating costs and sales, making profit studies, and getting approvals which, because of the lower risk, are easier to obtain. Prior to getting approval, editors and authors need to agree on the changes to be made in the new edition, including any significant increase in size. All changes agreed upon should be confirmed in writing.

If you are asked to prepare a revision, you should receive a letter from your publisher confirming that a revised edition has been authorized and stating when the manuscript is to be delivered. If you are revising a book originally written by someone else, you should get a contract as for a new work, except that the contract will specify the portions of the overall royalties to be paid to you for each subsequent edition.

The projected delivery date of revised manuscripts is of great importance to the publisher because he must coordinate the stock of the old edition with the projected publication date of the new one. On trade and professional books, publishers usually want to sell out all copies of the old edition four to six months before bringing out a new one, because customers buying the old edition a few weeks before the new one is available would feel cheated. However, college textbook publishers want to avoid running out of stock between editions, because that may force an instructor to switch textbooks and stay with the substituted text for several years. Because of these coordinating problems, it is imperative that you keep your publisher advised of any changes in the projected delivery dates of revisions.

Chapter 19

Terminating a Publishing Agreement

When you are enjoying the heady feeling of signing an agreement for the publication of your work, the last thing you are likely to think about is the termination of that agreement. Yet all good things come to an end, and bad things should come to an end sooner.

There are a variety of circumstances under which one or more parts of a publishing contract are, or should be, terminated and these should be provided for in the contract itself.

One of these circumstances is always provided for by the publisher—that is, the failure of the author to deliver a satisfactory manuscript by the date specified. This issue has already been discussed at length in Chapter 10.

A second situation is not normally covered in the standard publishing agreement, and you should ask that it be added, especially in a contract for a trade book. The author usually grants the publisher a bundle of rights, including reprint rights for trade and mass paperback editions, translation rights, dramatic rights, serialization rights, and book club rights. If the author has an agent, the agent will normally retain rights to a British edition, translation rights, and dramatic rights, with the balance of the rights being granted to the publisher. If after eighteen months your publisher has not sold one or more of those rights, or has not agreed to exercise those rights himself (for example by bringing out a trade paperback edition), then you should be able to terminate the license to those rights that have not been sold or exercised. When the time comes, you may be confident that the publisher is making a good faith effort to sell those rights and choose not to recover them. However, you should have that option.

Why would a publisher not try to sell rights that would bring him additional income? The person in charge of rights may be swamped with a number of big deals, and may not have the time to pursue little ones. But these can be very important to the average author. The option to recover those rights puts the publisher on notice that the rights are at risk if not pursued aggressively.

A similar option to recover rights should also apply to rights granted to but not exercised by an agent.

Another situation requiring termination of the agreement is when your book is no longer in print in any U.S. edition (that is, no longer available for sale from a publisher) or not under license for a reprint edition in the U.S. and is in fact out of print. When this occurs, the publishing agreement should be terminated and all rights granted to the publisher should revert to you. But there may be licenses granted by the publisher that are still in force. In other words, if the publisher has arranged for the publication of a Swahili edition, termination of the original agreement does not affect that edition nor the publisher's share of the income from it. However, most licenses are granted for a specific number of years. When such a license expires, the decision on any renewal or extension should be made by you, and any royalties resulting from the renewal need not be shared with the publisher, unless the publishing agreement states that the right to such renewal income is to survive termination. Most do not and should not.

Many publishers' contracts provide for termination only when there is no edition in print or under license. In that event, the existence of a license for a Swahili edition may keep you from recovering control of the work. You should request that the contract permit termination when there is no U.S. edition in print or under license to be printed.

At the time of termination, you should ask your publisher for copies of all licenses still in force, so you can know when each license terminates, and respond intelligently to any requests for licenses or attempt to market them.

Many trade contracts spell out an elaborate procedure for termination, requiring the author to notify the publisher that the book is not in print (as if the publisher didn't know), and giving the publisher six months or more in which to put the book back in print rather than have the contract terminated. Such clauses are designed to protect the publisher from a termination triggered by a temporary out-of-stock situation, and to give him time to decide whether to reprint or not. These circumstances arise with trade books when all the copies printed have been sold, but the publisher is uncertain about the continuing demand, and does not want to reprint until enough new orders have come in from bookstores and wholesalers to demonstrate that there is still a market for it. As a result, a trade book may be "out of stock" for several months until the publisher decides either to reprint or declare that edition "out of print." The termination clause enables authors to force that decision within a specified period of time if there is no other U.S. edition available for sale.

Most textbook and professional book publishers usually decide to let a work go out of print while there are still copies available, and notify the author of their decision.

When a book goes out of print, if you have assigned the copyright in the work to the publisher, the copyright should be reassigned to you, and that reassignment should be registered with the copyright office by the publisher.

The publisher's obligation to pay you any accrued royalties or shares in income from the prior sale of rights should survive the termination. Publishers usually want the author's indemnification against costs arising out of any legal action also to survive the termination.

If a book is selling very slowly, it is not uncommon for the publisher to declare it out of print even though copies are available in the warehouse. The remaining copies will either be sold as remainders or destroyed. At this time, you should be given the right to acquire any number of the remaining copies either free of charge, if they are to be destroyed, or at the remainder price, if they are to be remaindered, provided you pay the shipping costs.

If you wish to do so, you can continue to make your book available by having it listed in the *Buckley-Little Catalogue* of out-of-print books available directly from their authors. Your contract should also give you the right at this time to purchase the negatives used by the printer to make plates, so that you may, if you wish, have additional copies printed. Negatives do not cost much to buy or ship, and can easily be stored in a drawer.

Termination is also provided for in the new copyright law which states that thirty-five years after the book's publication or forty years after the agreement for publication is signed, the author has the right to terminate any agreement transferring copyright or any licenses granted under its copyright without regard to any agreement made to the contrary. If the author is deceased, then the author's spouse, children and grandchildren can exercise that right of termination. However, this termination does not apply to derivative works (translations, dramatizations, condensations) that were licensed by the publisher prior to such termination.

For works published prior to 1978 and under the old copyright law, the right of termination may be exercised fifty-six years after the date of first publication, if the copyright was renewed.

A 1984 court case dealt with the rights of the original publisher to a continuing share of the royalty income from the sale of derivative works after termination. In *Fox Agency v. Mills Music and Snyder*, the court ruled that upon termination, royalties continuing to be due from the sale of derivative works should be paid in their entirety to the author or his heirs, rather than shared with the original publisher who granted those derivative rights. This decision would seem to give an author or an author's heirs a financial incentive to exercise the right of termination and gain the full share of any royalty income still flowing from derivative works.

Unfortunately, most works are not durable enough to have much value thirty-five or fifty-six years after publication, and even fewer of their authors are around to reap benefits from the recovery of rights to their works. However, there are exceptions. A *New York Times* article on July 25, 1983, by Edwin McDowell reported that "Every Hemingway title is still in print and sales of his books in the United States total almost 750,000 copies annually . . . with his estate said to be earning $80,000 a year in foreign royalties." That is surely a record to inspire the Muse in the most slothful of us.

Negotiating a Book Contract

Success in negotiating depends in part on the strength of one's negotiating position (how badly one party wants what the other party has), in part on an understanding of what may be negotiable, and in part on the skill of the negotiating parties. Certainly all three of these elements come into play in negotiating a book contract.

Your negotiating strength as an author depends almost entirely on the commercial potential of your work, or more precisely, the amount of income it is likely to generate for the publisher. There are exceptions, of course. In some cases, a work is sufficiently important and prestigious to be sought after despite limited commercial potential, but these situations occur so infrequently that for all practical purposes they can be ignored.

Among all authors, poets are in the weakest negotiating position, for there is such a small market for books of poetry that even the works of our finest poets enjoy at best a modest sale.

Previously unpublished authors of fiction also negotiate from a position of extreme weakness. They generally have no reputation and no following or track record. And even if an editor is impressed by an author's talent and the quality of his work, the editor has no assurance that it will be reviewed favorably, if at all, no assurance that the average retail bookstore will order it, and certainly no assurance that enough persons will buy the book to generate a profit. Since most first novels lose money, publishing one is a blend of faith and folly—faith that, if not the first, then at least succeeding works by the same author will prove to be profitable. (And this, of course, is why publishers want options on authors' subsequent works.)

Morever, unpublished fiction authors whose works have already been rejected by a number of publishers and who are nurturing grave doubts about ever getting published are not likely to be in a mood for negotiating. The word that a book has been accepted for publication is such overwhelmingly good news that the publishing terms are almost irrelevant. If this is your situation, it may make sense for you to obtain the services of an agent to handle negotiations, in order to be assured that your publisher is not taking advantage of you.

Unpublished authors of trade books on recreational and practical subjects, such as hobbies, sports, travel, investing, and other practical how-to books are in a stronger negotiating position, because it is easier for editors to estimate sales. If one editor is interested in such a work, the likelihood that another would also be interested is high, and this gives you some negotiating strength. This is also true if you are writing a technical or professional book.

Among unpublished authors, college instructors are in the best negotiating position. They are regularly called upon by publishers' representatives who are promoting textbook sales and at the same time looking for new trends and new authors. It is relatively simple to find half a dozen textbook publishers who are "interested" in a new textbook project—meaning that they would like to see some material and have an opportunity to offer a publishing contract if the project seems promising. If you are the author of a sound project, you are likely to receive offers from several publishers, and are in a good position to negotiate a favorable arrangement. If you are at a large institution and can control or influence the use of the text in the course for which it is written, so much the better. And if it is an "influential" institution, better yet, since there is a tendency for smaller colleges to use the same texts as the larger, more prestigious schools in the same region.

It would be wrong, however, to suggest that textbook authors are without problems. There are a great many texts already available in all the traditional college courses, and it is no easy task to write a text that will win a sufficient share of its markets to be profitable for the publisher and the author. But notwithstanding the difficulties in writing a successful text, it is relatively easy for authors to have textbook proposals seriously considered by several publishers.

ISSUES AFFECTING THE NEGOTIATION

A factor that makes negotiating difficult is that you may establish a relationship of sorts with your editor over the period while the project is under review. If you then feel the contractual terms offered are unsatisfactory, and your editor is intransigent or able to make only minor changes, you are faced with the unhappy choice of accepting the unsatisfactory terms or starting all over with an unknown editor who may or may not be willing to publish on better terms—if at all.

It would be good, of course, if you could know the terms at the outset. However, the terms that can be offered are determined as part of the process of deciding if a project can be published profitably, and this process cannot readily be short-circuited. Still, there is no harm in asking about publishing terms early on, and the response may be sufficient to cause you to look elsewhere immediately. For example, if you need a sizable advance, and the editor says "We rarely give advances," that may be the end of that.

Unfortunately, it is only by submitting proposals to several publishers simultaneously that you can increase your chances of having practical and acceptable alternatives. Publishers, of course, prefer that you not do this because it establishes a competitive situation both with respect to terms and the time available for making a decision. Furthermore, if an editor knows a manuscript has been submitted to several publishers, and considers it from the outset a marginal project, he may be inclined to reject it without giving it serious consideration, since he may feel it is not worth gambling his time on its evaluation. Notwithstanding this risk, it's a good idea to tell publishers about multiple submissions, both in fairness to them, and so the author may derive some benefit from the potentially competitive situation.

Authors without—and even some with—prior experience also have the problem of determining what fair and reasonable terms might be for their specific projects. If multiple submissions result in more than one offer, then the author has a better feeling for the fairness of the offers received.

As stated earlier, multiple submissions can also greatly reduce the time it takes to find a suitable publisher, especially in trade book publishing where it is not uncommon for a project to be turned down by ten publishers only to be accepted by the eleventh. What is the best way to tell a publisher about multiple submissions? Very matter-of-factly. "I am also sending this proposal to several other publishers." No explanations or apologies are needed.

It is also a challenge to negotiate acceptable terms without appearing to be a "problem author"—that is, one who is going to be an unreasonable nuisance about everything from contract signing until the last copy of the book is sold. Because problem authors consume vast amounts of an editor's time that should be spent on other projects, editors prefer not to deal with them, unless the author is so potentially valuable that he or she must be endured.

If an editor senses that you are going to be an ongoing problem, he will take this into account and may turn down a project that he might otherwise accept. A reasonable and cooperative attitude on your part is very much in your own interest.

PRACTICAL STEPS

Following are some additional suggestions for negotiating satisfactory terms:

• First and most important you should submit as excellent a proposal and as polished a selection of sample material as possible. By presenting the project effectively, you make it much easier for the editor to see its virtues, thereby improving your negotiating position. (See also Chapter 5 on preparing publishing proposals).

The more material available for a publisher's consideration, the better the project can be evaluated, and the less risk for the publisher. Since it frequently helps to have the publisher's guidance in developing a project, one useful approach is to submit material during the early stages of its development in order to get helpful suggestions, but not to contract for its publication until a much larger share of the material has been prepared, so that its potential can be more effectively evaluated.

• If at all possible, you should meet face to face with your editor to negotiate terms, especially if you are asking for major changes from what has been proposed. Negotiating without being able to watch the other party's expression or body language is like driving a car blindfolded, i.e., you can't tell when you should slow down or change direction. If a meeting is impractical, the next best approach is a letter, followed by a phone call. The letter should mention the terms you feel are unacceptable, without mentioning exact monetary amounts. Instead, leave the editor in doubt, expecting the worst. Then when you phone several days later to discuss the changes you would like made, the editor may be surprised at how reasonable your requests are—if they are—and accept them with relief.

• Although almost every paragraph in a publisher's contract is potentially negotiable, they are not all negotiable in a single contract. Be judicious and selective in asking for changes, picking the issues that are of greatest importance.

● On certain issues it may help to have a rationale for the desired change or improvement in terms. For example, if a larger advance is needed to take the place of other income you must give up in order to complete the book, or to cover the cost of illustrations, the editor may be more responsive than if you simply request more money up front. For example, the editor may propose that the publisher arrange for the illustrations and charge them to your royalty account, solving your immediate financial problem, but giving the editor more control over the project.

● If the editor is unwilling or unable to meet your requested changes, don't accept "no" for an answer, but press instead for a counterproposal—either a tradeoff or a compromise. Look for signs that the editor can make concessions in some areas and not in others; that is, he may be required to get special approval for certain items, such as royalty terms in excess of a certain amount, but may have no restrictions on others. Listen carefully to what the editor has to say and try to think of ways of meeting his or her needs. There may be concessions you can make to get what you want. Remember that the editor probably wants a deal almost as much as you do.

● Publishers cannot afford to pay high royalty rates on lower levels of sales, and authors will find it difficult to negotiate better rates for the first twenty-five hundred or five thousand copies sold. Publishers don't have the margin to permit them to make concessions at these levels. However, when sales reach or exceed the publisher's own expectations, then the book becomes very profitable. If you can determine the number of copies the publisher expects to sell, you may be able to negotiate a somewhat higher royalty rate on sales beyond that point. This is especially true for textbooks, since marketing costs do not increase in direct proportion to sales. If you believe your editor is underestimating the probable sale of your work, and if you are a gambler, you might propose a lower royalty rate on a certain number of copies in exchange for a higher rate after sales exceed a certain amount, but this is not a game for an inexperienced author.

● Subsidiary rights income is another potentially negotiable area, especially on trade books. The costs associated with selling subsidiary rights are relatively low, and as a result, the income should be almost all gravy. Nevertheless, many publishers, and especially trade book publishers, count on at least some income from this source. You may find it difficult to get an increased share of the lower levels of subsidiary rights income, but it would not be unreasonable to ask for a larger share after a certain level has been reached.

● Sometimes an enterprising author can presell a major quantity of a book to a nontraditional book market, especially if he or she has good contacts in that market. Examples are the sale of a book on investing to a brokerage firm to be used as a premium or for sale to its clients; or a book on woodworking to a power tool company for sale to owners of power tools. Such a special sale, arranged in advance, virtually eliminates the publisher's risk and in so doing, strengthens the author's negotiating position considerably. It may be difficult to get a firm order for such a sale until proofs are available, but even an expression of strong interest by a company may be enough to encourage an editor to improve his or her offer. Most publishers offer 10 percent of net receipts on special sales of this type. If you are fortunate enough to have a major customer for your work, ask for 15 percent of net receipts for that specific sale, representing a sales commission as well as a royalty.

● There are times when editors reluctantly turn down projects because they fall a bit short of yielding sufficient profit margins. An author who is eager for commercial publication may wish to suggest foregoing a portion or all of the royalty on some initial number of copies sold. While this is not a satisfactory solution for someone trying to earn a living by writing, if you want the material published at all costs, it is a better solution than publication by a vanity press, and probably a better solution than self-publication.

● In negotiating with two publishers, keep in mind that a better deal with a less enthusiastic or less qualified company may not really be a better deal. But don't hesitate to use the better offer to try to get improved terms from the publisher you prefer.

● Be careful not to close out the negotiation by threatening to take you project elsewhere, unless you really mean to. If you still believe you are not getting a fair deal, tell the editor you are not happy with it and want to think about what to do. Maybe he'll call you in a few days with a compromise. Maybe you will call him and accept his final offer. One never knows.

It is perhaps not surprising that many authors do no negotiating at all with their publishers. They are pleased to have their work accepted for publication, and publishing terms are detailed and somewhat complex. However, those authors who do negotiate are generally well rewarded for their time and effort.

Chapter 21

Preparing and Submitting the Final Manuscript

After you have signed your publishing agreement, your publisher will probably send you information on the physical form in which the final manuscript should be submitted. However, if you prepare the final manuscript without a publisher, or if your publisher fails to tell you what is wanted, here are typical requirements.

USE OF HEADINGS

The same system of headings and subheadings should be used throughout the manuscript to indicate clearly the relationships within the material.

- Major headings are normally typed in capital letters on a separate line.

- Secondary headings, used to designate material that is subsidiary to the subject indicated by a major heading, are usually typed in initial capitals followed by lower case letters on a separate line.

- Tertiary headings are typed in capital and lower case letters, but are typed on the first line of the body of text and are underlined.

FRONT AND BACK MATTER

Every book has material that precedes the main body of text, called front matter, as well as material that follows the text, called back matter. Many books also have references to source materials and bibliographies. It is your responsibility to prepare most of this material and submit it with the final manuscript or, in the case of front matter, shortly thereafter.

Front Matter

The front matter consists of a number of components, some of which are optional or included only in certain situations. Among the elements, the first three are prepared by the publisher.

● The half-title page, which contains only the main title of the work.

● The title page, which contains the title and subtitle, if any, the author's name and affiliation (where appropriate), and the name of the publisher.

● The copyright page, on the reverse side of the title page, contains the copyright notice, Library of Congress cataloging data, the International Standard Book Number (ISBN) which is the industry identification number for the specific edition of each work, the number of the printing, and the date made.

If you have had other books published, the titles may be listed on the right-hand page facing either the half-title or the title page. In the past, books frequently had an illustration, called a frontispiece, on the left-hand page facing the title page, but these are relatively rare today.

A dedication provided by the author may appear on the first right-hand page following the title page. Dedications are optional, and it's up to you how to word them and whom to honor—wives, children, parents, friends, associates, and even an occasional dog, have all been so chosen.

● A foreword, which may be the next element in a book, is an introduction by someone other than the author. Such an introduction would be appropriate, for example, when the work has been sponsored by some organization, or if the work is part of a series. The sponsoring organization, or the editor of the series, may wish to write a foreword. If you are a relatively unknown author, a foreword by an established authority will help attract attention to the book, and may be arranged by your publisher.

• The preface, which follows the foreword, is the author's personal statement about the book—who it is for, why it was written, and what it is designed to achieve. The last paragraph of the preface may also contain acknowledgements to persons who helped with the book, or they may be presented under a separate heading on the following page. The preface is generally concluded with the author's name, and the date and place where the preface was written.

• The table of contents contains, at the least, a list of the chapter titles and the pages on which they begin, but it may also include the names of sections within each chapter, and sometimes even subsections (i.e., the headings and subheadings).

• If the book is illustrated, there may be a list of illustrations and their page numbers on the page following the table of contents.

• A book may also have a prologue or an introduction, if a separate introduction to the work itself seems desirable, as distinct from your more personal remarks in the preface. Or the first chapter may be the introductions.

References

Academic and scientific works, and some trade books, have references to source materials to support the author's statements. References can be handled in a number of ways. Most commonly, the relevant statements are numbered to refer to a single listing of source materials (by chapter and in numerical order) placed at the end of the book. However, lists of references may be placed at the end of each chapter. Or references may be handled as footnotes at the bottom of each page.

The conventional way of presenting references is essentially the same whether it is done in a footnote or in a reference listing.

If the source is a book, the reference should contain the name(s) of the author(s), including first names or two initials, the title and edition of the work, the publisher, the date of publication, and the page on which the source material occurs. For example:

Kirk Polking and Leonard S. Meranus, editors, *Law and the Writer*, Third Edition, Writer's Digest Books, 1985, p. 57.

If the source is a periodical, the reference should include the name(s) of the author(s), the title of the article, the name of the periodical, the date of the issue, and the page on which the article or reference appears. For example:

> Judson Jerome, "Big Opportunities in the Small Press," *Writer's Digest*, June, 1984, p. 24.

The same basic styles are used for serial publications, reports, theses, and symposia, except that if no author or editor is given credit for the material, the subject will be the first item in the reference.

If your book contains a large number of references, you may find it helpful to refer to one of the style manuals that are listed in the bibliography of this book

Bibliographies

Most scholarly, professional, and reference books, and some nonfiction trade books, contain bibliographies, listing other books dealing with the same subject matter. For an academic work, the list should be quite complete, but for other works, you can be more selective. Most textbooks have suggested readings listed at the end of each chapter, which are essentially bibliographies for each chapter.

A bibliography should be set up in the same way as a reference list, except that the first author's last name should be listed first, and the bibliography is alphabetized by that author's last name. Bibliographies can be simple lists or they can be annotated to indicate the special contribution or appeal of each work. If the bibliography is long, it may be more useful to organize it first by subject matter, and then alphabetically.

Glossaries

In certain books, glossaries of special terms can be very useful to readers, so they do not need to search back through the text for the place where the term was first used and defined. The glossary should define the terms only as they are used within the work itself. Occasionally a glossary is integrated with the index into a single alphabetical listing.

Appendixes

You may want to provide detailed material to support or elaborate on the text without interrupting the flow of the discussion. Such material is normally included in appendixes at the end of the book immediately before the index. These may be documents, mathematical proofs, tables of data, legal extracts, or any other relevant material. Nothing should be put in an appendix that the reader must know in order to understand the text, and nothing should be left in the main body of the text that most readers will not want to read.

All of the front matter and other supplementary material should be sent to the publisher with the final manuscript, or shortly thereafter.

Index

Except for works of fiction, authors are usually also responsible for developing indexes for their works. Most indexes are alphabetical listings of topics and the pages on which they are discussed in the book. However, supplementary indexes may be included that are organized in different ways, such as geographically, or on special subjects. For example, a book on plant pathology may have an index of plant diseases, and a survey of literature may have an index of authors. Indexing cannot be done until page proofs are available. The preparation of indexes is discussed in greater detail in Chapter 22 on the Publishing Process and the Author's Role.

PAPER & TYPING

The final manuscript should be typed on a good grade of 8½x11 white bond paper, preferably 20-pound or heavier, so that it will stand up under heavy handling. Erasable-finished paper should not be used, because it smudges easily, and resists ink markings that the copy editor or the editor may want to make on the manuscript.

The manuscript should be typed, double-spaced, on one side of the sheet only, allowing at least a one-inch margin on all four sides of the text so that there is plenty of room for editorial notations. It is important also that the type is clean and clear, since the manuscript will probably be duplicated several times.

While writing successive drafts of the manuscript, it is helpful to use two numbers to identify each page—the number of the chapter and the page number within the chapter, so that page 8-13 will be the thirteenth page in chapter eight. This makes it easier to rework individual chapters without regard to where they occur in the book. However, most publishers prefer to have the final manuscript numbered sequentially from beginning to end. If pages are added after the final manuscript has been typed, they can be marked as alphabetic extensions of the page they follow—e.g., pages added after 137 become 137a, 137b, 137c, and so on.

If footnotes are to be used, they can be typed at the foot of the page on which the reference occurs, or within the text on the line immediately following the reference, separated from the text by spaces or lines—an easier solution. Or if there are a great many footnotes, they may be submitted in a separate listing.

Minor corrections can be written on the final manuscript, provided they are neat and legible. However, if they are extensive, it is better to retype the page on which they occur.

If the manuscript contains mathematical equations, any Greek letters should be easily identifiable, and subscripts or superscripts should be clearly differentiated.

If you prepare the final manuscript on a word processor, the publisher may want to have duplicates of the diskettes. This may save the publisher the expense of keyboarding, and it would not be unreasonable for you to be compensated for a portion of that savings. If the publisher is interested, the compensation should be negotiated as part of the contract, and the publisher should give you instructions regarding the format and coding to be used in preparing the final manuscript.

Illustrations should be submitted separately from the text, and each should be numbered to indicate the chapter in which it is to appear, and its illustration number within that chapter. Figure 12-3, for example, is the third illustration in Chapter 12. The manuscript should be marked in the margin (Fig. 12-3) to show where that numbered illustration is to appear. Glossy halftones should be numbered on the back with a felt-tipped pen or grease pencil, so that the surface of the halftone is not marred. Do not use paperclips on photographs, since they can easily damage the glossy surface.

Captions for illustrations should be typed in a separate, double-spaced listing, each numbered to identify the illustration to which it belongs.

In submitting the final manuscript, send the original to your publisher since he will be duplicating it, but be sure to retain a copy, since it is always possible that the original will be lost in transit. In addition, you may need to refer to the copy in discussing the manuscript with the editor. If practical, also keep a copy of the illustrations.

The manuscript and illustrations may be mailed by fourth-class "book rate," which is considerably cheaper than parcel post. First-class mail is much more expensive, but also faster.

Since mail service is not infallible, it is wise to insure the manuscript and illustrations for the cost of their replacement—that is, the cost of retyping the text if necessary and obtaining new photo prints or other illustrations. In addition, for peace of mind, it may be worth the extra cost to send the manuscript "Certified, return receipt requested." That alleviates the concern about its possible loss when there is no early word from the publisher.

UPS is a good alternate choice for delivering manuscripts. The service is less expensive than first-class mail, faster than fourth-class mail, the chances of damage are less, and UPS shipments are traceable and automatically insured up to $100.

Whichever method you choose, the manuscript should be packaged securely so that it will not come open en route. Extra care should be taken with illustrations, and especially photographs, to assure that they will not be bent. Either a corrugated box or heavy cardboard or corrugated board on both sides of the package of illustrations should do the job.

PROTECTION AGAINST LOSS OF MANUSCRIPT

Nothing can be more devastating to an author than the loss of a manuscript. It is far worse than just the economic loss. It is the loss of ideas that have been carefully developed and honed. They may be tediously reconstructed, but will they ever be constructed as well?

Although the incidence of lost manuscripts is low, it is a risk, that should be avoided, especially when photocopying and computer printing make it so easy to do.

First, it always a good idea to retain the draft of each chapter prior to the final draft, so that if anything happens to the final draft, the prior draft, including all of its editorial changes, is available for retyping.

Second, in sending partial or complete manuscripts to publishers for consideration, you should retain the original, and send out clear photocopies. If the manuscript copy is lost either in the mails or at the publisher's (it occasionally happens), the loss is of no significance.

Third, it is prudent to protect against fire, which can easily destroy all copies of the manuscript that may be in your home or office, as well as all the notes and materials you have amassed as the foundation for your work. Keep an additional copy of your manuscript, either a photocopy or the last draft copy, at a separate location—at your home or office, or at the home of another member of the family, or in a safe deposit box. Or if the work is under contract, you may ask your publisher to retain a copy, and provide additional batches as chapters are completed or rewritten.

A few simple precautions can give you greater peace of mind, and eliminate the possibility, however remote, of a major disaster.

The Publishing Process and the Author's Role

The first word you are likely to receive from your publisher after submitting your final manuscript is a brief acknowledgment of its receipt. In your elation at having completed the project, you will probably find your editor's acknowledgment lacking in proper enthusiasm. But there is a reason for this editorial restraint. Until your manuscript has been carefully reviewed, your editor does not want to suggest that it is satisfactory, since he or she may have to reject it, or ask you to rework it. So the acknowledgment is likely to be nothing more than that.

REVIEW OF COMPLETED MANUSCRIPT

If the manuscript is for a trade book, the final review may be by the editor. If it is a professional book, scholarly book, or textbook, the review is almost always by an outside adviser, possibly the same adviser who recommended publication. If your editor is not satisfied with the quality or the thoroughness of the first review, a second review may also be obtained. This reviewing process may take four to six weeks.

Your editor will then either write or telephone you to discuss the comments and suggestions for changes. These may include adding or eliminating material, or changing the sequence of chapters or sections within chapters. The review may have identified language problems that are too complex for the copy editor to correct. Your editor may also question the quality of the illustrations, or the accuracy of certain statements that may need to be verified. If the manuscript is longer than originally agreed on, surgery may be required. In any event, it is not uncommon for a manuscript to require more work of either a minor or a major sort before it is accepted for publication.

When the revised manuscript is resubmitted, it will be reviewed again. If all the problems have been resolved, the editor will be able to authorize the payment of any advance due upon acceptance of a complete, satisfactory manuscript. However, because several people may need to approve the advance before it is paid and because accountants are reluctant to disburse money any sooner than necessary, it may be a month or so before you receive the advance.

Your manuscript is now finally ready for the tortuous passage through the book production process, and although you may think that you are finally finished, there is more work to be done.

PRODUCTION SCHEDULES

The process of converting a manuscript into a book takes a long time, usually between six months and a year, depending primarily on the size and complexity of the book. Since large newspapers are produced daily from reporters' notes to printed newspaper in less than twenty-four hours, six months to a year for the publication of a book might seem unreasonable. But there are significant differences in the processes.

First, in style and terminology, a book must be consistent and coherent in order not to confuse the reader. A description of an event in the tenth chapter should relate clearly to mention of the same event in the third chapter. The system of headings and subheadings should be the same throughout the book. In fiction, the names of the characters and places must be consistent throughout, and the dates and times of events must be in proper sequence. As a result, a book cannot be divided up among a group of editors, but must be worked through by a single person.

Second, making a book involves a large number of separate operations, most of which must be performed sequentially. For example, typesetting cannot begin until the entire manuscript is edited, because the editor may find something in the last chapter that affects the content of the first chapter; and the index cannot be prepared until the book is pasted up onto pages, because the indexer must know the number of the page on which the indexed item appears.

Third, about half the time required to produce a book is actually waiting time—that is, the manuscript or proofs or whatever are waiting for someone to finish working on another project. If everyone drops everything else to work immediately on one book, it can be produced in half the time otherwise needed, but all the other books on the publisher's schedule will take longer. The waiting time could be eliminated if all operations, including compositors, printers, and binders, were so lavishly staffed and equipped that books would never have to wait. Unfortunately, the cost of this approach is prohibitive.

MARKETING INFORMATION

Sometime after the manuscript is accepted for publication, your publisher will ask for marketing information: biographical data to be used in promotional material; a reaffirmation of the specific market or markets for which the book is written; a statement about competing works and how your work differs from them; and any ideas you may have about marketing the work. The author's ideas are especially important for professional and special-interest trade books, for the publisher may not be familiar with all the dealers that might handle the book, or all the publications in the field that might review it, or special interest mailing lists that may be used in promotion. An author of a book of this type should provide the publisher with this kind of information even if it isn't asked for.

Textbook publishers usually are much more interested in the comparative evaluation of competing works, since the new textbook will have to supplant current texts. The questions to be answered, therefore, is why should instructors, whose class notes are written based on those texts, go to the trouble of dropping them in favor of the new one?

TITLE

The title for the book must be decided well in advance of publication, and most contracts state that it is to be "mutually agreed upon." Authors often are reluctant to give up whatever title they've been using, but publishers who look at the issue from a marketing viewpoint, usually want a change. There are several criteria for a good title for a nonfiction work. First, it must describe the content of the book clearly and accurately so the prospective buyer has no doubt about what the book covers. Second, it should do this in as few words as possible, certainly not more than six.

Third, it should be sufficiently different from the titles of other books so there is little danger of confusion. The book may also have a subtitle to further clarify what the book is about. An example of an effective title is *MEGATRENDS: Ten New Directions Transforming our Lives*. Sometimes publishers are attracted to titles that are catchy and read well, but which don't accurately describe the book. These titles should be vigorously resisted.

It is difficult to find a distinctive title for a college textbook. There is a limited number of descriptive titles one can give, for example, to an introductory text in economics. As a result, textbooks are always referred to by their author's name instead of by their title.

For fiction, there is a tendency to pick titles from lines in the Bible, or Shakespeare, or from one of the better-known poets—lines that represent the theme of the work—but any title that seems to capture the essence of the work will do.

DESIGN & JACKET

Every book must be designed. Someone must determine how the inside and the outside of the book are to look. The book designer, working from the manuscript, develops specifications for the type faces and sizes to be used for the text, for headings and subheadings, captions and chapter titles, trim size, page size, and how illustrations will be handled in relation to text. Having done this, a designer will usually select samples of material from the manuscript to be set by the compositor as sample pages to show how the interior of the book will actually look. You should ask to see these sample pages as a precaution against the designer having come up with a design solution that you dislike intensely. You have put a lot of yourself into the project, and you ought to be satisfied with the visual appeal of the finished book. Be especially wary of over-design. Occasionally designers strive to achieve striking graphic effects when a simpler solution would be better for the reader.

Trade books and professional books normally have dust jackets that are the book's wrap-around promotion piece. Because they are also used separately by the sales force in selling to retail bookstores and wholesalers, jackets are usually designed and produced well in advance of the book's publication. Make a point of asking to see both the jacket artwork and jacket copy. In reviewing the artwork, remember that the jacket is really a poster advertisement for the book, and needs to be visually strong so that it will stand out when displayed in a bookstore or shown in a catalog or promotional circular. Check all text carefully for misspellings. Be sure to approve material or discuss changes immediately in order not to delay publication.

COPY EDITING

While the designer is at work, the editor or copy editor is reviewing the manuscript in order to prepare a style sheet for the book, that is, an alphabetized, itemized list of points of editorial style to be used in editing. For example, in a book on investments, will the price-earnings ratio be presented as *the price/earnings ratio*, or *the P/E ratio*, or *the P/E multiple?* Will the text refer to *one dollar*, or *$1*, or *$1.00? Five thousand dollars*, or *$5,000?* The more technical and complex the editorial content of a book, the greater the need for a style sheet. If you are interested in such issues, ask to see the style sheet as soon as it is available. It is too late to make changes in these basic elements once the book has been set in type.

The copy editor, who may be a freelancer, checks the manuscript for grammatical errors, discrepancies in fact, awkward or confusing language, as well as establishing consistency in style throughout. At the same time, the copy editor marks the various elements in the manuscript (heads, extracts, footnotes, etc.), so that the compositor can set the type for them in accordance with the design specifications and sample pages.

so they can see and approve changes, catch any errors that may have been made while resolving language problems, and answer any queries the copy editor may have about the author's meaning in certain places. Other publishers believe authors resent the changes made by copy editors, but are much less likely to dispute them in proofs, so they prefer to let authors review the copy editing in proofs. In either case, you should not accept changes that alter your meaning, or that you find awkward.

GALLEY PROOFS

As your manuscript is being typeset, you will receive galley proofs. These are long sheets of typeset material not yet divided into book pages. They will probably have been proofread against the manuscript by the compositor and a proofreader, but you still need to read them very

Proofreading & Copyediting Symbols

rom change <u>italic</u> to roman

e delete this letter/words

⌢ close up, join let⌢ers

e delete and join wit⌢hout space

∧ caret, insert∧here *word*

insert∧space

stet stet, Latin; let ᵢ̈t stand (as set) *stet*

tr trans⌢se

¶ new paragraph

sp spell out, ⑤ hours

u.c. upper case (capital)

l.c. lower case (small letter)

s.c. Small Capitals

b.f. boldface type

= hyphen, blue=green

$\frac{1}{m}$ em dash, he tried∧and failed

✓ superscript, footnote 3/

∧ subscript, Vitamin B₁₂

↗ comma

⊙ period

↗ semicolon

⊙ colon

᛭ ᛭ quotation marks

∤ ∤ parentheses

carefully and make corrections. Galleys are normally sent in batches, and you should correct and return each batch to your publisher as promptly as possible.

Standard proofreaders' marks are shown on p. 166. You should use ink or pencil of a different color from that used by the compositor so that your corrections can be properly identified. If the copy editor's queries have not yet been answered, they will be transferred to the galleys by the compositor, and should be resolved by you as galleys are read. Since the cost of your alterations (as distinct from corrections of the compositor's errors) in excess of a certain amount will be charged to you as spelled out in the publishing contract, you can frequently save money by being meticulous about the accuracy of the final manuscript you submit to your publisher.

The compositor makes all the corrections noted on the galleys and then divides the galleys into pages, adding running headings, page numbers, footnotes, and illustration captions, but leaving spaces for illustrations. A set of these page proofs will also be sent to you. These need to be read carefully again for errors still remaining in the text as well as mistakes in placement of captions for illustrations (where errors are very common), footnotes, and the other elements making up the page. Although it is important to correct mistakes, make no unnecessary changes, since alterations in page proofs are even more costly than changes in galley proofs. When changes are necessary, try to compensate for them by adding or deleting words in order to maintain the same number of letters in the corrected line as before, eliminating the need to reset more than a single line.

ILLUSTRATIONS

If your publisher is to prepare final drawings from your rough sketches, or if illustrations need lettering or labelling, this work is assigned to a draftsman. When completed, copies of all final illustrations, including any photographs that you have marked for cropping, are sent to you for checking and approval. Again, these must be reviewed carefully for errors, and returned promptly to your publisher. Be especially alert to errors in the wording added by the draftsman, to misplaced captions, and to photos that have been reversed so that what the caption says is "on the left" is now on the right.

THE INDEX

With the exception of fiction, every book should have an index. Authors are best qualified and usually make the best indexes for their own books, because they know what is significant and what is not. However, if you can't do the job well in the time available, your publisher can arrange for the index to be prepared by a professional indexer and charge the cost to your royalty account. Many trade publishers prefer to have the work done by a professional in order to avoid delays caused by inexperience, but be forewarned that this may cost you $500 or perhaps even more.

The simplest way to make an index is to prepare an index card for each entry and subentry to be indexed, together with the numbers of the pages on which the entries are to be found. Each subentry card must also include the main entry, so that the index can be assembled correctly. In selecting words for entries, you must anticipate the words the reader will use in looking for information. Care should be taken not to over-index. Entries leading the reader to text where the word is used without providing any additional information is not helpful. When cards have been completed for all the entries, they can be alphabetized. When in doubt about alphabetical sequence, any good dictionary can be used as a guide. The final step is to type the index double-spaced on 8½x11 white paper.

The index has to be prepared quickly, usually within ten days from the receipt of the last page proofs, or publication may be delayed. It may help to review indexes in similar books and to practice selecting topics before actually receiving page proofs.

FROM PAGES TO BOUND BOOKS

After the compositor has corrected the errors identified in the page proofs, final reproduction or "repro" proofs of pages are made on high-quality coated paper, and sent to the publisher. These are pasted up on cardboard flats together with all line illustrations, usually two pages to a board. These boards, called mechanicals, are then sent to the printer, who photographs them to make the negatives that are the first step in the plate-making process. Halftone illustrations are photographed separately with a fine screen imposed on them, and the negatives for these illustrations are then stripped into the negatives for the appropriate pages. Next, prints (known as blueprints or "blues") of the negatives are made that show all the pages together with illustrations, just as they will appear in the finished book. These are sent to the publisher for final checking, and the publisher may send them to you for final approval as well. This is not a time for any changes in the book. Rather it is a check to see that everything has come together correctly into pages, that illustrations are in the right place and are not upside down. It is really the publisher's responsibility to catch these errors, but the publisher may choose to share the burden and responsibility with you.

LAST TASKS

After receiving the blueprints back from the publisher and making any necessary corrections, the printer will proceed to make plates, and print and bind the book, and about six or seven weeks after the blueprints are returned, you should receive an advance copy of your book, with the balance of your author's copies coming along within ten days. At this point, you will probably experience a great sense of satisfaction and relief that you have finished the project, but it is still not time to relax.

Courtesy Copies

As soon as your author's copies are received, you will probably want to send a copy to each of the persons who gave you substantial help in writing the book, and you may want to autograph these "in appreciation." If you have received help from a fair number of persons, your author's copies will not go very far, and you may have to purchase extra copies from your publisher.

Corrections

After publication, you should set up a file for corrections. Despite all the manuscript checking and proofreading, errors will be discovered—typographical errors, factual errors, and perhaps conceptual errors, some of which will be discovered by you, some by reviewers and readers. Most will be sent to the publisher who will forward them to you. If the book does well enough to require a second printing, the significant errors should be corrected, but some may have to await a new edition. It is a good idea to discuss correction procedures with your publisher. Some publishers systematically check for corrections before making a second printing. Others may not, in which case the burden of seeing to it that corrections are made will rest with you.

As in reading page proofs, great care should be taken in making a correction to see that the number of characters in the line is not changed by the correction, so that the minimum amount of type will need to be reset.

Now that your book is published, you will probably be concerned about how it is marketed. Although the marketing will have begun during the early stages of production, it is dealt with separately in Chapter 24. The next chapter explains the details of book production for those authors who are curious about how books are made.

Chapter 23

How Books Are Produced

Many authors do not want to know any more about book production than they need to, but others are interested in having a fuller understanding of the whole process. This chapter is written for them.

DESIGN

Book designers are the architects of book production. They are responsible for writing the specifications that determine how the book will look, from the exterior jacket and cover to the interior layout of the pages. Designers work not only with the edited manuscript itself, but also with information regarding the book's market, the expected length of the press runs, the number of colors of ink to be used internally (usually one), for the cover (usually two) and jacket (two, three, or four), and how the book is to be bound. All these issues affect the design of the book.

Trim Sizes

One of the first decisions that must be made about a book is the size in which it will be produced, otherwise known as its trim size. This is the size of the pages after three sides have been trimmed in the binding operations.

The range of trim sizes commonly used is dictated by readability, cost, and custom. First, the length of lines on a printed page affects how easily the text can be read. If the line is very short, many words need to be hyphenated, which slows the reader. If the line is very long, the eye has difficulty picking up the next line to be read. A four-inch line of type seems ideal for the type sizes used in most books, although a three- or five-inch line is still readable. If you add 1½ inches for the inside and outside margins to the ideal four-inch line, you have a 5½ inch width for your page. It is not surprising, therefore, that one of the common sizes of trade books is 5½x8 inches. However, if it is a long book, a 6x9 trim size may be used with a somewhat longer line length, in order to get more words per page and keep the book from getting too bulky. A 6x9 trim size is commonly used for college textbooks and reference books.

It is possible to use a four-inch line of type on a wider page, allowing generous margins for occasional notations or illustrations, but the additional paper required increases the cost of production considerably.

Some books containing a large number of illustrations are designed for two columns on a page, which permits the illustrations to be in either single or double-column width. The readable line length again tends to dictate the page width of the book. Although two three-inch columns can be crowded into a page that is 7¼ inches wide, pages that are eight or 8½ inches wide accommodate two columns more comfortably. For double column books, therefore, trim sizes are commonly 7¼x9⅞, 8x10, and 8½x11.

The length of book pages is determined by aesthetics—the pleasing relationship of length to width—and by what can be accommodated by contemporary printing and binding equipment.

Although many variations are possible, most publishers produce their books in a limited number of trim sizes, since this permits economies in ordering paper, and in presswork and shipping cartons.

Typefaces

Typefaces and their arrangement on the page are the basic elements in book design. The variety of typefaces available is enormous; there are literally hundreds of individual faces. Types used for text matter are available in sizes ranging from 6-point (which is usually found in dictionaries) up to 14-point, and display types, which are used for book covers and jackets, title pages and chapter openings, are available in sizes from 18-point to 72-point. A point is ¹⁄₇₂ of an inch, so that 9-point type is roughly ⅛ inch from the top of a tall letter (l) to the bottom of a letter that descends below the line (y). And in addition to the wide array of sizes, each face may also be available in capital, small capital, and lower case for italic and roman, lightface and boldface, and possibly semi-boldface, as well as condensed and expanded.

The styles of type available can generally be classified as serif or sans serif (without serif), a serif being a terminal flair of each line making up a letter. Many people find text set in sans serif faces harder to read, and in the United States at least, the sans serif faces are used primarily for display or for headings. See examples of two type faces and their variations in figure 23-1.

Although it is possible to set lines of text type without space between them, it is more common to allow between one and three points of spacing (called "leading," after the metal) between the lines, especially when the lines are long, as in a single-column book. Unless there is leading between long lines of type, the eye does not easily go from the end of one line to the beginning of the next when reading. Setting 10-point type with two points of leading between lines is described as setting "ten on twelve," usually written as 10/12. The text in this book is set 10/12 in the typeface called century expanded.

With many computer-driven composition systems, it is also possible to compress type faces so that there are more characters per inch, or "stretch" them so there are fewer characters per inch than the standard for that type. It is also possible to put fractional points of leading between lines, so that the text may be set, for example, 10/12.5.

With all these variables at their command, designers specify the type face, size, and style to be used for each element of the book, including the title page, contents pages, chapter openings, running heads, several degrees of subheadings, captions and legends for illustrations, footnotes, extract material, bibliography, and index. Because it is almost impossible for anyone, including designers, to know how the type specifications will look, it is customary to have sample pages set in type to show all the elements listed above. The editor reviews the sample pages, sometimes making minor modifications if not satisfied, sometimes sending them to the authors for approval as well.

When everyone is satisifed with the type specifications, the book is ready to be typeset.

TYPESETTING SYSTEMS

From the middle of the fifteenth century, when Gutenberg perfected the use of moveable type, until the 1950s, almost all books were printed by using molten metal to cast raised type characters, which were used to print directly onto paper, or to make electrotype plates which were used in printing by the letterpress process. However, the development

Serif typestyles

WITH ALL OF THESE variables at their command, designers specify the type face, size, and style to be used for each element of the book, including the title page, contents pages, chapter openings, running heads, several degrees of subheadings, captions and legends for illustrations, footnotes, extract material, bibliography, and index. Because it is almost impossible for anyone, including designers, to know how the type
CENTURY EXPANDED

WITH ALL OF THESE variables at their command, designers specify the type face, size, and style to be used for each element of the book, including the title page, contents pages, chapter openings, running heads, several degrees of subheadings, captions and legends for illustrations, footnotes, extract material, bibliography, and index. Because it is almost impossible for anyone, including designers, to know how the type
CENTURY EXPANDED ITALIC

WITH ALL OF THESE variables at their command, designers specify the type face, size, and style to be used for each element of the book, including the title page, contents pages, chapter openings, running heads, several degrees of subheadings, captions and legends for illustrations, footnotes, extract material, bibliography, and index. Because it is almost impossible for anyone, including designers, to know how the type
CENTURY BOLD

WITH ALL OF THESE variables at their command, designers specify the type face, size, and style to be used for each element of the book, including the title page, contents pages, chapter openings, running heads, several degrees of subheadings, captions and legends for illustrations, footnotes, extract material, bibliography, and index. Because it is almost impossible for anyone, including designers, to know how the type
MELIOR

WITH ALL OF THESE variables at their command, designers specify the type face, size, and style to be used for each element of the book, including the title page, contents pages, chapter openings, running heads, several degrees of subheadings, captions and legends for illustrations, footnotes, extract material, bibliography, and index. Because it is almost impossible for anyone, including designers, to know how the type
PALATINO

WITH ALL OF THESE variables at their command, designers specify the type face, size, and style to be used for each element of the book, including the title page, contents pages, chapter openings, running heads, several degrees of subheadings, captions and legends for illustrations, footnotes, extract material, bibliography, and index. Because it is almost impossible for anyone, including designers, to know how the type
SOUVENIR LIGHT

All serif type samples set in 9 point type with 10 point leading

Sans Serif typestyles

WITH ALL OF THESE variables at their command, designers specify the type face, size, and style to be used for each element of the book, including the title page, contents pages, chapter openings, running heads, several degrees of subheadings, captions and legends for illustrations, footnotes, extract material, bibliography, and index. Because it is almost impossible for anyone, including designers, to know how the type
AVANT GARDE GOTHIC LIGHT

WITH ALL OF THESE variables at their command, designers specify the type face, size, and style to be used for each element of the book, including the title page, contents pages, chapter openings, running heads, several degrees of subheadings, captions and legends for illustrations, footnotes, extract material, bibliography, and index. Because it is almost impossible for anyone, including designers, to know how the type
AVANT GARDE GOTHIC BOOK

WITH ALL OF THESE variables at their command, designers specify the type face, size, and style to be used for each element of the book, including the title page, contents pages, chapter openings, running heads, several degrees of subheadings, captions and legends for illustrations, footnotes, extract material, bibliography, and index. Because it is almost impossible for anyone, including designers, to know how the type
OPTIMA MEDIUM

WITH ALL OF THESE variables at their command, designers specify the type face, size, and style to be used for each element of the book, including the title page, contents pages, chapter openings, running heads, several degrees of subheadings, captions and legends for illustrations, footnotes, extract material, bibliography, and index. Because it is almost impossible for anyone, including designers, to know how the type
HELVETICA LIGHT

WITH ALL OF THESE variables at their command, designers specify the type face, size, and style to be used for each element of the book, including the title page, contents pages, chapter openings, running heads, several degrees of subheadings, captions and legends for illustrations, footnotes, extract material, bibliography, and index. Because it is almost impossible for anyone, including designers, to know how the type
HELVETICA

WITH ALL OF THESE variables at their command, designers specify the type face, size, and style to be used for each element of the book, including the title page, contents pages, chapter openings, running heads, several degrees of subheadings, captions and legends for illustrations, footnotes, extract material, bibliography, and index. Because it is almost impossible for anyone, including designers, to know how the type
HELVETICA ITALIC

All sans serif type samples set in 9 point type with 10 point leading of photo-offset lithography in the early 1900s, and its gradual improvement over the decades, caused a revolution not only in printing books but also in typesetting methods. In letterpress printing, ink is applied to the raised type, and the raised type is then pressed against the paper, leaving an ink image of the type on the paper. In photo-offset lithography, which we'll refer to hereafter as "offset," the printing plate is made by the photographic process—that is, the plate is coated with a light-sensitive material, and exposed by passing light through a film containing the image to be reproduced. After the plate has been developed, only the image that has been transferred to the plate will hold ink. In printing by offset, the plate "offsets" the ink onto a rubber-covered "blanket" cylinder which in turn transfers the ink to the paper.

During the initial use of the offset process for printing books, type was still set by using hot metal to cast the type, and after all the corrections had been made in the typesetting, reproduction proofs were made, and these were photographed to create the negatives used in making the offset plates. However, the cumbersome process of casting metal to produce a type image on film was eventually replaced by typesetting systems that used the photographic process to create type images directly on film, thereby eliminating the casting and handling of type metal.

Phototypesetting today is actually a marriage of a computer with a machine capable of producing type images on photosensitive film or paper. In the first step, a typesetting operator keyboards the manuscript, adding codes within the text as typesetting instructions to the system. For example, a code may instruct the system that the material following should be set in italic, and another code tells the system when the italic should be discontinued. Text and instructions are temporarily stored on tape or disk. A printout is usually made to check for keyboarding errors.

If the author has used a word processor and can deliver the manuscript on diskettes as well as a typescript, the typesetting operator can load the manuscript into the typesetting system from the diskettes, make the editorial corrections marked on the manuscript by the editor, and add the necessary codes without having to rekeyboard the entire manuscript. However, the compositor must either have equipment compatible with the author's word processor, or be able to make the author's output compatible with his equipment.

In the next step, the manuscript data file is fed into the computer. However, the computer must also be given the typographical specifications established by the designer so that the computer "knows" what is wanted when it reads a code, and can translate that code into the detailed instructions needed by the typesetting device. The computer also has a hyphenation-justification routine in which it calculates the correct spacing between words in order to have the right-hand ends of all lines in alignment, but if that is not possible without spacing out the words awkwardly, it will hyphenate the last word on the line, usually by looking up the word in a hyphenation dictionary stored in the computer memory. As a result of these functions performed by the computer, the keyboarded manuscript that was entered into the computer comes out encoded with complete operating instructions for the phototypesetting device.

There are a number of different machines available to perform the typesetting, but they are basically of two different kinds. The first, operating on the computer's instructions, projects a beam of light through a negative image of the specific character called for, exposing an image of that character onto photosensitive paper or film in the precise position called for. In this fashion, character by character, the desired text is set in accordance with the specifications. The photosensitive paper or film is then developed, creating a master copy of the text material as it is to appear in the book. The first pass of this material is treated as proof copy to be checked by the compositor and the author for errors. The second pass creates reproduction proof copy which is to be photographed to make the negative for platemaking.

The second kind of phototypesetter generates the characters on a cathode ray tube, which exposes the photosensitive paper or film. Other than this different method of character creation, the two systems operate in essentially the same way.

Some systems simply create galleys—that is, long strips of text that must be cut up manually into pages, with page numbers and running heads then applied to the pages. Other systems make an additional pass through the computer using a paging program, which follows a complex set of rules for page makeup, such as that no partial last lines of paragraphs (known as widows) carry over to a new page, or that no page may end with a heading, or subhead, or that facing pages must be equal length. The output from these systems is full pages to be pasted up as mechanical artwork. A third alternative is to have a skilled operator intervene and tell the system page-by-page where to make the breaks between pages, to make decisions about the placement of artwork, legends, and tabular material, and to eliminate widows.

Once the phototypesetter has produced the master copy of the pages, the book is ready for platemaking and the press. In the meantime, the publisher's production manager has told the printer the specific paper to be used in the book, usually based on the recommendation of the designer. The production manager either arranges for the paper to be delivered to the printer, or asks the printer to provide it. Types of paper will be discussed after discussing presswork.

OFFSET PRINTING

In order to make plates for printing by offset, a set of negatives for each page of the book must be made and stripped into layout sheets, called "flats," representing one side of a printed sheet. The number of pages assembled in each flat depends on the trim size of the book and the size of the press, and may be as few as eight, or as many as thirty-two. The negatives for each page must be positioned in the flat so that when the sheet is folded, making what is called a "signature," the pages will fall in their proper numeric sequence.

If any of the pages contain halftone illustrations, they will be photographed separately through a fine screen that transforms the continuous tone of the halftone into small dots of varying sizes, but that still preserves the appearance of the original halftone illustration. These halftone negatives are then stripped into their proper positions on each of the pages on which they are to appear.

After the flats are assembled, blueprints are made of each flat, and these are usually sent to the publisher to be checked for errors in the positioning of illustrations, or other defects.

After the blueprints have been approved, the flats are ready to be used in the plate making. Offset plates consist of flexible sheets of aluminum, coated with a photosensitive material. Each flat is placed against an offset plate and the plate exposed and developed, much as one makes a photographic print from a negative. After the plate is exposed to light and developed, the image transferred to the plate is ink-receptive and water-repellent, and the nonimage area is water-receptive and ink-repellent.

There are a number of different kinds and sizes of offset presses, but the two basic types are sheet-fed and web-feb presses. As the name suggests, a sheet-fed press prints on individual sheets of paper, delivered on pallets from the paper manufacturer in sheet sizes specified by the printer or the publisher. A web-fed press prints on a continuous web of paper fed from rolls, and after the paper has passed through the printing cylinders, it is folded by the press and cut into signatures. Because paper is cheaper in rolls and because the press also performs the folding operation, the web-presses offer economy while running. However, because the press takes longer to set up for a press run, and because it spoils more paper while being set up, it is not economical for short press runs. Usually runs of ten thousand or less are done on sheet-fed presses and longer runs on the web-fed presses, although there are some small web presses that are economical for short-run work. In addition to coming in different widths and cylinder sizes, both types can be one-color, two-color, or four-color presses.

The basic printing unit in an offset press consists of a plate cylinder, a rubber-covered blanket cylinder, and if it is a sheet-fed press, an impression cylinder. As the cylinders rotate, a light film of water is applied to the plate cylinder followed by an application of ink, with the ink adhering only to the image areas of the plate. The inked images are offset to the blanket cylinder, and then transferred to the paper as it passes between the blanket cylinder and the impression cylinder. If the press is constructed for four-color printing, there are four separate printing units linked together, each printing one color on the paper in the precise position required as the paper passes through the press.

If a sheet-fed press prints on both sides of the sheet in a single pass through, it is called a perfecting press, and has two printing units with a tumble device between them that turns the sheet over as it passes from one unit to the other. However, many sheet-fed presses print only one side, in which case the sheets are turned over and passed through the press a second time.

Since the web press folds the web of paper and cuts it into signatures as it comes off the press, it must print both sides of the web as it passes through the press. To accomplish this, web press printing units are constructed with a plate cylinder on the top, and a second plate cylinder on the bottom, with two blanket cylinders between them, each applying ink to one side of the paper and acting as the impression cylinder to the other as the web of paper passes between them. As in the sheet-fed press, the web press will contain separate printing units for as many colors as the press is constructed to print at one time.

Sheets delivered by sheet-fed presses must be folded by a folding machine, but after that, the binding of the signatures from the two types of offset presses is identical.

PAPER

With the possible exception of the written word, no part of a book is as unappreciated as the paper on which it is printed. The product of an advanced technology, and available in infinite variety, it usually passes through the hands of readers almost unnoticed.

Fundamentally, there are two kinds of paper: (1) Groundwood paper, in which the wood content is mechanically ground, and therefore the paper actually contains natural wood fibers. This is the type of paper on which most newspapers and mass market paperbacks are printed; (2) Free-sheet paper, in which the wood has been chemically processed, eliminating everything but the free cellulose wood fibers. This type of paper is more expensive than groundwood paper because much more wood is required to make the same amount of paper. This paper is used in many books.

One of the major specifications of paper is its weight. In ordering paper, the publisher may specify, for example, that he wants 50-lb paper, which means that one ream of 25x38-inch sheets weighs 50 pounds. Papers are available in weights from 20 to 80 pounds, the lightest being used in dictionaries, bibles, and handbooks, where heavier papers would result in books too thick to be bound by most bindery equipment, and the heaviest used for book jackets and certain art books.

Paper is also priced by weight—that is, a given sheet will sell, for example, for $50 per hundredweight (cwt), so that using lighter-weight paper of the same quality will cost less than a heavier weight. However, the weight of the paper affects its opacity, or the extent to which images printed on one side do or do not show through the sheet. Publishers therefore often have to pay for heavier paper than they would otherwise like (say, 50 pounds) in order to get adequate opacity. The opacity of lighter-weight papers can be increased by adding titanium to the paper, but that also increases its cost.

There is also coated groundwood paper, which is a more economical solution to the opacity problem. As the name suggests, this paper is basically a goundwood sheet to which a coating has been applied, such that its appearance is similar to a free sheet. It is cheaper because of its groundwood content, but, because it contains unprocessed wood fibers, it has greater opacity than free sheets. Futhermore, although uncoated groundwood paper oxidizes and turns brown relatively quickly, the coating protects the paper from oxidizing, and gives it a life of many years.

Most free sheets contain a slight amount of acid, and as a consequence, will oxidize and deteriorate in fifty years or so. Some free sheets, however, are neutral and will last indefinitely. These are sometimes called acid-free or permanent papers. Libraries have a serious problem with the deterioration of books in their collections and would like to see permanent papers used in all books. However, most books are not retained by anyone for fifty years, and publishers are not as sensitive to this issue as libraries would like them to be.

Related to the weight of paper is its thickness, which is shown in number of pages to the inch. This number is critical to the designer who must design the cover and the jacket to fit the book's bulk. If a book is small, publishers will sometimes use a high-bulk paper to make it look like more book than it actually is. While high-bulk paper is more expensive, it is usually a cheaper way to increase bulk than purchasing a heavier paper.

Another characteristic of paper is its brightness or reflectiveness. A high level of brightness is considered desirable, because it creates a greater contrast with the type. Paper also comes in different shades of white, usually cream-toned or blue-toned.

Paper has a grain, or the direction in which fibers are aligned in the paper. Paper is made by flowing a slurry of material that is 95 percent water and 5 percent fiber and chemicals onto a fast-moving screen which allows the water to flow through but retains the fibrous solid materials. This process causes the fibers to align themselves with the flow of the materials. This web of solid materials then is fed through a series of cylinders that press and dry it, so that a relatively dry sheet comes off the paper machine and is collected in rolls. Paper delivered in rolls always has the grain running parallel to the web of paper, but in sheeted stock, the grain can run either way. Since paper has greater dimensional stability along the grain rather than across the grain, books should be made with the grain running parallel to the binding. This permits the book to lie flatter when open, and prevents waviness from developing in the pages when exposed to high humidity. Therefore, in ordering sheeted paper, the direction of the grain in the sheet must be specified so that the grain will be parallel to the binding in the finished book.

Finally, paper comes in a variety of finishes and surfaces. It can be made smoother by being pressed or calendered as it leaves the papermaking machine. The paper is passed between hard steel rollers that compress it to the required bulk specifications. Paper may also be coated with material that fills in all the surface irregularities, creating a very smooth printing surface. The coating may either be applied as an intregal part of the papermaking process, or in a separate operation. After the coating is dried, the paper is passed through a series of calendering and polishing operations to provide the surface and bulk required. Uncoated stocks are commonly used in straight-text books such as novels, and coated stocks are used for books with photographs, since the smoother surface of the paper results in sharper illustrations.

Obviously, there is almost an infinite array of papers. However, publishers generally use papers that are stocked at their printer's plant or by their paper merchant, so that if they need a reprint in a hurry, the paper need not be ordered from the mill.

Paper can sometimes give the printer a lot of grief. Occasionally, for example, the natural tackiness of the ink will pull away bits of the paper's surface, causing spots to appear in the printing. On web presses, breaks in the paper web while the press is running make it necessary to shut down the press and re-feed the paper through the press and folding equipment, reducing the productivity of the press. These problems make paper selection important to the printer as well as to the publisher.

BINDING

After folded sheets are available either from the folding machine or off the web press, the sheets are ready to be bound. Despite the many technological advances in book production, binding—especially for hardcover books—is still a series of mechanical, job-shop operations.

When the bindery has all the signatures for the book, the first step is to stack them on a long gathering machine that picks one signature from each stack to assemble a set of sequential signatures for each copy of the book.

Next, the signatures are fastened together at the spine, by one of several methods. School textbook signatures are usually side-stitched together—that is, a row of stitches is sewn down the side of the set of signatures about ¼ inch in from the back edge. This makes a very strong binding, but books bound in this fashion will not lie flat when open. If a book is to be side-stitched, the pages must be designed and printed to allow for the ¼ inch of the signature lost in the binding as well as an additional ¼ inch lost in the tight gutters.

If extra strength is not needed, signatures can be Smyth sewn. In this process, the stitches pass through the back folds in each signature, sewing the very back of all the signatures together. Books that are Smyth sewn will lie flat when open.

A third and increasingly popular alternative is adhesive (also called "perfect") binding. For many years, this method of binding was limited to mass-market paperbacks, where lower costs were more important than durability. However, improved adhesives and better methods of applying them have made adhesive binding a satisfactory alternative to Smyth sewing for trade books, professional books and college texts. If a book is to be adhesive bound, either ¹⁄₁₆ inch is ground off the backs of the signatures, or the backs of the signatures are notched, so that the adhesive reaches all the pages in the folded signature. Adhesive bound books will lie fairly flat when open, but the book should be designed and printed with an allowance for the space lost at the spine.

If the book is to have hard covers, these covers, or "cases," must first be made separately, and the sequence in which they are made depends on the method used in printing the covers. Most covers consist of boards similar to heavy cardboard, a backstrip that fits over the spine of the book, and a cover material of nonwoven plastic, or impregnated paper, or other durable material. The cover may be printed with an abstract design, or even a halftone illustration. If so, the cover material will be printed prior to being glued to the boards and the backstrip, and the printing may be done by offset in from one to five colors, or it can be printed by the silkscreen process. Following this, the material is glued to the boards and the back strip. Alternatively, if the covers are to be stamped with a metallic or ink foil, the cases are made first, and then stamped. This is the most common method used for books that are going to be jacketed and sold through trade bookstores.

If the book has been Smyth sewn, the sewn signatures next go through the "forwarding" operations. First, the book is "smashed" to force the air from between the pages and compress it. Then a layer of glue is applied to the spine. After the glue dries, the book is trimmed on the three open sides to the final page size. Following this, a "lining-up machine" rounds the back and forms the joint. Then, a layer of "crash" linen and kraft paper is applied to the spine between layers of glue. These are the steps that maintain the form of the book after it is bound. The book goes next to the "casing-in" operation where glue is applied to the endpapers that were previously applied to the first and last signatures of the book. The "case" or cover is then carefully placed over the body of the book, and subjected to heat and pressure. If the book is to have a jacket, the jackets (printed earlier) are now placed on the bound books.

If a book is to have a soft or paperback cover, the operations are much simpler. The signatures are adhesive bound, and previously printed paper covers are glued to the backbone of the book, with the cover becoming an integral part of the spine.

THE CAMERON BELT PRESS

Although this unusual printing system has some practical limitations, it is used often enough to justify some explanation of how it works.

First, the Cameron Press is a letterpress system, printing from flexible plastic plates with raised type. The plates are made from negatives by exposing a photosensitive polymer, and washing away the portions of the plate not hardened by the light.

All the plates for the book are mounted on two long belts, one holding all the plates to be printed on one side of a web of paper, and the other holding the plates for the reverse side. The paper feeds from a roll through the press where it is first printed on one side by one belt, then on the reverse side by the second belt. In contrast to offset presses that print one signature at a time, the belt press prints one complete book at each revolution of the belts. It then folds and cuts the book into signatures, and delivers complete sets of signatures ready to be bound. These signatures can be stacked off for separate casing-in operations if a hardcover edition is wanted, or the signatures can be fed directly into a softcover adhesive binding line. As a result, it is possible to have some bound books within an hour from when the press is started, as compared with several weeks later by offset.

Because it is difficult to produce good-quality halftone illustrations on the Cameron Belt Press, its use is generally limited to trade books containing type and simple line drawings.

Chapter 24

Book Marketing

Marketing is essentially the publisher's responsibility; however, authors naturally are often interested in following the marketing of their books. Sometimes authors of special-interest and professional books have a better market knowledge than their publishers, and can make helpful suggestions. And occasionally, with vacations and illnesses and turnover in jobs, some part of a marketing program will fall between the cracks and then be resurrected by the author.

Most publishers develop a marketing plan for each title several months before bound books are to be available. This plan serves as a checklist, and normally covers the basic markets for the book and the initial advertising and promotion planned to expose it to its markets. Request a copy of the marketing plan for your book, as well as a list of the publications and services that are scheduled to receive review copies. The marketing plan can then be compared with the marketing information that you gave your publisher. The plan should show that some combination of selling, advertising, promotion, and publicity is to be directed to each group that represents a market for the work, as well as to those organizations that are the channels of distribution to those markets. Marketing procedures differ, of course, for textbooks, trade books, professional books and scholarly books, but the common thread for all is that, as a bare minimum, some technique or combination of techniques must be used to let the markets for each book know that the book is available and why it should be bought.

There are two initial steps that must be taken for all books. Basic data on each book must be entered into your publisher's system so that orders can be processed and records maintained on sales and royalties. In addition, information on each book must be entered into the industry system. This is done by completing the Advance Book Information

185

(ABI) form and submitting it to R. R. Bowker Company, so that Bowker can add the book to its data base of some 600,000 titles that it uses to create reference volumes, including *Forthcoming Books in Print, Paperback Books in Print, Textbooks in Print, Scientific and Technical Books in Print*, and *Subject Guide to Books in Print*. These reference works are used by booksellers, wholesalers and librarians in identifying and ordering the specific editions of books that are wanted, and for all practical purposes a book does not exist unless it is listed in these volumes.

Also vital to all books is the promotional copy that appears on the jacket flaps and in catalogs. This description of your book is read by bookstores and wholesalers, by book reviewers, book clubs, and by customers examining your book in retail stores. Reviews and book announcements frequently pick up this copy, and your publisher will use it time and again in describing your book. The copy must accurately and concisely describe the book, emphasizing its unique features and its value to the buyer. You may want to ask your publisher to let you review the copy for accuracy before it is used, or even volunteer to help in its preparation.

Although there is some duplication in the marketing techniques used to sell various types of books, each type will be considered separately.

TRADE BOOKS

Marketing trade books, especially those for which there is no identifiable special-interest audience, is perhaps the most difficult assignment in publishing. Regular trade-book buyers are scattered so thinly through the population that bringing new books to their attention with modest marketing budgets is no easy task.

It is a common misconception among trade authors that advertising sells books, and that poor sales are the result of inadequate advertising. The hard reality is that advertising alone does not generate enough sales to cover the cost of the advertising. However, advertising, in conjunction with other marketing tools, will help sell books that the market is ready to buy.

Bookstores and Wholesalers

The bookstore is of paramount importance to trade books of all types. It is the one arena where buyer and seller meet, the first and frequently the only place a person goes when looking for a specific book, or a book on a specific subject, or a book in general. The trade publisher's primary mission, therefore, is to get its books into bookstores in sufficient quantities to meet whatever demand develops for those books. In addition to reasonable discount and returns policies, the publisher's principal tools are his sales representatives and advertising to the trade.

Trade sales representatives may be either employees of the book's publisher, or of a publisher acting as a distributor for the book's publisher, or commissioned salespersons representing a number of publishers. They call on store managers or buyers two or three times a year, with book jackets and a sales pitch for each book to be published in the coming season. Publishers usually establish as a goal the number of copies of each book that they want to have in bookstores prior to publication, and that goal is divided up among the representatives, who in turn allocate portions of their total among the stores they call on. So the representatives aim to sell a certain number of copies of each new book during each sales call. The store manager is, of course, under no obligation to take that quantity.

Part of the representative's pitch will be a recounting of the support the publisher has pledged for the book, including the advertising budget, special promotions, author tours and appearances, and so forth. These are all especially important if the representative is aiming for a large order.

Representatives also check the bookstore's stock of backlist titles, and recommend reorders of books that are out of stock or running low.

Perhaps nothing distresses authors more than to find bookstores that do not have their books in stock, and they usually hold their publishers accountable. But there are many reasons for stores not having stock, only a small portion of which are the publisher's fault. The manager may, because of limited space, choose not to stock certain titles. Or, he may have stocked the book, but not reordered when it sold out, either through an oversight or because it sold slowly. Or, the book may have been reordered, but not soon enough to get in more copies before running out. Or the publisher may be out of stock temporarily. Or the bookstore may be behind in paying for prior purchases, and the publisher is holding up on filling additional orders until payment is made. (Holding orders, by the way, is the only leverage publishers have in collecting from stores that are well behind in their payments.) All in all, there is not much point in asking bookstore managers why a given book isn't available, because it is most unlikely that they can remember why, and more often than not will blame the publisher regardless of the real reason.

Trade representatives also call on the wholesalers serving bookstores and libraries. Getting an adequate initial inventory to the wholesalers is critical, as many bookstores place their reorders with wholesalers because of the faster service they generally provide. So if the wholesalers run out of stock, bookstores ordering from them will be out of stock, perhaps at a time when interest in the book is running high.

Prior to publication, your book should also be promoted by advertising to the retail, wholesale, and library markets, most notably in *Publishers Weekly*, but also in *American Bookseller*, which is the journal of the American Booksellers Association, *Library Journal*, and the publications of the major wholesalers. Your book may be given a full page, or be one of several books on a page, or merely listed along with several dozen other books. The amount of money spent in this prepublication advertising to the trade is generally in proportion to the publisher's expectations for the book, since it would make no sense for a publisher to spend heavily in support of a book for which it has only modest expectations.

Publishers' catalogs are used to market both forthcoming titles as well as backlist books. Catalogs are produced for each of the selling seasons, and may include backlist and new titles together, or backlist books may be promoted in separate catalogs. Seasonal catalogs are usually mailed to bookstores (especially critical, since representatives may not be able to call on the smaller bookstores in their territory), wholesalers, libraries, book reviewers, book clubs, mass-market paperback publishers—in fact, to anyone who might influence the sale of copies or subsidiary rights in forthcoming books.

Reviews

Several media run prepublication reviews for the book trade, including *Kirkus Reviews*, *Publishers Weekly*, and the *Library Journal*. These are read by libraries, bookstores, wholesalers, and the publishing industry itself. They should therefore be sent proofs of your book as early as possible so that their reviews can stimulate interest prior to publication. It may be worth your while to check with your publisher to see that this has been done.

Having taken the necessary steps to get books to bookstores and wholesalers, your publisher's second mission is to get buyers into the stores. For literary works, probably the most important key to success is book reviews in the daily newspapers, especially in the *New York Times Book Review* section, which is, in essence, a national weekly magazine of book reviews. Aficionados of literary works regularly read book reviews, and are influenced more by them than anything else a publisher can do. Unfortunately, only a small percentage of the literary titles published are reviewed. Major daily papers at most carry on average one review a day, which means not more than 365 reviews per year, and many do not carry book reviews at all. The publisher's job therefore is to attract the attention and interest of book reviewers so that they will single out the publisher's books for reviewing from the many received. Here again, the jacket and jacket copy play a vital role, since this is the intial exposure that the reviewer has to the work. If they are attention-getting and interesting, the reviewer may look inside the book, and the book itself will then have to do the remainder of the selling. But if the jacket and copy do not interest the reviewer and the author is unknown, then the title has lost its first battle against anonymity. Publishers frequently send a set of bound proofs to key reviewers so they will have more time in which to prepare major reviews. The distribution of news releases, which are in effect canned reviews, is also important, especially for those publications that do not employ the services of a book reviewer, but who may run a story about a new book.

Media Appearances

For nonfiction especially, author's interviews on radio and TV are of great importance in selling books. Although in the early years of television, it was feared that TV would be the death of trade publishing, it has developed instead into the most influential medium for publicizing nonfiction books, and an author's appearance on a show such as *Donahue* can turn a languishing title into a bestseller overnight. Many books, including most novels, do not lend themselves to this type of publicity, but if a book has the potential and the author has an interesting personality, the publisher's publicity director may set up a tour of major cities and schedule as many appearances, including interviews and autographing parties, as possible in each area. Some publishers provide their authors with training before sending them forth. Although it can be taxing, many authors relish the opportunity to promote their books. However, since all such touring is at the publisher's expense, it is only done selectively for those books it will benefit most.

A less costly technique is to set up radio interviews across the country by telephone from the author's home.

Advertising

The next marketing step is consumer advertising, of which there are several types. There are the familiar space ads with a picture of the book and some compelling copy, urging buyers to get the book from their bookstores. There are similar ads with coupons to be clipped and mailed to the publisher. Most of the space advertising is placed in newspapers, but publishers place some ads for literary works in magazines such as *The New Yorker, Harper's,* and *Atlantic.*

Most publishers also have a cooperative advertising policy in which the publisher agrees to pay a share of the cost incurred by bookstores in advertising the publisher's books in either print or electronic media, but with the dollar amount limited to a certain percentage of the net value of the books ordered. For example, a typical policy will state:

> *Publisher allows 15 percent of net value of purchases of any title on its list to be used for cooperative advertising. Publisher will pay 75 percent of the cost of space in print media and of time in broadcast media. Bookseller must obtain prior approval of advertising manager.*

There are several advantages to these programs. First, the retail bookstore traditionally pays a much lower rate for space or time than a publisher, so its dollar buys more advertising. Second, the program virtually assures that books will be available in the bookstores that place the advertising when the ads appear or are aired, something that publishers find difficult to achieve when placing the advertising. Third, the ads list the specific bookseller from whom the books may be purchased, so the consumer does not need to hunt around for a store that has the book.

In addition to "co-op" advertising, for books of broad general interest with good potential sales, publishers place ads selectively in large metropolitan newspapers. The initial ads are timed to coincide with the official publication date, in the hope of reinforcing the impact of favorable reviews that may appear at that time. However, for the average book, the initial advertising budget is small—usually 10 percent of the sales of the first printing—and this must cover advertising to the trade as well as consumer ads. Thereafter, reorders from bookstores and wholesalers are monitored daily or weekly, and additional ads scheduled if the book appears to be moving out of the stores well. It is a very touchy game, however. If a book is not selling, no reasonable amount of advertising will sell it. On the other hand, if it develops some momentum of its own based on reviews and other publicity, and on the initial advertising, then additional advertising, judiciously placed, can help the book along. However, case histories abound in which titles produced large losses rather than modest profits because of the publisher's excessive zeal in advertising.

Special Promotions

For some titles, publishers develop special sales promotional materials, such as individual circulars to be mailed to bookstores and libraries or handed out at conventions, displays and posters for bookstores, bookmarks, and so on. Occasionally, sales kits are developed containing extensive biographical data on the author, or materials relating to the content of the book, photographs, and press releases. Although these materials can make a contribution, they tend to be of peripheral importance, and frequently are a waste of time and money.

Special-interest books (on sports, gardening, woodworking, knitting, cooking, and so forth) present marketing opportunities unavailable to most literary works, since they appeal to groups of consumers who are identifiable by virtue of subscribing to special-interest magazines, belonging to associations and clubs, shopping in specialty retail stores (sporting goods stores, pet shops, garden centers, and so forth), and, above all, by having bought books on the same subjects by mail in the past.

If your book has been written and published for direct-mail selling (of a size and price that will support the high costs of mailing), then mailings to lists of book buyers, and possibly to subscriber lists and associations, can also generate extra sales profitably. However, if a book will merely be of passing interest to such a group rather than provide useful information, or if its price is less than $15, it will not sell successfully by direct mail. In addition, if the publisher has little or no experience at direct-mail selling, and lacks an ongoing program, the company is not likely to be successful at direct mail even if the book is right for that type of marketing and good lists are available.

Special-interest books can also be sold through special retail outlets and service facilities—boating books through marinas, sports books through sporting goods stores, gardening books through garden centers, and so forth. If a publisher has a program of books that can be sold to a specific group of stores or facilities, then a major effort may be made to market your book to that group, including calls by sales representatives, special catalogs, promotional mailings, and even promotional displays. However, if your book is the only one on the publisher's list appealing to that group, it would be impractical for the publisher to do more than mail a circular to a list of such outlets and hope for a few positive responses. This points up again the importance of selecting the right publisher for each work in the first place.

Subsidiary Rights

In trade book publishing, subsidiary rights must be marketed with the same vigor and attention to detail that is required for the sale of the books themselves. As mentioned earlier, if a literary agent is handling your book, the agent usually retains certain rights, including first serial, dramatic, and foreign rights in both English and foreign languages. However, if there is no agent, it is the publisher's responsibility to market all the subsidiary rights.

First serial rights, that is, the right to use portions of the work on an exclusive basis in a magazine or newspaper before the book's publication, are important for two reasons: the income earned and the interest that this material can generate in the book not only among consumers but also in the sale of other rights. First serial rights are usually sold by the publisher's "rights" person getting in touch personally with editors of magazines or newspapers likely to have an interest in the material. Normally, a copy of the manuscript is made available to one editor at a time for consideration. If the first editor is not interested, the manuscript is sent to another editor, and so forth. Since this process can take time, efforts to sell first serial rights should begin as soon as the manuscript is available, or sooner.

Second serial rights, the post-publication sale of selections to newspapers and magazines on a nonexclusive basis, is usually handled by distributing seasonal catalogs to appropriate editors, rather than through the individual promotion of each book.

The sale of book club rights begins as soon as the manuscript is available. Copies of the manuscript are sent to the clubs, who are invited to bid for it, with the understanding that all bids will be made known to the other bidders, and of course, the highest bidder gets the book. For a special-interest book, however, there may only be one book club serving that interest, and therefore no competitive pressure.

Mass-market paperback rights are the most important subsidiary rights in that they bring in the most money for publisher and author. Although the mass-market paperback publishers now sometimes sign up authors themselves, rights purchased from hard-cover publishers still account for a majority of the books on their lists.

A publisher wants to sell mass-market paperback rights at the same time when the value of those rights is at its peak. If the author is well known, with a distinguished record on prior books, this may be before the manuscript is completed. In fact, if the author or agent is demanding an exceptionally large advance, the publisher may sell the paperback rights at the time of signing the author contract—in effect, sharing the risk of the large advance with the paperback house.

If the author is not well known, but the publisher has great confidence in the book's potential, the publisher may take time to enhance the book's value through the sale of first serial rights and a book club selection, or may even gamble on waiting for major reviews before concluding the mass-market paperback sale. In such cases, the publisher brings each favorable development to the attention of the mass-market paperback publishers as it occurs in order to build interest. The sale itself may be accomplished either by negotiation with a single mass-market publisher or through an auction. Auctions make sense only when there is broad and enthusiastic interest in a book. Without that kind of interest, an early low bid may take the book at a lower price than the winner would have been willing to pay as a result of a negotiation. In auctions, usually one publisher will establish a "floor" price prior to the beginning of the auction, in return for the right to make a final bid after bidding is completed without having participated in the bidding activity.

The sale of foreign rights is usually handled by the literary agent, but if there is no agent the publisher is responsible. Publishers (and agents) typically use agents located in the foreign markets. Two kinds of rights are normally involved. One is English language rights for other English language markets—Great Britain, Australia, and New Zealand. For these markets, the American publisher usually sells printed sheets of the book to local publishers who bind them up and sell them under their own imprint. The buyers usually also get the nonexclusive right to sell the works in other specified foreign markets. In the Canadian market, U.S. publishers usually sell books through a Canadian distributor or a Canadian publisher serving as a distributor, rather than selling rights.

The second kind of foreign rights is for foreign language editions. The advances against royalties that are paid for these rights are usually modest, but can be significant if many foreign language editions are undertaken. Most of these sales are initiated through the distribution of seasonal catalogs to foreign agents, who then request copies of the books in which they have an interest.

Dramatic rights are also usually retained by the literary agent, but again the responsibility falls to the publisher if there is no agent. The publisher markets appropriate titles in the same way an agent does—by arranging for a West Coast agent to handle them. As mentioned earlier, a producer normally purchases an option first and then tries to put together financing for the production. But it is difficult to locate the potential buyers of dramatic rights, and more often than not, the producer finds the material rather than the publisher or agent seeking out the producer.

MASS-MARKET PAPERBACKS

Although originally mass-market paperbacks were sold primarily to independent distributors for racks in non-book outlets, today the majority of these books are sold through trade and college bookstores.

Mass-market publishers usually employ two sales forces—one to call on retail bookstores, and a second to call on and work with the independent distributors.

The sales force calling on retail bookstores works in much the same way as the sales representatives for trade houses, except that they typically call on their accounts monthly or every other month, because the mass-market publishers produce on monthly instead of seasonal schedules.

The sales representatives calling on the independent distributors who maintain and stock the racks in drugstores, airports, supermarkets and other high-traffic areas are one step removed from the actual retailing of the books, and concern themselves primarily with the allocation of inventory among the distributors for which they are responsible. In determining the appropriate quantities of each title for each distributor, they take into account the nature of the market served by the distributor, and the kinds of books that have done poorly or well in each area in the past. Allocation is perhaps the critical operation in marketing these books, since a paperback's life may be very short, and a misallocation of stock can result in some distributors underselling because of insufficient stock and other distributors returning sizable quantities of covers of unsold books for credit.

Because mass-market paperbacks depend largely on impulse buying, the covers are a particularly important sales promotional tool. Competing in racks or displays with hundreds of other titles, they must seize readers' attention and quickly communicate what they offer in the way of information or entertainment.

Advertising and promotion of mass-market paperbacks is similar to that of hard-cover trade books and trade paperbacks. If a book has had a strong sale in hard cover, then the promotion will generally be built around its earlier success, including quotes from hard-cover reviews.

Mass-market paperbacks have found a good market on college campuses where they are frequently used as readings in liberal arts courses. Therefore they are selectively promoted to instructors in the appropriate disciplines, and sold to college bookstores both for course use as well as for impulse buying.

PROFESSIONAL BOOKS

Books written for the professional markets usually must be sold both through bookstores and by direct mail. Neither technique alone is satisfactory, since some professional-book buyers like the convenience of ordering by mail, and others prefer to examine books in a bookstore before buying. Unfortunately, however, the more specialized a book is, the fewer the bookstores that will stock it. Sales to libraries, predominantly to college and university libraries and special libraries, account for about 12 percent of the copy sales, and about 60 percent of those library sales are made through wholesalers.

The sales representatives who call on bookstores and wholesalers are the keys to successful bookstore sales. Because of the technical nature of many of the books, bookstores must rely more heavily on the recommendations of the representatives, but experienced representatives will only sell a bookstore the titles and the quantities that they believe the store can sell. To load up a store with books it cannot sell is counterproductive both for the store and the publisher, since the books will ultimately be returned at some cost and inconvenience to both. Representatives call on bookstore managers or buyers at least twice a year and sell titles prior to publication, normally using a copy of the book's jacket as a selling tool. Many representatives also check the store's stock and recommend reorders of backlist titles that are out of stock, and in some cases recommend the return of overstock. However, these activities have become less important as more stores install effective inventory control systems.

Some bookstores do not stock professional books, some stock a few of the more popular titles, while some have large departments devoted entirely to professional books. This is determined at least in part by the community that the store serves. If it is located near a large corporate facility employing many engineers, for example, it is much more likely to carry engineering books than a store in a suburban shopping mall.

To some degree, the publisher predicts and determines the extent to which bookstores will stock titles by the discounts they set on their titles. Professional titles of broad appeal (books on salesmanship or how to be a good manager, for example) are usually given the same discount as trade titles—40 to 46 percent depending on the quantity ordered. More specialized books usually carry a discount of 33⅓ percent, and highly specialized books are discounted at 20 to 25 percent. While the prophecy is self-fulfilling at least in part, higher discounts on specialized technical books do not measurably increase their sales.

Direct Mail

Of fundamental importance to professional books is direct-mail selling to the professions for which the books are written. Most direct-mail campaign packages consist of a circular containing a picture of the book and a description of its contents, plus a sales letter, promotional material on other books of interest to the same audience, plus a reply card and a business reply envelope. The promotional material is usually aggressive and packed with information and reasons why the books should be purchased. More tasteful, more professional sounding promotion normally does not do as well as the more aggressive styles. Some mail-order campaigns require cash with the order, but others will send a bill with the book if the publisher's credit experience with that professional group is good. Almost without exception, campaigns offering books on credit will sell more copies than those requiring cash with the order, but this is offset at least in part by a failure of some of the buyers to pay for them.

There are a large number and variety of mailing lists available from list brokers, as well as lists developed and maintained by publishers themselves, and list selection plays a large role in the success of any mailing. The more precisely the names on the list fit the group for whom the book is written, the fewer pieces of mail will be wasted, and the more successful the campaign will be. For example, a book on the structural design of buildings can be sold to a list of registered structural engineers, but it will sell better to a list of practicing structural engineers engaged in designing buildings rather than bridges and dams, and it will sell best of all to a list of buyers of books on structural design of buildings. In addition, because people move or change jobs, a new list will produce much better results than one that is several years old.

Professional books benefit from direct-mail campaigns, not only because of the sales made directly by mail but also because the campaign promotes indirect sales through bookstores, and through wholesalers to libraries. Those people who prefer to examine books before buying them will try to purchase the books from their local booksellers. Some may ask their companies to purchase the books for their personal use or for the company library. In all of these cases, the publisher has no way of knowing that the direct-mail campaign generated the sale, and there is no good data on the percentage of indirect sales that campaigns may generate. However, personal experience suggests that one can anticipate indirect sales of between 10 and 30 percent of the direct-mail responses, with the amount depending on the nature of the audience and the book.

Unless the available mailing list is very small, publishers normally make test mailings before making mailings to entire lists. The size of the tests will usually be in the range of 3,000 to 5,000 pieces, which is a large enough sample if the names are selected carefully. If the mailing list is very large, the publisher may test several different approaches to the copy to determine which will produce the best results. Frequently publishers use a benchmark for determining whether the sales generated by a test justify mailing to the entire list. For example, they may want $3 in sales for every dollar spent on the mailing, or alternatively a 2½ percent response. However, these rules of thumb are based on the direct responses, and do not take into account indirect sales through bookstores and wholesalers, company purchase orders, or projected returns and bad debts, all of which may differ from book to book, and should be considered on each campaign.

If the test results are not good enough to justify mailing the entire list, the publisher may try a different approach to the copy, or simply include the book in direct-mail campaigns on other titles. In all campaigns, it is important that the promotional copy not promise more than the book delivers, since this results in a greater number of books being returned for credit, and if the book is sold on credit, a higher level of bad debts. A book buyer who feels cheated feels no obligation to pay for the book.

Jackets are almost as important to professional books as to trade books. The jacket front is the point-of-purchase display for the book in bookstores, in mail-order circulars, in space advertising, and in the reviewer's pile of books, so it must get the viewer's attention and quickly communicate its subject matter, and the flap copy must provide sufficient detail to close the sale.

Reviews, Advertising, and Catalogs

Review copies and accompanying news releases are sent to all the trade and professional journals serving the audiences the book addresses. Even if a publication does not review books, it may announce their publication.

Reviews in trade and profesional journals may not appear for several months after the book has been received because it takes time to prepare the review, other books may be scheduled ahead of it, and monthly periodicals have closing dates as much as a month before publication. In fact, some reviews may appear as much as a year or more after publication. However, the chances of a review ultimately appearing are much better than for trade books.

Professional books are not likely to be reviewed in newspapers and other general interest publications, but it is usually worthwhile to send news releases to newspapers since they are frequently used as fillers. Of course, if there is anything truly newsworthy in the book, it is more likely that the release will be used.

Space advertising plays a minor role in marketing professional books, because the sales potential is not sufficient to support the cost of major advertising campaigns even in specialized journals. However, if the publisher also publishes professional or trade journals and will run book advertisements at special house rates or use them as fillers in making up pages, then space advertising can play a larger though secondary role. Otherwise, one or two single-column ads with coupons, sometimes including more than one title, is about all that is appropriate.

Annual or semiannual catalogs listing new and forthcoming books are essential in marketing professional books, and should be mailed to bookstores and wholesalers as well as to special libraries, college and university libraries, and large public libraries. If the catalogs are limited to a single discipline such as business or electronics or physics, then it may also be used for direct-mail promotion to the academic community and sometimes even as a mailing to professional audiences.

Depending on the subject of the book, international markets may be a significant source of sales. Generally speaking, the more specialized and advanced a book is, the greater the percentage of its sale in international markets. Scientific and technical books, for example, may have as much as half their sales in foreign countries. As pointed out in chapter 2, most publishers have a patchwork of arrangements for the sales of books in international markets, using small subsidiary companies or foreign publishers as distributors in some countries and book export agencies in others. It is critical that this network of organizations be provided with promotional material of all sorts—circulars, catalogs, jackets, news releases, and so forth, so they can perform their assignments effectively.

With the exception of medical books, professional books are seldom adopted as texts. However, they may be of value as references, and promotional material should be mailed to appropriate academic audiences. This may result in a sale to a departmental library or the college library, and occasionally to its selection for course use.

Subsidiary Rights

Among the subsidiary rights possibilities, there are only two that are worth pursuing vigorously for professional books—book clubs and foreign language rights, although some professional books may be suitable for trade paperback editions.

Many professional fields are served by one or more book clubs. For example, there is a Lawyer's Book Club, a Sales Book Club, several management book clubs, several electronics book clubs, several computer book clubs, and so on. Publishers of professional books generally make an effort to place books with clubs. However, many publishers do not allow their books to be offered as selections until six to twelve months after publication, since the club offering may diminish the publisher's own sales of the work. This is also good for authors, since they make higher royalties from copy sales by their publishers than from copies sold by an outside book club. If it is the publisher's own book club, the offering will probably be made shortly after publication, since the income is shared only with the author.

As stated earlier, sales of foreign language rights can be valuable for many professional books, especially those that deal with issues of worldwide interest and concern. Generally speaking, the higher-level books dealing with theory rather than practice are better prospects for direct translation, although some practical books can be modified and translated to meet the interests of foreign markets. These sales are best pursued through correspondence with foreign publishers with programs in the same subject areas.

If a professional book appeals to a large enough audience, a trade paperback edition may be published several years later by the original publisher, or the publisher may sell the rights to a trade paperback edition to another publisher.

COLLEGE TEXTBOOKS

The primary objective in marketing college textbooks is to have the books selected as required texts in the courses for which they were written and published. There are essentially three steps in this process: (1) identifying the instructor who will be giving the course; (2) getting a copy of the book into the instructor's hands; and (3) getting the instructor to examine the book and seriously consider its use.

The main burden of this assignment falls on college representatives who visit the colleges and universities in their assigned territory. They must find the appropriate instructors, tell them about forthcoming or recently published books that might be used in their courses, arrange for sample copies to be sent to them, and encourage them in every way possible to consider their use.

Publishers frequently enclose in the sample copies a "comment card," which is a postcard asking the instructor for comments about the text, whether he is considering adopting it, and if so, the size of the enrollment, and when the course is given. This gives the publisher an immediate feedback on the book's prospects.

Because representatives can't be in more than one place at a time, publishers often follow up on prospects by telephone from the office, occasionally even setting up an appointment for a visit by the representative. Or sometimes representatives themselves will make follow-up phone calls.

Publishers support these field activities with advertising and promotion. Prior to publication, circulars are prepared on each book and usually mailed to all the instructors teaching in a given discipline. These mailings invite the instructors to request an examination copy. Publishers also produce and mail out separate subject-matter catalogs including published as well as forthcoming books. In addition, publishers normally place advertisements in the professional or academic journals serving the various disciplines, but these ads do little more than help to establish the identity of the new book.

Some publishers also send out a news release on a newly published textbook, but this is done more to please the author than in the hope of it selling any textbooks.

Publishers are cautiously generous in their distribution of sample copies. On the face of it, the cost of a single copy of a work is modest compared with the potential revenue that may be generated by its selection as a required text. However, many of these books are sold to the local bookstores by instructors who receive them and have no use for them. Publishers, of course, decry this practice, but what is an instructor to do with the annual flood of books and limited shelf space? Texts at the senior-graduate level are given out even more cautiously, since sales to instructors and to libraries for reference use are considered a part of the market for these works, and a generous distribution of samples can seriously hurt those sales.

Conventions of academic associations, held annually or semiannually, provide textbook publishers with another opportunity for selling, and most publishers send exhibits, representatives, and sometimes editors to these conventions to promote books and to meet prospective authors.

As soon as instructors decide which texts they will use in the next semester or quarter, they tell the bookstores serving the college which texts have been selected and the expected enrollment in each course. If it is a new text, the store will order the text from the publisher in a quantity less than the estimated enrollment since some students will share texts or use library copies. If it is not a new text, the store will probably order a portion of the books needed from one of the secondhand textbook dealers, and a portion as new texts from the publisher.

After all orders for the season are in, publishers create and mail out a promotion piece listing all the colleges that are using the text. These lists are usually based on firm orders received rather than promises, since some promised adoptions do not materialize. Obviously, the more distinguished the colleges are that are using each text and the longer the list, the better the promotion will be.

Review copies are sent to the appropriate academic and professional media, and favorable reviews are collected and quoted in a circular mailed prior to the beginning of the second season for the text in an effort to stimulate additional adoptions.

Publishers usually continue to promote successful texts each year, but if a text has not been successful in the first two years, publishers generally give up on it. In the face of the flood of new books being published in each succeeding year, the chances of a textbook catching on after two years is fairly remote.

The availability of supplementary materials—readings, instructors' manuals, tests, and so forth—can be very important to the success of a textbook in a highly competitive market, and authors should cooperate fully in personally developing any materials suggested by their publishers, or by arranging for others to develop them.

Because textbooks have no point-of-purchase sales, they do not normally have jackets. Instead, they are produced with attractively designed printed covers, which cost less than the covers plus jackets used on trade and professional books.

There is a good international market for most U.S. textbooks, good enough in fact that the production of unauthorized editions in Taiwan, Singapore, and the Philippines has been a major problem. There are strong sales of U.S. editions not only in English-speaking countries but also in the many countries where English is the second language, and good sales of foreign language rights. Sales of U.S. editions are handled through a combination of export agents, distributors, foreign publishers, and foreign subsidiaries of U.S. publishers.

Other than foreign language editions and an occasional sale to a special-interest book club, there are few opportunities for the sale of subsidiary rights in textbooks.

SCHOLARLY BOOKS

Scholarly books are sold by most of the same marketing techniques that are used for other books, except they must be used with great restraint. If a book has a potential sale of only one thousand copies, there are very few dollars available for marketing, and they must be spent with great care and precision.

Remember, there are essentially two types of scholarly books: works in the physical and biological sciences and technology that are published by a small group of commercial publishers (who also usually publish journals for the same audiences); and works in the humanities that are published by nonprofit university presses.

Notwithstanding the differences, the two types of scholarly books are marketed in much the same way, except that much more attention must be given to international markets for technical books.

A majority of these books are bought by libraries—academic libraries, by corporate libraries, research facilities, and government agencies, and larger public libraries. These purchases are made primarily from wholesalers.

Catalogs are the cornerstone of the marketing program for scholarly books, and must be distributed regularly both to libraries and wholesalers.

Publishers of scholarly books also use commissioned sales representatives for calls on those few trade bookstores that handle specialized books, calls on college and university bookstores serving the academic market, and of course on the wholesalers serving the library market.

Ultimately, however, the key to sales to libraries and through bookstores is reviews in professional, academic, and technical journals, and direct mail to professional and academic groups for whom the books are written, who may either purchase the books directly from the publisher, request their library to acquire the books, or purchase the books from their college bookstore.

Foreign sales are an important component of the total sales of scholarly books, and, as indicated earlier, are of paramount importance to scientific and technical works. Marketing is handled through book export agencies, and arrangements with foreign publishers of similar types of books.

Subsidiary rights sales are limited to foreign language editions, and these sales are relatively infrequent since the academic community in other language groups is small and can usually work with the English language editions.

Chapter 25

Alternatives to Commercial Publication

In view of the hundreds of commercial book publishers, it would seem that authors would never exhaust the list of candidates for their works. However, most of the medium-sized and small publishers have programs that are limited to certain types of books—textbooks, or religious books, or juveniles, or technical books, and so forth. Therefore, the number of publishers who might publish a specific work are not as great as it might seem; and there are even fewer if you consider only those who have a demonstrated capability of reaching a specific market. As a result, after collecting a sizable file of rejections, you may well run out of viable candidates for commercial publication. Are there alternatives available to commercial publication? Yes, within limits, and at a price.

Before examining these alternatives, however, it may be worthwhile to discuss the types of books being rejected. At one extreme is the book for which there is really no market at all. A typical example is an autobiography of a person who led a normal life, graduated from the local schools, married a high school classmate, ran a shoe store in town, grew vegetables on weekends, raised a family, and felt compelled to write it all down so the world would know. The market for this book consists of members of the family and a few close friends, and they already know most of the story. This is the kind of book that is best left to be read in manuscript by any present and future members of the family who want to. It will not be read often enough to smudge the typescript.

At the other end of the spectrum is the book which has a clearly definable market, and which may even make a contribution to the knowledge in its field, but for which the market is too small or too difficult to reach for it to be profitable for a commercial publisher. It could be a medical book on a rare tropical disease, or a detailed study of the barn owl, or a survey of the wild flowers of Nebraska. It could even be a good first novel that commercial publishers did not feel could successfully compete in the marketplace. These are the types of works for which alternative publishing solutions are needed.

UNIVERSITY PRESSES

Literary Market Place lists ninety-two presses in this country that are nonprofit, most of them associated with a university. In recent years, as commercial publishers have set higher sales criteria for books, university presses have begun publishing works that would have been published commercially in the past. However, for a project to be considered by a university press, it must be a work of some distinction. If it is a work with a primarily regional market, say, the Northwest or New England, then a university press in that region may not only be interested in publishing it, but may very well do a better job of marketing it than a large commercial publisher.

University presses occasionally publish fiction, but they are primarily interested in nonfiction works, and it is probably not worthwhile to submit fiction unless there is some special reason for the press to be interested in it, such as its local or regional setting.

Occasionally university presses even publish best sellers. In 1980, the Louisiana State University Press published a novel by John Kennedy Toole entitled *A Confederacy of Dunces* which won the 1980 Pulitzer Prize for fiction and became a best seller in its paperback edition. And more recently, Harvard University Press published Eudora Welty's *One Writer's Beginnings* which, to the astonishment of both the author and the press, achieved best-seller status.

VANITY PUBLISHERS

There is a small group of publishers who specialize in books that are subsidized by the author. You pay a fee up front to cover all the costs of producing a small printing of the book plus a profit for the publisher. The fees can range from $5,000 for a book of less than 100 pages to $15,000 for a large one. Then the publisher pays you a high royalty rate, usually 40 percent of the list price on all copies sold, which in theory permits you to earn back the money paid for publication. In practice, however, these books rarely sell enough copies for you to earn back your investment. The vanity publisher sends out review copies to a small group of book reviewers and does some perfunctory promotion to bookstores—all paid for by your fee. However, since reviewers and booksellers know that you have paid for publication, reviewers don't review the books and bookstores don't stock them. The annual output of commercial publishers and university presses alone vastly exceeds the number of books that can be reviewed by the press and stocked by bookstores, so it is not surprising that books published by the vanity publishers get little or no attention. Furthermore, since their product is essentially unsalable, there is no point in the vanity publishers maintaining a strong marketing organization.

Since you have paid to have your book produced, you might think you own the copies. Not so. If you want copies, you must pay for them again.

It would be financially unsound for vanity publishers to publish salable books on the conditions outlined above. For example, if the book were priced at $10, it would be sold to bookstores at a 40 percent discount, so the publisher would get $6 for each copy sold. In addition, the author's royalty would be 40 percent of $10, or four dollars a copy sold, leaving the vanity publisher with only $2 to cover the costs of producing the book, billing and shipping, and the general administrative costs of the business. Since the cost of paper, presswork, and binding is usually at least 15 percent of the list price, or in this example, $1.50, and billing and shipping costs at least $.60, there is no practical way in which $2 can cover all those costs. In order for a vanity press to succeed, its books must fail.

There is nothing wrong with paying a vanity press to publish your book, so long as you understand what you are getting and have no illusions about earning back the money you paid the publisher. In fairness to the vanity presses, they are reasonably candid about what they will do and what they won't do as publishers. However, although they warn you that you may not earn back the money you pay for publication, they fail to indicate that this is almost a certainty, and that the shortfall will be sizable. An example of a vanity press contract is presented in the Appendix.

The book industry seems to be missing a type of publisher somewhere between the commercial publisher and the vanity press, who will publish a book with a modest sales potential if you contribute to the cost of publication, but whose profit is derived only from sales of the book. For example, assume a book is priced at $15, and costs $3 to manufacture a first printing of 5,000 copies. Assume also that you pay the publisher $15,000 to cover the cost of making the books, with the understanding that the publisher will pay you $3 plus a royalty of 10 percent, or $1.50, for each copy sold until the first 5,000 copies were gone. At $4.50 a copy, you recover the cost of the books when 3,555 copies are sold, and if all 5,000 copies are sold, you have cleared $7,500 and the publisher has made a normal return on the sale for the relatively small investment in managing the publication of the book. If there appears to be a continuing demand after the sale of the initial printing, either the arrangement can revert to the more traditional relationship, with the publisher paying for the printings and paying you a 15 percent royalty, or you can pay the cost of the second printing as well, and be repaid as books are sold. Perhaps some publishers make such arrangements from time to time, but avoid publicizing them for fear of attracting too many unpublishable works or being thought of as a vanity publisher. In any event, if you've been unsuccessful in getting a standard contract and are willing to share more of the publishing risk, there is no harm in proposing such an arrangement to a publisher. Nothing ventured, nothing gained.

THE SMALL PRESSES

Another alternative for authors of trade-type books in particular is one of the several thousand small presses that have sprung up across the country during the last twenty years.

Because of the great variety of small presses, it is difficult to define them except to say that they publish books that commercial publishers would not.

Some of the small presses seem to have grown out of the anti-establishment movements of the late sixties and seventies, and many of them today still publish on single issues such as lesbianism, or environment, or disarmament, but many simply publish fiction, nonfiction, and poetry for which no commercial publisher could be found. Some publish chapbooks, or small pamphlets containing poetry, short stories, or tracts on issues, publications that because of their small size don't generate enough revenue to cover a commercial publisher's overhead costs.

Many small presses have been started as self-publishing ventures by authors who have not been able to find publishers for their works, and who, having published their own books, then take on additional projects. Some publish one book a year or less, and a few publish as many as ten a year and are indistinguishable from small commercial publishers.

Press runs are generally short, usually between one and five hundred copies, but some presses that have developed effective editorial and marketing programs print from three to five thousand copies of the works they publish.

As one might expect, the biggest problems confronting the small presses are marketing and distribution. With the flood of trade books published annually by commercial publishers, small presses have difficulty in getting their books into the marketplace. Nevertheless, many succeed, principally through the services of distributors specializing in small press books. These distributors may operate regionally or nationally, usually on a nonexclusive basis. They select books they feel they can sell effectively, and take copies on consignment with the understanding that they will receive a discount of 50 to 60 percent from the list price on all copies they sell. They distribute catalogs to bookstores and libraries known to be interested in small press publications. And the distributors handle shipping and billing of the consigned stock at discounts of between 40 and 45 percent. Some distributors make sales calls on selected bookstores. Several major book wholesalers and the Waldenbook and B. Dalton chains also handle selected small press books.

Publishing terms are as varied as all the other aspects of small press activities. Some will pay a royalty based on the list or net price; some require a subsidy of some sort; many give the author a number of copies of the book, usually 10 percent of the quantity printed, as compensation.

Arrangements are usually informal. In dealing with a small press, however, you should at least protect yourself by having some written agreement regarding what rights are granted to the press, what compensation, if any, is to be paid for each of those rights, and when those rights are terminated. Occasionally, a small press book becomes a commercial success of some magnitude, and you should be assured of getting a fair share of the income if that happens.

Most small presses are unprofitable in a strictly business sense. Some are run part-time as a hobby, some receive personal financial support from the publisher, and some are supported, at least in part, by grants.

If you are interested in considering publication by a small press, you should review the *International Directory of Little Magazines and Small Presses*, edited by Len Fulton and Ellen Ferber and published annually by Dustbooks, Paradise, California. The directory describes the types of books published by each press, and has a subject-matter index and a geographical index to the presses, as well as a list of distributors handling small press books. In addition, *Small Press* magazine, published by R. R. Bowker Company, has useful information regarding small presses as well as guidance for authors considering the self-publishing alternative.

SELF-PUBLISHING

Although effective book publishing involves hundreds of important steps and functions, it is possible to publish your own works, and it has been done many times. Such distinguished authors as William Blake, John Bartlett (*Familiar Quotations*), Walt Whitman, Upton Sinclair, Anaïs Nin, and Carl Sandburg, among many others, published their own works with varying degrees of success, and thousands of others who remained relatively unknown have also done so.

Before proceeding, two points must be stressed. First, self-publishing requires a great deal of time and effort and attention to detail. It will take about as much time to publish your book as to write it. Second, it can cost a good deal of money that may not be recovered. The actual cost will depend on the size of the book and the number of copies printed, but $10,000 would not be an unreasonable amount to spend to produce three thousand copies of a two-hundred-page book.

Furthermore, every book published is a risky venture. A commercial publisher succeeds not because he doesn't have failures, but because he publishes enough books to have his successes offset them. He statistically eliminates the risk that is inherent in publishing a single book. If you are publishing your own work, you cannot do that, and must recognize the high risk in the undertaking, a risk that is even greater if you have no prior publishing experience. In short, you should put no money into self-publishing that you cannot afford to lose.

The extent of the risk is partly a function of your objectives, and how they are pursued. If you wish to produce a small book of poetry in an edition of a few hundred copies to distribute to friends and a few critics, then you are faced simply with a small known cost. On the other hand, if you plan to publish your own six hundred-page novel and are aiming at a sale of five thousand or more copies, then the risk is great indeed.

In days past, self-publishing often meant literally doing all the operations yourself, including setting the type, and operating a hand press. Although one must admire the determination of an author willing to learn typesetting and printing in order to publish a work, this is perhaps carrying self-publishing a bit far.

Today, virtually every phase of the publishing operation can be subcontracted out. You can act as general contractor of the project, assigning functions to others and monitoring their performance. However, the more work given to others, the larger your investment in the project will be, and the greater the financial loss can be. Therefore, the best approach is to find out what it will cost to have someone else perform given jobs and decide on the basis of that cost whether you wish to do them yourself.

Before starting production work on any book, commercial publishers have the final manuscript reviewed by some competent person. And if you are publishing your own work, you should make every effort to do the same. A second mind will see errors, omissions, and ambiguities that you will never see. Certainly, no one undertaking the onerous job of self-publishing would want to bring forth a seriously flawed work. You should offer a fee for this service which may range from $50 for a small, simple work to $500 for a large, complex work. If the reviewer is a friend or a member of the family, the fee may be declined, but the offer establishes the fact that you are looking for professional help and are expecting a detailed critique.

Producing the Book

The whole process of producing copies of your book can be handled in a variety of ways. *Literary Market Place* has a section on services and suppliers which lists organizations and individuals who handle all aspects of book production. There are organizations that take the manuscript, handle all the editing, design, and composition work, arrange for printing and binding, and deliver bound copies. Others do the work up to the printing and binding, and in that case you need to arrange for these operations to be done separately. Alternatively, you may work individually with a free-lance editor, with a designer, with a compositor, and finally with a printer and binder. This clearly requires more work on your part in negotiating for each of the services and in coordinating the work so that the compositor gets the manuscript in a form with which he can work, the printer gets reproduction proofs in the form needed for making plates, and so forth.

It is impossible to suggest the best approach for you to take in producing your own book, because the best approach depends on the complexity of the book, your objectives in producing it, your own particular aptitudes and interests, and the specific suppliers you select. Perhaps the best way to attack the problem is to begin by talking with several printers. These should be firms who advertise that they do short-run work (one thousand copies or less) and preferably also do composition and binding, so that those three functions can be handled by a single organization. Discuss the project with the printers, getting their advice on how you should proceed and their recommendations for people to do the jobs that have to be completed prior to composition. At the same time, it may be worthwhile to discuss the project with one or more of the organizations providing a complete service from manuscript to bound books to get a fuller understanding of how they work, and what their charges would be. Examine the quality of the work done in each case. Check references, get bids in writing that specify the work to be done, and, wherever possible get bids from three sources for each assignment—not necessarily to give the work to the lowest bidder, but to have a financial basis for making a decision.

Marketing

Marketing is not a problem if you are producing a small number of copies of a work to give to friends, but if you are interested in getting the widest possible distribution of your work, marketing is of paramount importance. In fact, before making a firm decision to proceed with self-publication, you should have a marketing plan that you believe can be executed.

In developing such a plan, be aware of some hard facts.

Fact one: Self-published authors find it difficult, if not impossible, to get their books into bookstores nationally on their own initiative. The stores will not purchase books for stock based on a circular mailed to them by authors. More books are published commercially and by university presses than can be stocked by retail stores, and as a result, they simply won't bother with books published by vanity publishers or by authors themselves. If you have an attractive jacket for your book, an interesting subject, and some selling ability, you have a fighting chance of getting your book into some stores by making sales calls personally, but that is an enormous undertaking, and the sales will not cover the traveling expenses.

Fact two: Reviewers of general interest books are not going to review books published by authors themselves unless there is some extraordinary reason for them to do so. A book reviewer will review, at most, 365 books a year, out of thousands of candidates. The vanity press books and the self-published books are the first to be set aside.

How, then, can you reach the audience for your self-published book? With difficulty.

If it is a trade book for which bookstore sales are essential, and if a trade publisher has rejected it with favorable comment rather than with a form rejection letter, then it is worthwhile to ask if the same publisher would handle distribution of the book. In that event, you either sell copies to the publisher or make copies available to him on consignment (You still own them, and the publisher only pays for them when they are sold). The publisher undertakes the selling and filling of orders just as though the book were one of his own. Under a distribution arrangement, the publisher should pay you about 30 percent of the list price for the books, which should cover the cost of production, plus a small profit or royalty. Such an arrangement can be negotiated when proofs of the book are available, but before books are printed, so that the publisher's name can be printed in the book as distributor, and so that he can have a voice in the jacket design, and perhaps even in minor changes in the book's content, for example, if there are risks of libel or other legal problems.

You may also want to check with some of the smaller, independent trade publishers to see if they would be interested in distribution. Many of these publishers are anxious for additional product to sell, especially in a year when their own list is not particularly strong, and the opportunity to distribute a book without having to make an investment in it can be appealing.

In such arrangements, you can retain all the subsidiary rights in the work, or arrange for the distributing publisher to handle one or more of these rights with some agreed-upon split in the income.

If it is not possible to make an arrangement for distribution, then the next option is to approach several of the distributors specializing in small press books to learn if they will serve as distributors. There really is no distinction between a small press and a self-publishing author, so you may find it advantageous to identify yourself as a small press in seeking distribution arrangements. For a list of small press distributors, you should look in the back of the most recent edition (there being a fairly high mortality rate among distributors) of the *International Directory of Little Magazines and Small Presses* mentioned earlier. The distributors will want to see a copy of the bound book before making a decision. If a distributor is willing to handle your book, he will want copies on consignment, and a discount on sales of between 50 and 60 percent.

One of the dilemmas facing self-publishing authors who must depend on small press distributors for sales is the number of books to produce. You should know how the books are to be marketed before making a printing, but distributors want to see bound books before deciding whether to distribute them. The best solution to the problem is to make a small first printing—perhaps as few as five hundred copies. It is expensive to make small printings, but not nearly so expensive as having one thousand unsalable copies on hand. If there is an error common to the book publishing industry, it is printing too many copies in order to get the cost per copy down, only to find that it actually costs more when the books cannot be sold. Your first printing should be only enough copies to test the market. If the market is responsive, you can always print more.

If your book is for a business, technical, professional or other special-interest audience, then it may be possible to sell the book by direct mail. This possibility is enhanced if you have access to a current directory or membership list of key prospects for the book. If the list has more than five thousand names, you should make a test mailing of about three thousand, in order to be sure that there will be an adequate response to cover expenses. Above all, remember that a 3 percent response is good, and ten thousand names will therefore generate sales of only about three hundred copies. *Trade Book Marketing*, edited by Robert A. Carter, and published by R. R. Bowker Company, has an informative chapter on direct-response marketing, as well as other aspects of marketing trade books.

Publicity is every bit as important to the self-published book as to the commercially published book, but harder to obtain. However, this should not deter you from trying in every practical way to bring your book to the media's attention by means of news releases, letters, and personal calls. But remember that your book must be newsworthy or have a human interest angle for you to be successful.

About a year after publishing your book, it will be time to take another crack at the commercial publishers. It is much easier for an editor to evaluate a book than a publishing proposal, or even a complete manuscript, and if your book has achieved any kind of acceptance, so much the better. In addition to a copy of the book itself, put together a package of any favorable reviews or letters you have received. (If you have little to show, you can send your book to a few people, asking for comments.) Any information you have about sales should also be included. Are any bookstores or wholesalers stocking the book? Have there been sales to libraries? Have you been able to sell any by mail? Editors will be impressed by even minor successes, mentally converting them into major successes in the hands of their professional staff.

To editors, another attractive feature of a self-published book is that it can be put into production almost immediately, and be generating sales for the company in less than a year—a real plus for a hungry publisher. A publisher actually has two choices. He can either reprint your book with a few minor changes, including the addition of his name as publisher, or he can make a larger number of changes, including revisions you may wish to make, and reset the book as a new edition. In either case, you will sign a standard publishing agreement as though you were submitting a manuscript for publication. And don't forget to negotiate with your publisher for favorable terms. You've earned them.

Chapter 26

Writing Software for the Personal Computer Market

With personal computers now commonplace in homes, schools, colleges and businesses, a whole new kind of "authorship" has developed—creating programs, or software, for them. And an increasing number of book authors with a knowledge of programming are writing them.

Computer programmers have been around as long as computers, but until recently, most have been employed by companies or software houses developing large-scale programs to meet the special needs of a single client—systems for accounts receivable, billing, scheduling, inventory control, and so forth. The advent of the personal computer has created a demand for small-scale programs on diskettes or cassettes. Today many programmers are writing this type of software as freelancers, and arranging for its production and distribution much as authors write books and arrange for their publication.

Software development houses are creating most of this software for software publishers, using either staff programmers or freelancers, or a combination of both. However, book publishers are also publishing software for the personal computer market, including Hayden, McGraw-Hill, Scott, Foresman, and Xerox Education. Book publishers produce only a small portion of current software, and much of it is actually being developed for them by software development companies.

However, since these publishers are already producing and marketing books to the same groups who are the markets for software, both marketing capability and economies of scale suggest that they will be able to compete successfully with software publishers, if they can effectively adjust to the requirements of this new medium.

TYPES OF SOFTWARE

As with books, software can generally be classified according to the markets for which it is created.

There is, for example, the home/personal-use market which includes the educational and entertainment games. This software is created for a mass market and must be priced accordingly, usually around $30. There are also programs for more adult home use, including software for computing income taxes and personal finances, and for word processing. This software is likely to be priced in the $40 to $60 range, although some is priced considerably higher.

In the elementary and high school market, the objective is to teach skills, such as spelling or reading or math, through software consisting of carefully crafted instructional systems. However, there is no limit to the subjects that can be taught with instructional software. In this market, the software is sold directly to the school systems to operate on their computers, frequently IBM or Apple. Software developers for this market need professional programming skills as well as a thorough knowledge of teaching methodology. Publishers developing software for the school market already publish textbooks for this market.

The college and university market is more amorphous than the school market for a variety of reasons. The subjects being taught are both more diverse and more complex, the instructional methods and content less standardized, and the marketing methods not yet fully developed. Most colleges and universities have a computer center with personal computers available for student use. These may be under the direction of the computer science department, the engineering department, or even the library. The computers are usually IBM PCs or Apples, although more powerful machines, such as those made by Hewlett-Packard and Digital Equipment, are also used. The software must be promoted to the course instructors and department heads, although the sale may be handled either by direct mail or through the campus bookstore. The programs are likely to lead the student through the problems and exercises in a given text. The best software is being developed by course instructors who have had formal training in programming. Publishers of college textbooks such as McGraw-Hill are developing software for this market. In an effort to forestall the illegal copying of software, publishers are also exploring the licensing of departments at schools that wish to duplicate software packages for students.

The professional and small business market includes doctors, lawyers, real estate offices, contractors, retail stores, smalltown governments, and libraries. These tend to be application programs which perform the required calculations on data entered by the professional person, or programs that handle the bookkeeping, mailing lists, and word processing needs of the office. The equipment used ranges from the mid-priced IBM, Apple and Radio Shack models to the more powerful minicomputers.

Book publishers are taking two approaches to developing software. One is to develop independent, or stand-alone, packages. The other is to design "wrap-around" packages, or software that is integrated with a specific book, and which may be either packaged with the book or sold separately. Book publishers are attracted to the wrap-around approach, because each of the two media has its strengths, which, when used together, complement each other, and because each tends to promote or reinforce the use of the other. Many publishers who have become active in the field of software are reviewing their backlists looking for books that will lend themselves to software development. The availability of this source material is an advantage that book publishers have over software houses.

Another field writers may wish to consider is software design—that is, writing the specifications for what a program is to do, without doing the actual programming. Of particular interest may be the design of interactive stories, a program containing a story with multiple outcomes that are determined by a player's response. Mysteries, fantasies, science fiction, and juveniles are all good candidates for interactive programs.

GETTING SOFTWARE PUBLISHED

The author-publisher relationship for software is very similar to that for books. Creators of software seek out publishers in much the same way as do book authors, sending out query letters and proposals similar to those prepared for books. If a software publisher wants a project, he will give the creator a contract for the development of the software either in return for royalties on the sales and an advance against royalties, or for a fixed fee. The software publisher may acquire all or limited rights. The software is protected by copyright in much the same way as books.

The differences, however, are more important than the similarities. First, unlike books, software for a given market must be written for specific makes and models of computers that are most commonly used in that market. Because there are several different models in use in each market, software publishers usually want to issue several versions of a program, each written for one of the popular models. If the programmer has written for only one model and is not equipped to write other versions, the software publisher will probably want to acquire the rights to other versions and arrange for their development by someone else. Multiple versions of each program are vital to the publisher, since he cannot afford the high cost of promoting a software package to a small segment of the potential market.

In addition to providing a working program on a diskette or cassette, the programmer may also be required to provide the software publisher with documentation of the software, and copy for a user manual. Or the publisher may choose to have the documentation and manual prepared by companies or freelancers specializing in this work. The documentation must include information on the equipment for which the software was designed, the operating system used, a flow chart of the logic of the system, a list of the source codes and variables used, and information on how the data files are designed. This information is needed by the software publisher in eliminating any bugs that materialize during testing procedures, or in preparing additional versions and enhancements. The user manual, of course, must provide detailed instructions on how the program is to be operated. It is vital that these instructions are accurate, unambiguous, and easy to understand.

Software is also different from written text material in that it can contain hidden flaws, referred to as bugs or glitches. The flaws are hidden in that the program may operate correctly under one set of circumstances, but not under another, because the programmer has not taken into account the full range of possibilities. Because of these potential problems, programs must be thoroughly tested before being made available to the public, and it is not uncommon for software publishers to employ two sets of tests—a series of in-house tests, known as alpha testing, and a series of outside tests, called beta testing. There are several organizations which perform outside testing for a fee, including the National Educational Association's Educational Computer Service, which runs an elaborate series of tests not only on the operation of educational software, but also on the instructional techniques, the completeness of the material, the quality of the language, the methods used to hold the student's interest, and so forth.

Furthermore, because it is so difficult to completely debug software, some problems arise even after the software has been put on the market. As a consequence, software publishers must be willing to accept and deal with phone inquiries regarding operating problems and provide further debugging as needed. User manuals that are not absolutely thorough and clear also generate inquiries that must be answered by experienced people.

The royalty arrangements on software are similar to those made for books, but rates are much more variable, ranging from 5 percent to 20 percent of either net or list price. Royalty terms given are closely guarded secrets, and unlike book contracts, software contracts usually contain a nondisclosure clause prohibiting the programmer from telling others the financial terms of the agreement. Advances against royalties can range from $15,000 to amounts in excess of $100,000, depending on the complexity of the program, the number of models for which versions are prepared, and the size of the market. The advance is usually paid in installments, for example, four equal payments made on signing the publishing agreement, on submitting the first draft for in-house testing, on submitting the second draft for outside testing, and on the acceptance of the final program. Some software publishers prefer to purchase the software outright, rather than pay a royalty. In each such case, the programmer must decide if the purchase price is adequate to justify forgoing royalty income on sales that may continue for many years. In addition, as in book publishing, it is not necessary to sell all rights, or to sell them forever. The programmer may sell the rights to selected versions to one software publisher for a specified number of years, and sell the rights to other versions to other software publishers for a different number of years.

Contracts for software usually contain a detailed specification of the program to be delivered, as well as requiring the programmer to be available for consultation during the testing and debugging stages, and for preparing enhancements and updated versions.

Several software agencies have been established to represent software creators in their search for and negotiations with software publishers, just as literary agents represent book authors. Among them, John Brockman Associates is working primarily with software houses, helping them negotiate distribution deals with publishers. The Software Agency, Inc. is covering some of the same ground, but is also interested in representing software programmers. The Steven J. Axelrod Agency is working with programming groups in creating products and arranging for their publication. The Electronic Media Association is a software agency seeking companies, institutions, and programmers as clients. All of these agencies are located in New York City.

Although software can be protected by copyright, it is not entirely clear what the copyright protects, and there have been few court cases to clarify the issue. It seems that copyright protects the specific details in the program itself, but not necessarily the results that appear on the monitor or in print form. In any event, computer software, its documentation, and the user manual accompanying it, can and should be copyrighted in the name of the programmer rather than in the name of the publisher. Critical to copyright protection is placement of a copyright notice (Copyright © 1985 John Doe) at the beginning of the program itself, as well as on the first page of the documentation and the user manual. Registration with the Copyright Office is also recommended, and is usually handled by the software publisher on behalf of the programmer. See also the separate chapter on copyright.

A useful reference for the freelance programmer is the annual *Programmer's Market*, published by Writer's Digest Books. This publication lists over five hundred software publishers, giving the types of software they are interested in, their requirements, and information on what they look for in submittals. It contains a variety of useful indexes, including a list of publishers by the hardware for which they handle software, and a list of publishers by the subject matter in which they specialize. And it also includes articles on writing and selling software.

Bibliography

GENERAL REFERENCE BOOKS

Adelman, Robert H. *What's Really Involved in Writing and Selling Your Book.* Los Angeles: Nash, 1972.

Appelbaum, Judith, and Nancy Evans. *How to Get Happily Published.* New York: Harper & Row, 1978.

Balkin, Richard. *A Writer's Guide to Book Publishing.* 2nd ed. New York: Hawthorn, 1981.

————. *How to Understand & Negotiate a Book Contract or Magazine Agreement.* Cincinnati: Writer's Digest Books, 1985.

Belkin, Gary S. *Getting Published: A Guide for Businesspeople and Other Professionals.* New York: Wiley, 1984.

Carter, Robert A. (ed.). *Trade Book Marketing: A Practical Guide.* New York: Bowker, 1983.

The Chicago Manual of Style, 13th Ed. Chicago: University of Chicago Press, 1982.

Chickadel, Charles J. *Publish It Yourself,* 2nd ed. San Francisco: Trinity, 1980.

Cleaver, Diane. *The Literary Agent and the Writer: A Professional Guide.* Boston: The Writer, 1984.

Crawford, Tad. *The Writer's Legal Guide.* New York: Hawthorn, 1978.

Curtis, Richard. *How to Be Your Own Literary Agent.* Boston: Houghton Mifflin, 1983.

Dessauer, John P. *Book Publishing: What It Is, What It Does,* 2nd ed. New York: Bowker, 1981.

Fischel, Daniel N. *A Practical Guide to Writing and Publishing Professional Books.* New York: Van Nostrand Reinhold, 1984.

Geiser, Elizabeth A., and Arnold Dolin (eds.). *The Business of Book Publishing.* Boulder: Westview Press, 1984.

Gunther, Max. *Writing and Selling a Nonfiction Book.* Boston: The Writer, 1973.

Hawes, Gene R. *To Advance Knowledge: A Handbook on University Press Publishing.* New York: AAUP Services, 1967.

Henderson, Bill (ed.). *The Art of Literary Publishing: Editors on Their Craft.* NY: Pushcart, Wainscott, 1980.

————. *The Publish-It-Yourself Handbook: Literary Tradition and How-To,* 2nd ed. New York: Harper & Row, 1980.

Hill, Mary, and Wendell Cochran. *Into Print: A Practical Guide to Writing, Illustrating and Publishing.* Los Altos, California: Kaufman, 1977.

Johnston, Donald F. *Copyright Handbook,* 2nd ed. New York: Bowker, 1982.

Jordan, Lewis (ed.). *New York Times Manual of Style and Usage.* Times Books, 1976.

Larsen, Michael. *How to Write a Book Proposal.* Cincinnati: Writer's Digest Books, 1985.

Lee, Marshall. *Bookmaking: The Illustrated Guide to Design/Production/Editing,* 2nd ed. New York: Bowker, 1979.

Longyear, Marie, (ed.). *The McGraw-Hill Style Manual.* New York: McGraw-Hill, 1983.

Madison, Charles A. *Irving to Irving: Author-Publisher Relations, 1800-1974.* New York: Bowker, 1974.

Mayer, Debby. *Literary Agents: A Writer's Guide,* New York, Poets & Writers, 1983.

Meyer, Carol. *The Writer's Survival Manual: The Complete Guide to Getting Your Book Published Right.* New York: Crown, 1982.

Nicholson, Margaret. *A Practical Style Guide for Authors and Editors.* New York: Holt, Rinehart & Winston, 1970.

Pocket Pal: A Graphic Arts Production Handbook, 12th ed. New York: International Paper Co., 1979.

Polking, Kirk, and Leonard S. Meranus. *Law and the Writer,* 3rd ed. Cincinnati: Writer's Digest Books, 1984.

Ross, Tom, and Marilyn Ross. *The Complete Guide to Self-Publishing.* Cincinnati: Writer's Digest Books, 1985.

Wincor, Richard. *Literary Rights Contracts: A Handbook for Professionals.* New York: Harcourt Brace Jovanovich, 1979.

Wittenberg, Philip. *The Protection of Literary Property,* 2nd ed. Boston: The Writer, 1978.

DIRECTORIES AND ANNUALS

Books in Print. New York: Bowker.

Burack, Sylvia K. (ed.). *The Writer's Handbook.* Boston: The Writer.

Fulton, Len, and Ellen Ferber. *The International Directory of Little Magazines and Small Presses.* Paradise, CA: Dustbooks.

Literary Agents of North America. New York: Author Aid Associates.

Literary Market Place. New York: Bowker.

Subject Guide to Books in Print. New York: Bowker.

Writer's Market. Cincinnati: Writer's Digest Books.

APPENDIX: SAMPLE PUBLISHING CONTRACTS

This appendix contains three sample publishing contracts: for a trade book, for a college textbook, and for publication by a vanity press. Although no two publishers' contracts are alike, they all cover the same issues, and these examples show how one publisher handles each of those issues.

No professional book contract is presented because they are usually very similar to college textbook contracts in that they do not normally contain option clauses, provision for agents, or separate royalty terms for the sale of each of the subsidiary rights. In addition, the royalty payments in both are usually based on the net price rather than the list price of the book.

The vanity press contract was offered for a small book of about 80 pages—actually a few preliminary chapters from this work. The publication fee for a larger work would be proportionately greater.

(PUBLISHING AGREEMENT)

T-050185

Name:

(the "Author") shall prepare and deliver to the McGraw-Hill Book Company, a division of McGraw-Hill, Inc. (the "Publisher") a manuscript for a work entitled

(the "Work") or such other title as may be mutually agreeable to the Publisher and the Author, and the Publisher shall publish the Work, in accordance with and subject to the provisions of this Agreement dated   , 19

1 RIGHTS CONVEYED TO PUBLISHER AND PAYMENTS TO AUTHOR

a. Rights and Royalties. The Author grants and assigns exclusively to the Publisher the following rights, for which the Publisher shall pay to the Author the royalties indicated:

(1) *Sale by Publisher of the Work in the United States, Philippines, and Canada.* The right to reproduce and distribute the Work in the English language, and all revisions and future editions of it, in the United States of America and its territories and dependencies, the Philippines, and Canada.

Royalty. On all copies sold, a royalty of:

of the Publisher's domestic list price, except:

(i) On copies sold in Canada, one-half the applicable royalty payable on sales in the United States.

(ii) On copies sold by mail direct to consumers by the Publisher, 5 percent of the Publisher's domestic list price.

(iii) On copies sold to wholesale or retail distributors or booksellers, or to such groups as schools, reading circles, and newsdealers, when Publisher's net receipts are less than 50 percent of the Publisher's domestic list price, 1 percent less than the royalty percentage which would otherwise be applicable.

(iv) On copies sold after two years from the date of first publication from a reprinting of 2000 copies or less where the regular sales in the six-month period preceding such reprinting did not exceed 500 copies, one-half the royalty percentage which would otherwise be applicable.

(v) On copies sold through the Publisher's own book clubs, 5 percent of the club's member price.

(vi) On paperback copies reproduced and sold by the Publisher, 5 percent of the Publisher's domestic list price.

(vii) On copies of hardbound reprints of the Work which shall sell for no more than two-thirds of the Publisher's domestic list price of the original hardbound edition, 5 percent of the Publisher's domestic list price.

(viii) On copies sold in bulk for premium or promotional use, 5 percent of the Publisher's net receipts.

(2) *Sale and License of the Work by the Publisher in the Exclusive Territory.* The right to reproduce and distribute, and to license others to reproduce and distribute, copies of the Work in the English language, and all revisions and future editions of it, for use in the United Kingdom, the Republic of Ireland, the Republic of South Africa, Australia, and/or New Zealand (all such countries constituting the "Exclusive Territory").

Royalty. On all copies sold by the Publisher or the Publisher's subsidiaries, one-half of the applicable royalty payable on sales of the Work in the United States. On all copies sold by the Publisher's licensees: if sold from an edition separately manufactured and published abroad, 50 percent of the Publisher's receipts; if sold from exported Publisher's sheets or bound books, 10 percent of the Publisher's receipts, less manufacturing and shipping costs.

(3) *Sale of the Work by the Publisher in the open market.* The right to reproduce and distribute copies of the Work in all parts of the world other than the United States of America, its territories and dependencies, the Exclusive Territory, Canada, and the Philippines.

Royalty. On all copies sold, one-half the applicable royalty payable on sales of the Work in the United States.

(4) *Translations.* The right to translate, reproduce, and distribute and to license others to translate, reproduce, and distribute the Work in French, Spanish, German, Italian, Japanese, Arabic, and all other foreign languages.

Royalty. On all copies sold: if sold by the Publisher or its subsidiaries, 5 percent of the translation's list price; if under license to others, 50 percent of the Publisher's receipts.

(5) *Reprint editions.* The right to license a publisher to reprint and distribute the Work in a paperback, hardbound, and/or anthology edition.

Royalty. 50 percent of the Publisher's receipts.

(6) *License to book clubs.* The right to license recognized book clubs to reproduce and distribute the Work, either in whole or as a condensation.

Royalty. 50 percent of the Publisher's receipts, less one-half of the unreimbursed cost of any reproductive materials required by the book club and furnished by the Publisher.

(7) *First serialization.* The right to license others to publish first serializations of the Work (which shall comprise all serializations published before publication of the Work).

Royalty. 50 percent of the Publisher's receipts.

(8) *Second serialization.* The right to license others to publish digests, abridgments, selections, and second serializations of the Work (which shall comprise all serializations published after publication of the Work).

Royalty. 50 percent of the Publisher's receipts.

(9) *Database and electronic rights.* The right to exercise, and to license others to exercise, database and electronic rights to the Work, including but not limited to videotex, teletext, and computer programs based on the Work.

Royalty. If such rights are exercised by the Publisher, 10 percent of the Publisher's net receipts; if such rights are licensed and the Publisher does not provide services to its licensee, 50 percent of the Publisher's receipts; if such rights are licensed and the Publisher provides services, including but not limited to data formatting, storage, product development, or marketing, to its licensee in connection with the licensee's exercise of these rights, the percentage payable to the Author may be reasonably adjusted by the Publisher to reflect the cost of these services but in no event shall be less than 25 percent of the Publisher's receipts.

(10) *Dramatization.* The right to license others to exercise stage, motion picture, television, and radio rights to the Work, and allied rights licensed in connection with any of those rights.

Royalty. 75 percent of the Publisher's receipts, except as provided in Section 1a(11) with respect to Derived Works.

(11) *Video Rights.* The right to exercise and to license others to exercise video (including but not limited to video cassettes and video disks) rights to the Work.

Royalty. If such rights are licensed, 50 percent of the Publisher's receipts. If such rights are exercised by the Publisher, acting by itself or in conjunction with any third party, 5 percent of the net receipts from the distribution of the work based on or derived from the Work (the "Derived Work") and 5 percent of the receipts from licensing rights to the Derived Work, in either case less the reasonable production costs of the Derived Work.

(12) *Audiovisual rights.* The right to license others to exercise any or all of the other mechanical, visual, audiovisual, sound-reproducing, and recording rights to the Work.

Royalty. 50 percent of the Publisher's receipts.

(13) *Commercial rights.* The right to exercise and to license others to exercise all commercial rights to the Work, which shall mean the exploitation of the Work itself, all material contained in it, and all rights in connection with merchandise and/or use of the Author's name in connection with the merchandise.

Royalty. If such rights are exercised by the Publisher, 10 percent of the Publisher's net receipts; if such rights are licensed, 50 percent of the Publisher's receipts.

b. Other Matters Relating to Grant of Rights

(1) *Recordation.* The Author appoints the Publisher as the Author's attorney-in-fact to execute any documents the Publisher deems necessary to record any of the rights granted in this Agreement with the United States Copyright office or elsewhere.

(2) *Permissions.* All requests for permission received by the Author to reproduce, exploit, or otherwise use any material from the Work for those rights granted to the Publisher in this Agreement shall be submitted to the Publisher for written approval and grant of permission.

(3) *Copies of agreements.* Each party to this Agreement shall, upon request of the other party, furnish to the other party a true copy of any agreement which either party may make with any third party for the disposition of any rights affecting the Work.

c. Other Matters Relating to Royalties and Payments

(1) *Royalty-free distributions.* No royalties or other payments shall be due with respect to (i) free copies furnished to the Author; (ii) any copies of the Work, or selections from it, furnished by the Publisher to others without payment for the purposes of review, promotion, or publicity, or publication or broadcast (but not dramatization) by radio or television, without charge, of such selections from the Work as in the opinion of the Publisher may benefit its sale; (iii) any copies destroyed or sold at the Publisher's manufacturing cost or less; (iv) any not-for-profit publication of the Work in Braille or in special editions for the physically or visually handicapped.

(2) *Advances.* The Publisher shall pay the Author, or the Author's duly authorized representative, an advance of $, which shall be a charge against all sums accruing to the Author under this Agreement, payable to the Author as follows:

(3) *Settlement.* Within 90 days after June 30 and December 31 each year, the Publisher shall render a statement of the number of copies of the Work sold and the amount payable to the Author under this Agreement semiannually through June 30 and December 31 and make settlement for the amount due, except as follows: (i) For the first two semiannual accounting periods following the publication of the Work, the Publisher may withhold from payment to the Author a reasonable reserve for returned copies not to exceed 15 percent of the amount payable to the Author under this Section 1 as reflected on the statement. The balance of the reserve at the close of the second accounting period shall be paid to the Author with the payments for the following accounting period. (ii) Any sums due and owing from the Author to the Publisher, whether or not arising out of this Agreement, may be deducted from any sum due or to become due from the Publisher to the Author under this Agreement. For the purposes of this paragraph, a nonrecoverable unearned advance made to the Author under another agreement shall not be considered a sum due and owing unless the Author is in default under the other agreement.

(4) *Definitions.* As used in this Agreement, "Publisher's net receipts" shall mean the Publisher's applicable domestic list price less discounts, credits, and returns. "Publisher's receipts" shall mean the total amount received by the Publisher less agency commissions. For royalties that are based on the Publisher's domestic list price of all copies sold, the total of these sales shall be reduced by the amount of credits and returns. If the Publisher adopts a freight pass-through policy, royalties based on the Publisher's domestic list price shall be based on the Publisher's invoice price, which shall mean the price shown on the Publisher's invoices to its customers on the basis of which the Publisher's discounts to its customers are calculated.

2 MANUSCRIPT PREPARATION AND DELIVERY
 a. The Author shall prepare and deliver to the Publisher on or before   ,19   , two complete, clean copies of a manuscript for the Work in double-spaced typewritten form on 8½- by 11-inch or metric size A4 sheets or as may otherwise be specified by the Publisher. The manuscript for the Work must be acceptable to the Publisher in both form and content for publication. It shall be between   and   words in length and shall include such materials as the Publisher may reasonably specify for the Work, including but not limited to copy for the title page, table of contents, index, tables, and bibliographies, and copy for drawings, illustrations, and charts. The Author shall supply these in finished form to the Publisher within a reasonable time after the delivery of the completed manuscript; if the Author shall fail to do so, the Publisher may supply them and charge the expense to the Author.

b. The Author shall obtain, without expense to the Publisher, written permission to include in the Work any copyrighted material which is not in the public domain as well as any other material for which permission is necessary in connection with the Author's warranty in Section 3 of this Agreement. These permissions must be consistent with the rights granted to the Publisher in this Agreement so that they may cover all the uses to which the material may eventually be put. The Author shall deliver to the Publisher a copy of all these permissions with the complete manuscript.

c. If the Work or any subdivision of it contains a significant portion of material taken from documents prepared and published by the United States government and therefore not subject to copyright, the Author shall notify the Publisher in writing of the existence and location of all such material in the Work.

d. If the Author fails to deliver the complete manuscript within 90 days after the delivery date specified in this Agreement, or if the Author fails or refuses to perform any correction or revision of the manuscript within the time or as otherwise specified by the Publisher, the Publisher shall have the right in its discretion: (1) to give the Author written notice of its intention to terminate this Agreement, in which event the Author shall promptly reimburse the Publisher for all sums advanced to the Author against royalties under this Agreement, and upon such reimbursement this Agreement shall terminate; or (2) to make such other arrangements in connection with this Agreement as the Publisher deems advisable to complete, correct, or revise the manuscript, in which event the reasonable cost of such arrangements may be charged against any sums accruing to the Author under this Agreement.

e. If requested by the Publisher, the Author shall correct proof of the Work and return it promptly to the Publisher. If the Author makes or causes to be made any alterations in the type, illustrations, or film which are not typographical, drafting, or Publisher's errors and which exceed 15 percent of the original cost of composition and artwork independent of the cost of these Author's alterations, the cost of the excess alterations shall be charged against any sums accruing to the Author under this Agreement.

f. The Author shall retain one copy of the manuscript submitted to the Publisher until the Work is published. The Publisher shall have no liability of any kind to the Author by reason of the loss, destruction, or mutilation of the manuscript delivered to the Publisher. This provision shall also be applicable to the original artwork, illustrations, and photographs, unless such loss, destruction, or mutilation is covered by insurance of the Publisher, in which case the Author shall look only to the insurance carrier for replacement or reimbursement.

3 **AUTHOR'S WARRANTY**

a. The Author represents and warrants to the Publisher that the Author has full power and authority to enter into this Agreement and to grant the rights granted in this Agreement; that the Work is original except for material in the public domain and those excerpts from other works as may be included with the written permission of the copyright owners; that the Work does not contain any libelous or obscene material or injurious formulas, recipes, or instructions; that it does not infringe any trade name, trademark, or copyright; and that it does not invade or violate any right of privacy, personal or proprietary right, or other common law or statutory right.

b. The Author agrees to indemnify the Publisher and its licensees and assignees under this Agreement and hold them harmless from any and all losses, damages, liabilities, costs, charges, and expenses, including reasonable attorneys' fees, arising out of any breach of any of the Author's representations and warranties contained in this Agreement or third-party claims relating to the matters covered by the representations and warranties in this Section 3 which are finally sustained in a court of original jurisdiction. If any action or proceeding is brought against the Publisher with respect to the matters covered by the representations and warranties in this Section 3, the Publisher shall have the right, in its sole discretion, to select counsel to defend against this action or proceeding. In addition to other remedies available to the Publisher, the Publisher may charge the amount of these losses, damages, liabilities, costs, charges, and expenses against any sums accruing to the Author under this Agreement or any other agreement currently existing between Author and Publisher.

c. If there is an infringement of any rights granted to the Publisher or rights which the Publisher is authorized to license or in which the Publisher is to share in the proceeds, the Publisher shall have the right, in its sole discretion, to select counsel to bring an action to enforce those rights, and the Author and the Publisher shall have the right to participate jointly in the action. If both participate, they shall share equally the expenses of and any sums recovered in the action, except that if the Author retains separate legal counsel, the Author shall be solely responsible for the legal expenses of the Author's counsel. If either party declines to participate in the action, the other may proceed, and the party maintaining the action shall bear all expenses and shall retain all sums recovered.

The provisions of this Section 3 shall survive any termination of this Agreement.

4 **COMPETING WORKS**

While this Agreement is in effect, the Author shall not, without the prior written consent of the Publisher, write, edit, print, or publish, or cause to be written, edited, printed, or published, any other edition of the Work, whether revised, supplemented, corrected, enlarged, abridged, or otherwise, or any other work of a nature which might interfere with or injure the sales of the Work or any grant of rights or licenses permitted under this Agreement by the Publisher, or permit the use of the Author's name or likeness in connection with any such work.

5 **PUBLICATION OF THE WORK**

After giving written notice to the Author that it has accepted the Work for publication, the Publisher shall within 12 months of written acceptance of the manuscript publish the Work at its own expense and in such style and manner and with such trademarks, service marks, and imprints of Publisher, and sell the Work at such prices, as it shall deem suitable. The Publisher shall publish the Work with a copyright notice and register the Work in accordance with the United States copyright laws in the name of the Publisher or Author as the Author may elect.

6 **AUTHOR'S COPIES**

The Publisher shall give the Author ten copies of the Work upon publication, free of charge, and sell to the Author as many additional copies as the Author may wish for personal use and not for resale, at a discount of 40 percent of the Publisher's then list price, f.o.b. the Publisher's warehouse.

7 DISCONTINUANCE OF PUBLICATION
   a. When in the judgment of the Publisher the demand for the Work is no longer sufficient to warrant its continued publication, the Publisher shall have the right to discontinue the publication and declare the Work out of print, in which event the Author shall be so advised in writing.

b. If the Work is not for sale in at least one edition (including any revised edition or reprint edition) published by the Publisher or under license from the Publisher and, within eight months after written demand by the Author, the Publisher or its licensee fails to offer it again for sale, then this Agreement shall terminate and all rights granted to the Publisher in it shall revert to the Author (except for material prepared by or obtained at the expense of the Publisher which shall remain the property of the Publisher).

c. The termination of this Agreement under this Section 7 or otherwise shall be subject to (1) any license, contract, or option granted to third parties by the Publisher before the termination and the Publisher's right to its share of the proceeds from these agreements after the termination and (2) the Publisher's continuing right to sell all remaining bound copies and sheets of the Work and all derivative works which are on hand at the time of termination.

8 RIGHTS OF REFUSAL

a. Other Rights. The Author grants the Publisher the "right of first refusal" to exercise or license any dramatization, video, audiovisual, and commercial rights in the Work to the extent that any of these rights have not been granted to the Publisher. The Author shall not enter into an agreement with another party relating to such rights upon terms equal to or less favorable than the last offered by the Publisher.

b. Author's Next Work. The Author grants to the Publisher the "right of first refusal" to publish the Author's next full-length book and shall submit the manuscript for it to the Publisher before submitting it to any other publisher. In no case shall the Publisher be required to exercise this option before publication or within three months following publication of the Work. The Author shall not enter into a contract for the publication of this next work with any publisher upon terms less favorable than any offered by the Publisher.

9 AGENT
   The Author hereby authorizes as agent:

of:

(1) to collect and receive all sums payable to the Author under this Agreement, the receipt of such sums by the agent being a full and valid discharge of the Publisher's obligation for the payment made, and (2) to act on behalf of the Author in all matters in any way arising out of this Agreement.

10 OTHER MATTERS
   a. Assignments. No assignment of this Agreement, voluntary or by operation of law, shall be binding upon either of the parties without the prior written consent of the other, provided, however, that the Author may assign or transfer any sums due or to become due under this Agreement without the Publisher's consent.

b. Law to Govern. This Agreement shall be interpreted and governed by the laws of the State of New York and the United States of America.

c. Bankruptcy. In the event of bankruptcy, receivership, or liquidation of the Publisher, this Agreement shall terminate without further procedure and all rights granted in this Agreement to the Publisher by the Author shall revert to the Author.

d. Notices. Any written notice required under any of the provisions of this Agreement shall be deemed to have been properly served by delivery in person or by first-class mail, postage prepaid, to the last known address.

e. Binding Agreement. This Agreement shall be binding upon the parties signing it and on all their heirs, personal representatives, successors, and permitted assignees.

f. Complete Agreement. This Agreement constitutes the complete understanding of the parties and supersedes all prior agreements of the parties relating to the Work. No amendment or waiver of any provision of this Agreement shall be valid unless in writing and signed by all parties affected by the amendment or waiver.

11 **SUPPLEMENTARY PROVISIONS (IF ANY)**

The following parties have executed this Agreement.

McGraw-Hill Book Company
A Division of McGraw-Hill, Inc.

By _____

_____
TAX OR SOCIAL SECURITY NUMBER   AUTHOR

_____
CITIZENSHIP

_____
TAX OR SOCIAL SECURITY NUMBER   AUTHOR

_____
CITIZENSHIP

PUBLISHING AGREEMENT

C-2-050185

Name(s):

(the "Author") shall prepare and deliver to the McGraw-Hill Book Company, a division of McGraw-Hill, Inc. (the "Publisher"), a manuscript for a work entitled

(the "Work") or such other title as may be mutually agreeable to the Publisher and the Author, and the Publisher shall publish the Work, in accordance with and subject to the provisions of this Agreement dated , 19

1 MANUSCRIPT PREPARATION AND DELIVERY

a. The Author shall prepare and deliver to the Publisher on or before , 19 , two complete, clean copies of a manuscript for the Work in double-spaced typewritten form on 8½- by 11-inch or metric size A4 sheets or as may otherwise be specified by the Publisher. The manuscript for the Work shall be acceptable to the Publisher in both form and content for publication. It shall be approximately pages in length and shall include illustrations, including parts, as well as such other material as the Publisher may reasonably specify for the Work, including copy for the title page, table of contents, preface, index, tables, and bibliographies. The Author shall retain at all times before publication of the Work one complete copy of the manuscript for the Work.

b. The Author shall obtain, without expense to the Publisher, written permission to include in the Work any copyrighted material which is not in the public domain as well as any other material for which permission is necessary in connection with the Author's warranty in Section 4 of this Agreement. These permissions must be consistent with the rights granted to the Publisher in this Agreement in order that they may cover all the uses to which the material may eventually be put. The Author shall deliver to the Publisher a copy of all these permissions with the complete manuscript.

c. The Author shall notify the Publisher in writing of the existence and location of all material taken from documents prepared and published by the United States government, and therefore not subject to copyright, when it constitutes a significant portion of the Work.

d. Within a reasonable time after receipt of the complete manuscript, the Publisher shall either accept it or, if it is not acceptable in form or content as provided by this Agreement, return it to the Author for correction or revision within the reasonable time specified by the Publisher.

e. In the event the Author fails to deliver the complete manuscript within sixty days after the delivery date specified in this Agreement, or the Author fails or refuses to perform any correction or revision of the manuscript within the time specified by the Publisher, the Publisher shall have the right, in its discretion: (1) to give the Author written notice of its intention to terminate this Agreement, in which event the Author shall promptly reimburse the Publisher for all sums advanced to the Author against royalties under this Agreement, and upon such reimbursement this Agreement shall terminate; or (2) to make such other arrangements as the Publisher deems advisable to complete, correct, or revise the manuscript, in which event the reasonable cost of such arrangements may be charged, in the Publisher's discretion, against either any sums accruing to the Author under this Agreement or the Author's royalty percentage (Section 7) or both.

f. The Publisher shall have the right to make such editorial revisions and changes in the manuscript as it deems necessary, but the Author shall be given an opportunity to review these changes.

g. The Author shall read, correct, and return promptly to the Publisher all printed proofs of the Work. If the Author makes or causes to be made any alterations in the type, illustrations, or film which are not corrections of typographical, drafting, or Publisher's errors and which exceed 20 percent of the cost of original composition and artwork independent of the cost of such Author's alterations, the cost of the excess alterations shall be charged against any sums accruing to the Author under this Agreement.

2 MULTIPLE AUTHORS

If there are multiple authors under this Agreement, the obligations of all the authors shall be joint and several unless otherwise expressly provided in this Agreement, but the Publisher reserves the right to exercise any or all of its remedies against only the author who does not perform as provided in this Agreement.

3 RIGHTS CONVEYED

The Author hereby grants and assigns exclusively to the Publisher each and every right in the Work throughout the world, which shall include but not be limited to all copyrights (and renewals, extensions, and continuations of copyright) in the Work and in all derivative works, together with all exclusive rights granted to an author under the copyright laws of the United States, foreign countries, and international copyright conventions and the right to grant these rights or any part of them to third parties. The Author appoints the Publisher as its attorney-in-fact to execute any documents the Publisher deems necessary to record any of these grants with the United States Copyright Office or elsewhere.

4 AUTHOR'S WARRANTY

a. The Author represents and warrants to the Publisher that the Author has full power and authority to enter into this Agreement and to grant the rights granted in this Agreement; that the Work is original except for material in the public domain and such excerpts from other works as may be included with the written permission of the copyright owners; that the Work does not contain any libelous or obscene material or injurious formulas, recipes, or instructions; that the Work does not infringe any trade name, trademark, or copyright; and that the Work does not invade or violate any right of privacy, personal or proprietary right, or other common law or statutory right.

b. The Author shall indemnify the Publisher and its licensees and assignees under this Agreement and hold them harmless from any and all losses, damages, liabilities, costs, charges, and expenses, including reasonable attorneys' fees, arising out of any breach of any of the Author's representations and warranties contained in this Agreement or third-party claims relating to the matters covered by these representations and warranties. In addition to other remedies available to the Publisher, the Publisher may charge the amount of any such losses, damages, liabilities, costs, charges, and expenses against any sums accruing to the Author under this Agreement. The provisions of this Section 4 shall survive any termination of this Agreement.

5 COMPETING WORKS

While this Agreement is in effect, the Author shall not, without the prior written consent of the Publisher, write, edit, print, or publish, or cause to be written, edited, printed, or published, any other edition of the Work, whether revised, supplemented, corrected, enlarged, abridged, or otherwise, or any other work of a nature which might interfere with or injure the sales or licensing of the Work by the Publisher as permitted under this Agreement, or allow the use of the Author's name in connection with any such work. If the Publisher reasonably believes that the Author has breached the provisions of this Section 5, the Publisher may retain, in addition to other remedies available to the Publisher, all sums accruing to the Author under this Agreement until the matter has been resolved.

6 PUBLICATION OF THE WORK

After giving written notice to the Author that it has accepted the Work as being in form and content satisfactory for publication, the Publisher shall publish the Work at its own expense at such time and in such style and manner and with such trademarks, service marks, and imprints of the Publisher, and sell the Work at such prices, as it shall deem suitable. The Publisher shall publish the Work with a copyright notice and register the Work in the name of the Publisher in compliance with the United States copyright laws.

7 ROYALTIES

a. As full payment to the Author, the Publisher shall pay to the Author the following royalties:

Domestic Sales   (1)   percent of the Publisher's net receipts for each copy of the Work sold by the Publisher for use within the United States (except as otherwise provided in this Section 7)

Foreign Sales   (2)   percent of the Publisher's domestic list price for each copy of the Work sold by the Publisher to the McGraw-Hill International Book Division or to third parties for use outside the United States

Direct Marketing   (3) 5 percent of the Publisher's domestic list price for each copy of the Work sold through the mails directly to consumers

Publisher's Book Clubs   (4) 5 percent of the Publisher's net receipts for each copy of the Work sold through the Publisher's own book clubs

Sale of Rights   (5) 50 percent of the Publisher's receipts from the sale, assignment, or licensing to others, including the Publisher's subsidiaries, of any rights to the Work or any part of it except (i) where the Publisher provides services to a licensee in connection with the licensee's exercise of database or electronic rights, the percentage payable to the Author may be reasonably adjusted by the Publisher to reflect the cost of those services but shall in no event be less than 25 percent; and (ii) on sales of International Student Editions by McGraw-Hill International Book Division subsidiaries, $7\frac{1}{2}$ percent of the subsidiary's list price of each copy sold

Exercise of Other Rights by Publisher   (6) 10 percent of the Publisher's net receipts from exercise by Publisher of any rights to the Work or any part of it for which a royalty is not otherwise provided in this Section 7

b. No royalty or other payment shall be due for (1) any copies of the Work, or a derivative work, which are sold by the Publisher at the Publisher's manufacturing cost or less; (2) supplementary materials distributed with but not sold separately from the Work; (3) any copies of the Work or a derivative work or selections from it furnished by the Publisher to others without payment for the purposes of promotion or publicity or for any other purpose deemed appropriate by the Publisher in its sole discretion; and (4) any not-for-profit publication of the Work or a derivative work in Braille or in special editions for the physically or visually handicapped.

c. For royalties that are based on the Publisher's domestic list price of all copies sold, the total of these sales shall be reduced by the amount of credits and returns, or a reasonable reserve for returns. The term "Publisher's net receipts" shall mean the Publisher's selling price, less discounts, credits, and returns, or a reasonable reserve for returns.

d. Within 90 days after June 30 and December 31 each year, the Publisher shall render a statement of the number of copies of the Work sold and the amount payable to the Author under this Agreement semiannually through June 30 and December 31 and make settlement for the amount due.

e. If there are multiple authors under this Agreement, the royalties to be paid shall be divided among them as follows:

If the division of royalties is not specified at the time this Agreement is made, the division may be specified later in a letter signed by all the authors and delivered to the Publisher before publication of the Work.

f. Any sums owing from the Author to the Publisher, whether or not arising out of this Agreement, may be charged against any sums accruing to the Author under this Agreement or under any other agreement between the Author and the Publisher. If there are multiple authors under this Agreement, sums owing from a particular author may be charged only against sums accruing to that author.

g. The rights for all portions of any royalties relinquished under Section 1 or 9 shall revert to the Publisher and shall be owned by the Publisher unless and until reallocated to new author(s).

8 AUTHOR'S COPIES
The Publisher shall give the Author 10 copies of the Work upon publication, free of charge, and sell to the Author as many additional copies as the Author wishes for personal use, and not for resale, at a discount of 25 percent off the Publisher's then list price, f.o.b. the Publisher's warehouse. If there are multiple authors under this Agreement, each author shall receive 10 copies.

9 REVISED EDITIONS
a. At the Publisher's request, the Author shall prepare and deliver a manuscript for a revised edition of the Work. Subject to the provisions of this Section, each revised edition shall be deemed to be covered by this Agreement to the same extent as if it were the Work referred to in this Agreement.

b. If the Author fails for any reason to prepare and deliver a manuscript for a revised edition within the reasonable time specified by the Publisher and as provided in this Agreement, the Publisher may make such arrangements for the preparation of the revision as the Publisher shall consider appropriate and charge the reasonable cost of doing so against sums accruing to the Author under this Agreement. In the Publisher's reasonable discretion, this charge may be in the form of a fee and/or a percentage of the Author's royalty for this revised edition or percentages for this revised edition and future editions. If failure to revise the work is due to the Author's death, the Publisher shall also have the right, in its discretion, to terminate this Agreement with respect to the revised edition and any future editions. In that event the Author's estate shall be paid one-half of the sums which would have otherwise accrued to the Author for the revised edition if published and one-quarter for the next future edition, if any. Thereafter the Author's estate shall have no proprietary interest in the Work and no further right to royalties for it. If there are multiple authors under this Agreement, the provisions of this Section 9b apply only to the author(s) who do not prepare the revised edition of the Work as provided in Section 9a. The Publisher shall retain the right, in its discretion, to use any Author's name in connection with any edition of the Work even though the Author has not participated in the preparation of that edition.

10 OUT OF PRINT
a. When in the judgment of the Publisher the demand for the Work is no longer sufficient to warrant its continued publication, the Publisher shall have the right to discontinue publication and declare the Work out of print, in which event the Author shall be so advised.

b. If the Work is not for sale in at least one edition (including any revised edition or reprint edition) published by the Publisher or under license from the Publisher and, within eight months after written demand by the Author, the Publisher or its licensee fails to offer it again for sale, then this Agreement shall terminate and all rights granted to the Publisher in it shall revert to the Author (except for any material prepared by or obtained at the expense of the Publisher, or for rights which have reverted to the Publisher under Section 1 or 9, which shall remain the property of the Publisher). If there are multiple authors under this Agreement, they shall take individual ownership, in proportion to their respective shares of the royalties under this Agreement, of all rights owned jointly by them at the time of termination.

c. The termination of the Agreement under this Section 10 or otherwise shall be subject to (1) any license, contract, or option granted to third parties by the Publisher before the termination and the Publisher's rights to its share of the proceeds from such grants after the termination; and (2) the Publisher's continuing right to sell all remaining bound copies and sheets of the Work and derivative works which are on hand at the time of termination.

11 APPLICABLE LAW

This Agreement shall in all respects be interpreted and construed in accordance with and governed by the laws of the State of New York, regardless of the place of its execution or performance.

12 ASSIGNMENTS

This Agreement may not be assigned by either the Author or the Publisher without the prior written consent of the other party, which shall not be unreasonably withheld. This Agreement shall be binding on the parties signing it and on all their heirs, legal representatives, successors, and permitted assignees.

13 COMPLETE AGREEMENT

This Agreement constitutes the complete understanding of the parties and supersedes all prior agreements of the parties relating to the Work. No amendment or waiver of any provision of this Agreement shall be valid unless in writing and signed by all parties affected by the amendment or waiver.

14 SUPPLEMENTARY PROVISIONS (IF ANY)

The following parties have executed this Agreement.

McGRAW-HILL BOOK COMPANY
A Division of McGraw-Hill, Inc.

By _____

_____
TAX OR SOCIAL SECURITY NUMBER

AUTHOR _____

_____
CITIZENSHIP

_____
TAX OR SOCIAL SECURITY NUMBER

AUTHOR _____

_____
CITIZENSHIP

_____
TAX OR SOCIAL SECURITY NUMBER

AUTHOR _____

_____
CITIZENSHIP

_____
TAX OR SOCIAL SECURITY NUMBER

AUTHOR _____

_____
CITIZENSHIP

_____
TAX OR SOCIAL SECURITY NUMBER

AUTHOR _____

_____
CITIZENSHIP

_____
TAX OR SOCIAL SECURITY NUMBER

AUTHOR _____

_____
CITIZENSHIP

_____
McGRAW-HILL EDITOR

𝕬𝖌𝖗𝖊𝖊𝖒𝖊𝖓𝖙 made and entered into by and between

Herbert W. Bell
3506 E. Yacht Drive
Long Beach, NC 28461

party of the first part, hereinafter called the Author, and VANTAGE PRESS, INC., a corporation duly organized and operating under the laws of the State of New York and engaged in the subsidy book publishing business, whose principal offices are located at 516 West 34th Street, New York, N.Y. 10001, party of the second part, hereinafter called the Publishers:

WHEREAS, the Author represents and warrants to be at least eighteen years of age and is the sole composer and/or proprietor of a literary work at present known as

AN AUTHOR'S GUIDE TO BOOK PUBLISHING

hereinafter called the Work, which Work the Publishers agree to publish in book form on the terms and conditions specified hereinafter,

IT IS HEREBY MUTUALLY AGREED between the Author and the Publishers as follows:

Grant
of
Rights

1. The Author hereby grants and assigns to the Publishers, during the full term of this contract, the exclusive right to print, publish, sell and export, or cause to be printed, published, sold and exported, the said Work in the English language (and in any foreign language, or languages, as the Publishers may deem desirable) in the United States of America, its dependencies and territories, and in the Dominion of Canada, and also the exclusive right to arrange for publication of the said Work in the British Commonwealth and in all other foreign countries.

Physical
Specifications

2. The Publishers agree to publish the said Work in the English language, in hard-covered book form, and in such format, type and style of paper, jacket and binding as they believe will make the volume attractive-looking. It is specifically understood and agreed, furthermore, that the said Work will contain all manuscript material originally submitted by the Author (unless otherwise designated hereinafter or provided for), and that the approximate size of the volume, when completed, will be 5½ inches by 8½ inches.

Author's
Copyright
Protection

3. The Publishers agree to take all steps necessary to obtain copyright in the said Work in the name of the Author, and thereby secure their own rights and those of the Author under the United States Copyright Acts. Both parties, furthermore, agree to execute, at any and all times when necessary, all such papers and/or other documents as may be required in order to protect, assign, renew or otherwise effectuate the rights herein. Copyright protection may also be taken out by the Publishers, in the name of the Author, in foreign countries, as the Publishers may consider to be necessary or desirable. The statutory United States copyright fees shall be paid by the Publishers.

Availability of
Copies and Filling
of Orders

4. The Publishers agree during the term of this contract to print and bind from time to time sufficient copies of said Work to fill all bona fide orders. Nothing contained herein shall be deemed to limit the right of the Publishers to produce printings and/or editions at any time during the life of this agreement if, in the Publishers' judgment, sales warrant. Furthermore, the Publishers agree to have a minimum of four hundred bound copies available prior to the official publication date for purposes of prepublication publicity, review, merchandising, promotion and sales.

Retail Price
and
Payments
to Author

5. The retail price shall be $. .9.95 . . . . . . per copy. The Publishers agree to pay to the Author $. .3.98 . . . . . per copy *(40% of the retail price)* on every copy of the said Work that may be sold and for which the Publishers shall receive payment. On all sales made at a discount of more than 40%, the Author's compensation shall be reduced by a percentage equal to the difference between 40% and the discount given. In no event, however, will the Publishers agree to give a discount of more than 50% without approval of the Author.

Copies Not Subject to Payment

6. The Author agrees that all copies of the said Work that may be used for review, merchandising sales and publicity purposes, or as samples to prospective customers (including dealers and whole salers), and all that the Publishers may deliver to the Author without receiving payment i money, and all that the Publishers may deliver to the Author at a discount from the establishe retail price, shall not be subject to any payment to the Author.

Author's Compensation for Subsidiary Rights

7. No payment shall be made to the Author for permission gratuitously given to others to publish extracts from the said Work with a view toward benefiting the sale thereof, or to create publicit or promotion thereon. But all compensation received by the Publishers for the sale of the follow ing subsidiary rights shall be divided in the proportion of 80% to the Author and 20% to th Publishers:

Soft Cover or Other Reprint Edition	Serialization or Syndication
Dramatic	British Publication
Radio and Television	Commercial Use of Title
Book Club	Merchandising Tie-Ins
Digest, Abridgment, Condensation or Extracts	Foreign Language Publication
Anthology or Quotation	Motion Picture

Should any revenue accrue from any other rights in the said Work, not specifically mentione above, such revenue shall also be divided in the proportion of 80% to the Author and 20% t the Publishers. This provision shall not be deemed a representation, warranty or guaranty o revenue from any or all such rights.

Author and/or Publishers May Negotiate Rights

8. The Author and the Publishers hereby agree that each shall have the right, during the life of thi contract, to negotiate for the sale, lease, license or other disposition of the said Work in the motion picture, dramatic, radio, television and/or all other fields. All gross compensation re ceived in payment for such sale, lease, license or other disposition shall be collected and dis bursed by the Publishers, and all contracts for such sale, lease, license or other disposition shal provide that such compensation is to be paid to the Publishers, and the Publishers are authorized to receive, collect and disburse same and to endorse and deposit all checks and/or drafts for such payments.

Review Copies

9. The Publishers agree to distribute, for purposes of publicity, sales, subsidiary rights, comment and review, from seventy-five to one hundred copies of the said Work to newspapers, magazines dealers and other outlets throughout the United States of America and/or in foreign countries as the Publishers may deem advisable. Distribution of these copies shall be to publications o the Publishers' choice, unless otherwise provided for hereinafter, and at no extra cost t the Author.

Author's Copies and Author's Purchases

10. The Publishers agree to deliver to the Author fifty copies of the said Work, without extra charge F.O.B. the Publishers' New York office, on completion thereof, after all sums of money that ma be due the Publishers, as hereinafter provided for, have been paid in full. Should the Author pur chase additional copies of the Work directly from the Publishers, same will be supplied at a dis count of 45% from the established retail price, F.O.B. the Publishers' New York office. Th Author may dispose of these copies in any manner and, if resold, may retain all funds de rived therefrom.

Statements of Account

11. The Publishers agree to render and forward to the Author, during the months of April and October next succeeding the official date of publication of the said Work, and continuing there after twice annually during such designated months while this agreement remains in full force and effect, statements of account setting forth the number of copies sold and paid for as of the previous six-month periods ending December 31st and June 30th, respectively, and also of any other income received from other sources to be accounted for hereunder, together with remit tances in full payment of all sums shown to be due to the Author thereon. Should the sale of the Work fall below fifty copies in any six-month period, the Publishers may, at their discretion defer issuing statements or making payments thereon, until total sales and receipts have reached minimum of fifty copies. Upon written request, the Author may examine, or cause to be exam ined through Certified Public Accountants, the records of account of the Publishers insofar as they relate to the sale or licensing of the said Work.

**Diligent
Collection**

12. The Publishers agree to pursue diligently the collection of funds due from the sale of the Work including, by way of description and not limitation, the use of an independent agency at prevailing and customary rates. The Author's compensation shall be based upon the net amount received by the Publishers.

**Editing of
Manuscript**

13. If, in the Publishers' opinion and judgment, the manuscript of the said Work requires copy-editing, or other editorial treatment, the Publishers agree to provide same without extra cost or expense to the Author. It is specifically understood and agreed, however, that the Publishers shall make no major revisions, changes, alterations or deletions therein without first consulting the Author and receiving written permission to do so. If the Author incorporates in the said Work any copyrighted material, he shall procure, at his own expense, written permission to reprint it. The Publishers shall not be required to include in said Work matter which they may consider to be obscene, offensive, indecent, libelous or against the public welfare.

**Author's
Alterations**

14. If the Author shall make any changes and/or alterations in the proofs of the said Work, which deviate from the manuscript of same as originally submitted to the Publishers and edited by the Publishers (other than corrections of printer's errors), or if the Author shall add new material thereto at any time following the signing of this agreement, the Publishers agree to make such changes and/or alterations, and/or to add such new material, only on condition that the said changes, alterations or new material shall be approved by the Publishers, and on condition that the Author shall pay to the Publishers, on request, all the additional costs and expenses involved.

**Sales Promotion,
Distribution,
Advertising**

15. Sales promotion, distribution, advertising and publicity shall be at the Publishers' election and discretion as to the extent, scope and character thereof and in all matters pertaining thereto, and same shall be at no extra cost to the Author, unless otherwise provided for. It is specifically understood and agreed, however, that the promotion, publicity and advertising recommendations in the *Author's Promotion and Production Report*, a copy of which is being submitted to the Author with this agreement, will be performed by the Publishers within a reasonable period of time following completion of the said Work, provided that the Author has fully and completely performed each and every term, covenant and condition to be performed by him under the terms of this agreement. It is agreed, furthermore, that the recommendations in the said *Author's Promotion and Production Report* represent the minimum promotion program allocated to the said Work and will constitute the Publishers' full and satisfactory compliance as provided for in this agreement.

**Design and
Production**

16. The Author agrees that all matters dealing with the design and production of the said Work shall be at the discretion and election of the Publishers, unless otherwise provided for.

**Author's
Original
Manuscript**

17. Should the Author desire that the original manuscript of the said Work, and/or any other material belonging to him, be returned following publication, application for its return should be made to the Publishers, in writing, within thirty (30) days after the signing of this agreement; failure on the part of the Author to make such application will automatically remove from the Publishers any and all responsibility or liability thereon.

**Production
Schedule**

18. The Publishers agree to complete production of the said Work within one hundred fifty to two hundred forty working days from the date of the receipt by the Publishers of the signed agreement, with the initial payment indicated in Article 31 below, provided that they are not hindered by causes beyond their control or by delays caused by the Author.

**Author's
Proofs**

19. The Author shall have the right to examine, approve and correct, if necessary, all proof sheets of the said Work that may be submitted by the Publishers during the period the said Work is in production, but the Author shall be required to return same to the Publishers within fifteen (15) days after receipt. The Publishers shall not be held liable or responsible for any delay in the completion and release of the said Work should the Author fail or neglect to return proof sheets, and/or other pertinent material relating to the said Work, within such fifteen (15) day period.

Infringement of Copyright

20. In the event of the infringement of the copyright, or other rights, in the said Work, the Publishers may, in their discretion, sue, or employ other remedies as they may deem expedient, and shall pay to the Author 50% of the net proceeds of any recovery.

No Termination of Contract for at Least Two Years

21. The Publishers shall not have the right to terminate this Agreement before two (2) years from the date of delivery of bound copies of the said Work to the Author. At any time thereafter, however, should the Publishers determine that there is not sufficient demand for said Work to enable them to continue to handle same profitably, they may then terminate this agreement by giving the Author notice thereof by first class mail at his last known address.

On Termination of Contract All Rights Revert to Author

22. Upon termination of this agreement, all rights in and to the said literary Work, including that of copyright, shall revert to the Author. Upon termination of this agreement, furthermore, the complete ownership of all remaining bound copies of the said literary Work shall be vested in the Author, and the Author shall have thirty (30) days to notify the Publishers, by registered or certified mail, to ship the above-mentioned material to him, F.O.B. the Publishers' New York headquarters. In the event that the Author fails to request said copies, or to indicate his intention of so doing, within thirty (30) days after notice of termination of contract has been mailed to the Author, the Publishers may then dispose of said copies in any manner without having to report to the Author thereon, and the Publishers shall then be free from any further responsibility or accountability to the Author.

Author Also Has Right to Terminate

23. Should the Author wish to terminate this agreement, he shall have the right to do so following the same two-year period mentioned in Article 21 of this agreement and under the same terms and conditions as set forth in Article 22 with respect to termination by the Publishers.

No Sales Guarantee

24. This agreement is entered into by both parties hereto in good faith, it being distinctly understood that neither party has guaranteed, or intends to guarantee, the sale of any specific number of copies of the said Work, or receipts from possible subsidiary rights, it being mutually recognized and acknowledged that it is impossible to predict what success any book may attain.

Complete Contract

25. The Author acknowledges that the Publishers have not made any prior pledges, promises, guarantees, inducements of whatever nature, either in writing or by word of mouth, or in any other form except as may be contained in this agreement. This agreement constitutes the whole and complete understanding of the parties, and no representations other than those expressly contained herein shall be binding. No alteration, modification, amendment, or waiver of any provision hereof shall be valid and enforceable unless it be in writing and signed by both parties.

Change of Address

26. The address of the Author shall be deemed to be that indicated in this agreement. All letters, communications and notices of whatever kind, nature and description sent to the Author to the address so indicated shall be deemed good and sufficient, unless and until the Author shall notify the Publishers in writing, by registered or certified mail, of change of address.

Performance by Author and Publisher

27. The Publishers shall not be in default of any provisions of this agreement if the Author has not fully performed all the terms and conditions thereof by him to be performed, it being understood that performance by the Publishers is based upon full compliance by the Author; nor shall the Publishers be responsible if any delay in their performance is occasioned by governmental restrictions on essential materials, supplies or services, war, strikes, delays in shipping, shutdown of industry affecting the printing or publishing industry, distribution or sales, acts of God, or by any other conditions beyond the Publishers' control. If the Publishers shall nevertheless fail to perform any of the conditions by them to be performed, then and in that event it shall not be deemed a breach of this agreement unless the Author shall have given the Publishers written notice thereof by registered or certified mail, and the Publishers shall have failed to cure said default within a reasonable time thereafter.

New York Law and Forum

28. Regardless of the place of physical execution of this agreement, or of its delivery, it shall be treated as though executed within the State of New York and shall be governed and interpreted according to the laws of that State; and the legal tribunals of or in the State of New York shall be the sole forum for resolving any questions or disputes or matters arising out of or pertaining to this contract, and/or any alleged tort that is related to this agreement. To achieve substantial justice for each, the parties acknowledge that New York is the proper, logical and convenient

forum for every purpose, including the fact that all records and personnel involved are there, and that it is the location of the publishing industry with availability of the knowledgeable experts in publishing and all of its areas relating to publicity, sales, printing, accounting, merchandising, promotion and exploitation.

Assignment of Contract

29. This agreement may not be assigned by either party without the consent of the other, in writing, but subject to the foregoing, the provisions of this agreement shall be binding upon and inure to the benefit of the heirs, executors, administrators and assigns of the Author and of the successors and assigns of the Publishers.

Author's Guarantee

30. The Author covenants and represents that the said Work has not hitherto been published in book form, or, if so published, has become and is now the property of the Author; that the said Work contains no matter that, when published, will be libelous or otherwise unlawful, or which may infringe upon any proprietary interest at common law or statutory copyright; that the Author is the sole proprietor of the said Work and has full power to make this grant and agreement and that the said Work is free of any lien, claim, charge or debt of any kind, and that he and his legal successors and/or representatives will hold harmless and keep indemnified the Publishers from any and all manner of claims, proceedings, losses, damages, costs, attorneys' fees and expenses which may be taken or incurred on the ground that the said Work is subject to any such lien, claim, charge or debt, or that it is such violation, or that it contains anything libelous or illegal.

Terms of Payment

31. In consideration of the expenditures, services and efforts to be incurred and undertaken by the Publishers in accordance with the terms of this agreement causing the said Work to be published, the Author agrees to pay to the Publishers in money of the United States of America the following sum, on the following terms:

Total sum to be paid...$ 5,850.00

$ 2,000.00   to be paid with the signing of this agreement;

$ 2,000.00   to be paid upon receipt of the galley proofs;

$ 1,850.00   to be paid thereafter in installments convenient to the Author, with the understanding that the balance still due when said Work has been completed and ready for delivery shall be fully paid at that time.

☐ *Check here if you wish to remit the entire sum when returning the signed contract. In appreciation for saving us bookkeeping costs, we shall send you, on publication, an additional fifty copies of the book, without extra charge.*

IN WITNESS WHEREOF, the parties hereto have executed this agreement as of the date indicated alongside the signature of the Author.

Author..(L.S.) Date ....

For the Publishers...(L.S.)

                          Authorized Signature

Please sign both copies of this agreement, retain one copy, and forward the other copy with your remittance to:

VANTAGE PRESS, INC., *Publishers*, 516 WEST 34TH ST., NEW YORK, N.Y. 10001
New York, N.Y. / Washington, D.C. / Atlanta, Ga. / Hollywood, Calif. / Chicago, Ill.

Index

Other Books of Interest

General Writing Books

Beginning Writer's Answer Book, edited by Polking and Bloss $14.95

Getting the Words Right: How to Revise, Edit and Rewrite, by Theodore A. Rees Cheney $13.95

How to Get Started in Writing, by Peggy Teeters $10.95

How to Write a Book Proposal, by Michael Larsen $9.95

How to Write While You Sleep, by Elizabeth Ross $12.95

Law & the Writer, edited by Polking & Meranus (paper) $10.95

Knowing Where to Look: The Ultimate Guide to Research, by Lois Horowitz $16.95

Teach Yourself to Write, by Evelyn Stenbock (paper) $9.95

The 29 Most Common Writing Mistakes & How to Avoid Them, by Judy Delton $9.95

Writer's Block & How to Use It, by Victoria Nelson $12.95

Writer's Encyclopedia, edited by Kirk Polking $19.95

Writer's Market, edited by Paula Deimling $19.95

Writer's Resource Guide, edited by Bernadine Clark $16.95

Magazine/News Writing

Complete Guide to Writing Nonfiction, by The American Society of Journalists & Authors $24.95

How to Write & Sell the 8 Easiest Article Types, by Helene Schellenberg Barnhart $14.95

Fiction Writing

Creating Short Fiction, by Damon Knight (paper) $8.95

Fiction Writer's Market, edited by Jean Fredette $17.95

Handbook of Short Story Writing, by Dickson and Smythe (paper) $7.95

How to Write Short Stories that Sell, by Louise Boggess (paper) $7.95

Storycrafting, by Paul Darcy Boles $14.95

Writing Romance Fiction—For Love and Money, by Helene Schellenberg Barnhart $14.95

Writing the Novel: From Plot to Print, by Lawrence Block (paper) $8.95

Special Interest Writing Books

The Children's Picture Book: How to Write It, How to Sell It, by Ellen E. M. Roberts $17.95

Complete Book of Scriptwriting, by J. Michael Straczynski $14.95

The Craft of Comedy Writing, by Sol Saks $14.95

The Craft of Lyric Writing, by Sheila Davis $17.95

How to Make Money Writing Fillers, by Connie Emerson (paper) $8.95

How to Write a Cookbook and Get It Published, by Sara Pitzer, $15.95

How to Write a Play, by Raymond Hull $13.95

How to Write & Sell (Your Sense of) Humor, by Gene Perret $12.95

How to Write the Story of Your Life, by Frank P. Thomas $12.95

Mystery Writer's Handbook, by The Mystery Writers of America (paper) $8.95

On Being a Poet, by Judson Jerome $14.95

Poet's Market, by Judson Jerome $16.95

Travel Writer's Handbook, by Louise Zobel (paper) $9.95

TV Scriptwriter's Handbook, by Alfred Brenner (paper) $9.95

Writing for Children & Teenagers, by Lee Wyndham (paper) $9.95

Writing After 50, by Leonard L. Knott $12.95

Writing and Selling Science Fiction, by Science Fiction Writers of America (paper) $7.95

Writing for the Soaps, by Jean Rouverol $14.95

The Writing Business

Complete Guide to Self-Publishing, by Tom & Marilyn Ross $19.95

Complete Handbook for Freelance Writers, by Kay Cassill $14.95

Editing for Print, by Geoffrey Rogers $14.95

Freelance Jobs for Writers, edited by Kirk Polking (paper) $7.95

How to Understand and Negotiate a Book Contract or Magazine Agreement, by Richard Balkin $11.95

To order directly from the publisher, include $2.00 postage and handling for 1 book and 50¢ for each additional book. Allow 30 days for delivery.

Writer's Digest Books, Dept. B, 9933 Alliance Rd., Cincinnati OH 45242
Prices subject to change without notice.